Myth
and
Modern Philosophy

Portrait of René Descartes painted about 1647 by Jan Baptist Weenix. Inscription in book reads, "Mundus est Fabula." © Centraal Museum, Utrecht. Used by permission.

Myth
and
Modern Philosophy

Stephen H. Daniel

Temple University Press
Philadelphia

Temple University Press, Philadelphia 19122
Copyright © 1990 by Temple University. All rights reserved
Published 1990
Printed in the United States of America

The paper used in this publication meets the minimum requirements of American
National Standard for Information Sciences—Permanence of Paper for Printed
Library Materials, ANSI Z39.48–1984

Library of Congress Cataloging in Publication Data

Daniel, Stephen H. (Stephen Hartley), 1950–
        Myth and Modern Philosophy / Stephen H. Daniel.
            p.   cm.
        Bibliography: p.
        Includes index.
        ISBN 0-87722-644-X (alk. paper)
        1. Philosophy, Modern—17th century.   2. Philosophy, Modern—18th
century. 3. Myth.   I. Title.
        B801.D36 1990
        190'.9'032—dc20   89-33534
                                                                              CIP

For Breaux

Contents

Preface

THE HISTORY OF PHILOSOPHY in the seventeenth and eighteenth
centuries is as much a report of what philosophers and literary
theorists now do as it is an account of classical modern philosophy itself. For what we today understand the source texts to
mean emerges in the context of a history whose techniques of
critical interpretation outline the possible meanings that a text
can have.

That history includes practices by early modern thinkers who
refuse to exclude myth and metaphor in favor of a narrower,
completely literal understanding of philosophic activity. Indeed,
these thinkers acknowledge the need to account for how philosophic and literal expressions originally become meaningful. To
do so, they point to the communal discursive practices and
particular expressions of relationships by which meanings emerge:
that is, they point to myth and metaphor as the means by which
all other expression or discourse becomes possible.

The initially implicit assumptions underlying such a discussion
of modern philosophy within the context of myth are probably
more controversial than many of the interpretations I put forward
in this book. From one perspective, even to raise the possibility
that philosophy in general, and seventeenth- and eighteenth-
century philosophy in particular, could be understood in mythic
ways gives rise to the disquieting suggestion that claims of truth
are jeopardized by adopting such an approach. For if philosophy
cannot be distinguished from "utter myths," then it would appear
to fail in its attempt to achieve truth. In short, to associate
philosophy with myth might be seen as undermining the very
advance beyond myth embodied in the move to philosophy.

From another perspective, to highlight mythic elements within
philosophy elevates myth to such a position of prominence that
philosophy, along with other forms of discourse, are at risk of
being subsumed under the heading of myth. By such means

myth takes on the status of a character found in all thought and writing. In fact, all thought and writing might be seen as mythic insofar as myth encompasses central discursive practices. Furthermore, this approach permits every expression to be understood not only literally but also metaphorically (i.e., as a moment of possible creative renovation in meaning).

Such concerns about the relation of myth and philosophy have recently crystallized in contemporary strategies for historiographic study. In particular, interest in the nature of myth and in the corresponding creative activity of metaphor has increased significantly, partly as a result of attempts by philosophers and literary theorists to identify the contexts out of which meaning and discourse emerge. Hermeneutics, semiotics, deconstructionism, and poststructuralism have all pointed to the need to understand the processes by which language becomes meaningful and introduces novelty into discourse. These methodologies portray mythic activity and metaphoric expression as providing not only the historical and conceptual background for philosophic reflection but also the means for revealing presuppositions and structures implicit within creative transformations of usage.

Such strategies present traditionally recognized functions of myth in contexts that invite renovation of prior interpretations. For example, classical myths and fables often are identified as sources of meaning and as guides for organizing experience within a linguistic community. In the contexts of contemporary approaches, this observation creates the possibility that myth presents the vocabulary and grammar by which subsequent rational discourse is made possible. Sensitivity to the presence of myth within and on the horizon of conventional philosophic discussion thus has to recognize this activity of creative ingenuity.

Much contemporary scholarship traces the philosophic recognition of the importance of myth to the nineteenth-century Romanticist reaction to modern (seventeenth- and eighteenth-century) philosophy. And while it is indeed the case that many modern thinkers ignore the question of the origins of meanings, language, and creative ingenuity or the philosophic importance of myth, others treat myth (or "fable," as it is often called) as the domain proper to the study of origins and the creative activity of the mind.

Certainly, the thematic treatment of philosophical creativity, ingenuity, and the mythic origins of language and meaning is more developed in the Romanticist thought of Herder, Schelling, or Coleridge than in earlier philosophies. But the attempt to provide such treatments of the historical and conceptual presuppositions of meaning only indicates how late-eighteenth-century Romanticist accounts reinstate the early modern philosophic concern for explaining something always in terms of its origins or genesis.

The purpose of this book is to indicate how modern thinkers ✓ incorporate an interest in the mythic or fabular into philosophic inquiry. Such a focus on the mythic highlights features in their thought that unite such thinkers within a tradition of mythic or fabular philosophizing. It likewise challenges contemporary approaches to the history of philosophy by revealing how the Romanticist emphasis on the mythopoetic genesis of philosophy can affect our own interpretation of early modern philosophers. My argument for the importance of myth in philosophy cannot, then, be divorced from my historical account of how myth functions in the works of various philosophers.

Even though they often limit their understanding of myth to Homeric myths, Burton Feldman and Robert Richardson *(The Rise of Modern Mythology: 1680–1860)* have provided researchers resource material for the study of myth during the modern period. Elizabeth Sewell *(The Human Metaphor* and *The Orphic Voice)* extends the conception of myth in ways that invite further examination of philosophic texts. Hayden White's *Metahistory* and *Tropics of Discourse,* Dominick LaCapra's *Rethinking Intellectual History,* and Timothy Reiss's *The Discourse of Modernism* indicate how contemporary literary theory affects the historiographic study of texts, though these writers have not generally pursued such an inquiry into the works of modern philosophy. Eric Gould's *Mythical Intentions in Modern Literature* and James Engell's *The Creative Imagination* address mythic or imaginative elements in the literature immediately after the modern period; however, they too do not consider classical modern philosophy as such. Ernst Cassirer's studies *(The Philosophy of Symbolic Forms* and *The Philosophy of the Enlightenment)* and Hans Blumenberg's *Work on Myth* indicate the epistemological presuppositions that make possible the analysis of myth within modern philosophy. And under the editorship of Richard Rorty, Jerome B. Schneewind, and Quentin Skinner *(Philosophy in History: Essays on the Historiography of Philosophy),* traditional procedures for doing the history of philosophy have been opened to the possibility of a sympathetic treatment of the rhetorical and literary aspects of philosophy.

Specific discussions of some of the individual philosophers with whom I deal do address mythic concerns. For example, Ernesto Grassi's research (especially in *Rhetoric as Philosophy*) highlights the Renaissance background for understanding myth, but he does not examine modern thinkers in an extended way. James Stephens *(Francis Bacon and the Style of Science)* and Lisa Jardine *(Francis Bacon: Discovery and the Art of Discourse)* point out mythic features in Bacon's writings. In *Descartes' Philosophy of Nature*, James Collins examines the significance of the fabular or mythic in Descartes in ways that are different from, but as provocative as, the deconstructive studies of the Cartesian cogito by Jean-Luc Nancy, Sylvie Romanowski, and Dalia Judovitz. Exemplary applications of the deconstructive technique in regard to myth and modern philosophy appear in Jacques Derrida's *The Archeology of the Frivolous: Reading Condillac* and in his extended article "White Mythology: Metaphor in the Text of Philosophy." Thomas Noel *(Theories of the Fable in the Eighteenth Century)* considers theoretical aspects of fabling that have implications for the study of myth. And Donald P. Verene appeals fruitfully to implications of Cassirer's project in *Vico's Science of Imagination* and *Hegel's Recollection*. No work with which I am familiar, however, attempts to draw out the mythic and imaginative connections I identify in the writings of Bacon, Descartes, Mandeville, Vico, Herder, and others—particularly within a context that requires reunderstanding how the history of philosophy is to be studied.

Accordingly, my Introduction examines the role of myth and metaphor in philosophic historiography. Bacon, Descartes, Mandeville, Vico, and Herder have different aims in their appeals to mythic thought, and, as such, their uses or discussions of myth differ. Likewise, a comparison of contemporary strategies of historical interpretation reveals how poststructuralism in particular captures the spirit of mythological exegesis essential for the appreciation of the genesis of meaning. Because the emergence of meaning is central to the mythic enterprise, it appears then most strikingly in just such a historiography.

Chapter One addresses Francis Bacon's contribution to mythic philosophy by examining his fascination with the myths of the ancients and the retrieval of philosophic ingenuity *(ingenium)*. Chapter Two indicates how Descartes' discussion of the rules regulating ingenium (e.g., in the *Regulae ad directionem ingenii*) is complemented by his "fable of the world" *(Le Monde)*; the turn to the meaning-constitutive character of myth recurs in the *Discourse on Method*, a work that Descartes also refers to as a fable.

The practico-moral aspect of fabling that appears in Descartes' treatment recalls the need to interpret the seventeenth-century use of fable in terms of both Aesopic fable and classical myth. Chapter Three considers how English theorists unite these two characteristics of fabling by emphasizing the social regulation of the emergence of ingenuity. Especially important in Mandeville's *Fable of the Bees*, this appeal to the mythic becomes evident when Mandeville's early interest in classical myth is balanced by his later recognition of the need to explore the historical origins of meanings and language—the topic of Chapter Four.

Chapter Five shows how Vico unites the discussions of the origin of language and the creative function of ingenium within a historical appreciation of the proto-philosophical requirements for creative reassertions of control over meanings. Chapter Six describes how the heterodox character of Vico's philological turn to the presuppositions of philosophy becomes incorporated into the linguistic mythologies of Herder and Hamann.

The final chapter (Chapter Seven) points out how Romanticist philosophies of myth redefine the historiographic appropriation of Renaissance fabulation and eighteenth-century treatments (by Berkeley, Shaftesbury, Diderot, and Condillac) of creativity. This reorientation toward the linguistic significance of myth by late-eighteenth-century thinkers (e.g., Schelling, Coleridge) permits accounts of what is identified as the biography of reason itself as well as the revision of interpretive methodologies characteristic of contemporary historiography of philosophy.

Acknowledgments

MATERIAL FROM THE FOLLOWING previously published articles has been revised and expanded in this work.

"Political and Philosophical Uses of Fables in Eighteenth-Century England," *The Eighteenth-Century: Theory and Interpretation* 23 (1982): 151–71.

"Myth and the Grammar of Discovery in Francis Bacon," *Philosophy and Rhetoric* 15 (1982): 219–37.

"Descartes on Myth and Ingenuity/Ingenium," *Southern Journal of Philosophy* 23 (1985): 157–70.

"The Philosophy of Ingenuity: Vico on Proto-Philosophy," *Philosophy and Rhetoric* 18 (1985): 236–43.

"Vico on Mythic Figuration as Prerequisite for Philosophic Literacy," *New Vico Studies* 3 (1985): 61–72.

"Myth and Rationality in Mandeville," *Journal of the History of Ideas* 47 (1986): 595–609.

"Metaphor and the Historiography of Philosophy," *CLIO: An Interdisciplinary Journal of Literature, History, and Philosophy of History* 15 (1986): 191–210.

"The Narrative Character of Myth and Philosophy in Vico," *International Studies in Philosophy* 20 (1988): 1–9.

Grants and fellowships supporting research for this study include the National Endowment for the Humanities (Residential Fellowship Program for College Teachers and Summer Stipend Program); the William Andrews Clark Memorial Library—UCLA (Andrew W. Mellon Postdoctoral Short-Term Independent Research Fellowship Program); Spring Hill College, Mobile, Alabama (Faculty Research Grant Program); and the College of Liberal Arts at Texas A&M University (Faculty Summer Research Grant Program). I am grateful for the support of all these programs.

Without the encouragement of my colleagues in the Department of Philosophy at Texas A&M University, I would not have been able to complete this book. To them I owe a sincere debt of gratitude. I also owe thanks to Ralph Cohen of the English Department at the University of Virginia for opening up my conception of myth to contemporary practices in literary theory. By permitting me to typeset this book myself, Temple University Press allowed me to participate in the figural activity that has always characterized myth. John Ziff contributed substantially to improving the clarity and consistency of the text.

As with all my endeavors, I am most indebted to my wife, Breaux, for all the things she does for me in making an academic life both possible and immensely fulfilling. Her understanding and enthusiasm, for my scholarly pursuits and even my passion for whitewater kayaking, astound all who know her. What good sense I exhibit in this work and elsewhere I trace back to her example. She deserves more love and admiration than I will ever give her.

Myth
and
Modern Philosophy

Myth and Historiography

PRESUPPOSITIONS IN MYTH

MYTH HAS COME TO MEAN so many different things that any initial definition that I might propose would surely be too broad or too narrow to serve any useful purpose. A more promising tack lies in noticing the various functions of mythic thought or expression. For when thought or expression exhibits certain characteristics, and especially when such characteristics appear in conjunction with one another, discourse becomes identifiable as mythic.

What I mean by myth is a particular mode or group of functions, operative within discourse, that highlight how communication and even thought are themselves possible. Certain functions of discourse are mythic insofar as they reveal how discourse itself is possible. This explains why we are fascinated with myth, because without myth, fascination itself lacks direction and coherence.

Myth designates characteristics found in all language and thought insofar as all discourse reveals presuppositions implicit within the possibility of discourse. The fact that some instances of discourse are labeled as myths indicates how they make explicit what is only implicit in most discourse—namely, the fact that communal structures of meaning themselves are grounded originally in the performance of discourse. That is, the act of speaking or writing as a public performance lays claim to meaning in virtue of its publicity. Prior to the regulative structures of speech or writing, no discourse is possible because no standards of meaning exist.

In the absence of such standards of meaning, it is impossible to identify not only the principles by which individuals are united socially but also the principles by which an individual would be able to become aware of himself or herself as an individual. The mythic mind does not exist prior to expression, because only in expressions (i.e., in "metaphors" or, more generally, "myths") do a vocabulary and a grammar emerge so as to make thought possible. The originator of a myth literally does not understand what he is saying because his saying what he does is what makes understanding possible. In fact, he does not even know that *he* is saying anything, because the concept of self-identity distinct from mythic expression depends on prior recognition of a system of meaning that itself exists only in expressive performances.

While mythicity may permeate all discourse and metaphoricity may reside within each expression, particular myths and metaphors explicitly acknowledge the ongoing generation of meaning-structures within discourse. Myths do not describe a world that is somehow distinct from discursive expressions themselves. Nothing other than chaos exists prior to the world that the myth reveals, and what the myth reveals is the ability of discourse to order experience and expression in such a way as to make possible a world to be known.

Instead of describing a world already meaningful apart from the description, myths present a world that only becomes meaningful in virtue of the account given in the mythic expression. The essence of a myth lies in its telling, for apart from the recounting of the myth there is no ordered world (or cosmos) about which one can speak.[1] Prior to thought are the discursive expressions that present the text by which the world is made accessible. Myths, as such discursive expressions, place us immediately in touch with the world because the world is the complex of expressions; it is the text.

This is why speaking the myth, performing the ceremony, engaging in the ritual, uttering the incantation, or saying the sacred name (e.g., Yahweh) must be reserved only for those who recognize how such discourse creates the world in which we live.[2] In myth, the word is made flesh, expression is identified as reality, and we become realized in virtue of dwelling within the expression. To lose touch with the immediacy of discourse— that is, to alienate ourselves from the world by distinguishing our discourse from a so-called objective world—is, in religious terms,

1. See Martin Heidegger, *What Is Called Thinking?* tr. J. Glenn Gray (New York: Harper and Row, 1968), 10; and Timothy J. Reiss, *The Discourse of Modernism* (Ithaca, N.Y.: Cornell University Press, 1982), 9–10.

2. Cf. Denis Tedlock, "The Spoken Word and the Work of Interpretation in American Indian Religion," in *Myth, Symbol, and Reality,* ed. Alan M. Olson (Notre Dame, Ind.: University of Notre Dame Press, 1980), 136. Cf. Hans Blumenberg, *Work on Myth,* tr. Robert M. Wallace (Cambridge: MIT Press, 1985), 37.

the Fall into sin.[3] Sin is nothing more than the affirmation of oneself as distinct from the communal, the communicative, the publicly expressive. Repentance from sin (in the mythic consciousness) must necessarily be public, then, because communal, public discourse is the reality into which the individual is to be reintegrated. To sin is to assert one's independence from discourse, to fall into the chaos of private meanings, to presume the priority of thought over expression. Redemption thus lies only in the return to the Word, which means that salvation from chaotic meaninglessness lies only in the mythic recognition of the preeminence of discourse.

Four characteristics of discourse in particular account for the influence of myths.[4] First, myths provide a narrative account by which the origins of events, beliefs, or practices are explained. But such a narration is not simply an imaginative fable or story that has a moral or that brings those who share in retelling the story closer together—though, no doubt, myths do have these features. More important for this first point is the recognition that mythic expression is justified in describing origins because mythic expression itself originally identifies events, beliefs, and practices as such. It is not simply accidental, then, that myths happen to tell stories about origins, for myths display the process by which meaning originates in the very mystique of their presentation.

Myths reveal grammar and vocabulary in precisely the manner in which the myths are expressed, for these expressions explain origins in the very act of showing the origin in expression. To say that myths describe something that happened long ago misses an essential point, for in the very way in which the elements of the recitation are associated, the reciting of the myth here and now shows how such elements come to be related. Their relations

3. See Gene M. Bernstein's comment on Coleridge in "The Mediated Vision: Eliade, Lévi-Strauss, and Romantic Mythopoesis," in *The Binding of Proteus: Perspectives on Myth and the Literary Process*, ed. Marjorie W. McCune, Tucker Orbison, Philip Withim (Lewisburg, Pa.: Bucknell University Press, 1980), 168–69; and William E. Abraham, "The Origins of Myth and Philosophy," *Man and World* 11 (1978): 166–67.

4. For similar summary accounts, see Eric Gould, *Mythical Intentions in Modern Literature* (Princeton, N.J.: Princeton University Press, 1981), 6; William Righter, *Myth and Literature* (London: Routledge and Kegan Paul, 1975), 15–24; Percy Cohen, "Theories of Myth," *Man*, new series 4 (1969), 338–53; and G. S. Kirk, *Myth: Its Meaning and Function* (Cambridge: Cambridge University Press, 1970), 254.

exist in no way prior to their embodiment in the grammar of the
story.   That is why it is so important that the myth be told in a
certain way, or that certain combinations of words be used in an
incantation, because to change the order of the account is to
change the order of reality.   Myths recall us to that stance of awe,
care, even terror before the word.   In the mouth of the unini-
tiated, myths are dangerous not only because careless expression
threatens the grammatical structure of the world but also because
insensitivity to the creative immediacy of discourse undermines
respect for the significance of expression.   Loss of respect for the
significance of discourse only encourages a proliferation of expression in an attempt to increase in quantity what has been lost in
reverence and impact.   But this, in turn, reintroduces chaos by
effectively multiplying structures of meaning to the point where
elements within structures are indiscriminately relatable to any
and all other elements.

A properly mythic expression, then, opens the possibility that
the relational or ontological character of the world might be
changed.   In his or her use of metaphor, for example, the poet
recognizes this fact in restructuring grammatical relations.   But in
doing so, the poet undermines hope for discovering a true and
stable description of reality and its origins.   Poetic expression
draws attention to itself as discourse, creating its own grammar in
the midst of other texts that are themselves engaged continuously
in alternative grammatical realignments.   Within this intertextual
discourse, myth combines the impulse to simplify expression in a
determinate grammar within the story with the admission of the
open-ended character of ongoing grammatical recommitments.[5]
It is no wonder, then, that Plato wanted to exclude poets and
mythologists from the Republic, for they espouse nothing less
than linguistic (and thus ontological and political) revolution.

The second function of myth extends the practice of providing
accounts of how things originate (i.e., genesis accounts) to the
recognition of how such accounts themselves can introduce order
or harmony into an otherwise chaotic situation.   Myths organize
experience in ways that validate claims, establish values, and
identify problems.   As such, discursive formations (e.g., the
human sciences) are mythic in characterizing their objects:
Humanity, society, and culture do not exist as distinct objects

---

5.   See Righter, *Myth and Literature,* 100–101.

other than as abstractions of the rules of discourse established in mythic expression.[6]

In like manner, philosophy (as the activity most sensitive to the presence of such foundations) discloses not the world but its own mythology, its own structures of metaphorical relations.[7] It does not interpret reality or the human condition as much as it presents a purified (self-disclosing) expression of its own mythic presuppositions. In this way all philosophy becomes a commentary or gloss on the history of philosophy, and all history of philosophy is nothing more than the historiography of philosophy. In the same manner, poetry is literary criticism, and all criticism or theory is emergent poetry insofar as all interpretations paraphrase expressions that themselves are aboriginally metaphoric. To identify all discourse as fundamentally mythic or metaphoric undermines all hope of discovering some ideal, literal language that truly describes the world without need for interpretation.

The mythologist or mythic poet, then, does not *interpret* the world through myth or poetry. Rather, by means of the explicit appeal to myth, the poet makes grammatical commitments that have meaning only in relation to other forms of discourse: *Poesis* interprets not the world but rather other texts by proposing itself as part of the constitutive network in which meaning is possible. Thus, in virtue of its own principles of expression, the study of the history of philosophy or literature is itself part of the discursive network that makes past texts accessible as meaningful texts. It even defines what the past is in virtue of its own discursive performance.

Perception operates in accord with this character of poesis and, as such, does not identify items existing in a world antecedently organized. This does not mean that prior to myth there is nothing, only that prior to myth there is chaos. Myths retrieve the possibility of a purified (*mundus*) world (*mundus*), insofar as a world is not any world as such unless it lends itself to some order made determinate. Through figurative (mythic, poetic) expression, chaos is refined accordingly into cosmos (a world).

6. See Hayden V. White, "Foucault Decoded: Notes from Underground," *History and Theory* 12 (1973): 24, 45, 53.

7. Cf. Carl R. Hausman, "Philosophical Creativity and Metaphorical Philosophy," *Philosophical Topics* 12 (1981): 204, 207; and Friedrich Schlegel's notebook entries quoted in A. Leslie Willson, "Romantic Neomythology," in *Myth and Reason: A Symposium*, ed. Walter D. Wetzels (Austin: University of Texas Press, 1973), 62.

The world the infant learns to perceive in terms of the myths of his community is a world in which everything is known with certainty. Falsity or truth, irony or displacement have no meaning in the world of the mythic because what is, is limited solely to that expressed in myth. Without myths, there are no commonplaces, no shared forms of experience, no vocabularies of landscape by which perception itself can be ordered and meaning generated.

A community thus becomes organized as a community in virtue of the shared experiences and expectations embodied in its myths. This socializing force is a third factor in understanding the impact of mythic expression. Initiation into a community involves learning and relying on the myths, for the myths identify what kinds of beliefs and events are of communal interest. The fact that a prayer must be said in a certain way, that presents are to be exchanged at certain times of the year, or that Santa Claus is invoked at Christmas serves to reaffirm one's participation in and re-creation of the community. Myths thus stabilize social structures and institutionalize the correct performance of rites in such a way as to guarantee the continued survival of the community as a unity.[8]

The recognition of the mythic basis of community reemphasizes the centrality of discourse as the source of unity among individuals. Conversely, it dismisses the belief that somehow individuals innately share basic common interests or perceptual structures. Just as the child must learn how to organize experience of an originally chaotic world according to mythic guidelines, so also does the child learn to adopt political and social concerns similar to those of others in virtue of shared myths. For example, Americans are united by their myths; it is not that their shared mythology is a product of some natural, prediscursive interests. Myths give focus and meaning to otherwise indiscriminate interest. In fact, it is only insofar as the same discursive formation or myth characterizes different individuals' experiences that we can say that they experience the same things or live in the same world.

This point raises the issue addressed by the fourth presupposition of myth, namely, that for the mythic consciousness there is

---

8. See E. O. James, "The Nature and Function of Myth," *Folk-Lore* 68 (1957): 477; and David Bidney, "Myth, Symbolism, and Truth," in *Myth: A Symposium*, ed. Thomas A. Sebeok (Bloomington: Indiana University Press, 1958), 9, 16.

no question about whether myths are true or false, only whether they are effective. Because there is no meaningful experience prior to the organization provided by the communal interests embodied in the myths, no myth can legitimately be judged true or false. Indeed, myth provides the vocabulary, the text, the grammar by which judgments are made possible in the first place. Without the certainty of determinate meaning, no question about truth can be asked.

This last point, however, is deceptive. For even if myth provides some determinacy in what can be said or thought, it does so by masking the fact that myth survives only in its repeated re-creations.[9] Each time it is recounted it introduces a new determinacy into the world by the sheer fact that the ritual of expression is what provides the order of the world. Insofar as discourse is the attempt to eliminate doubt about the survival of the individual or the community, it succeeds only to the extent that it is recalled intact and re-created anew. But each re-creation in ritual succeeds only in inviting further interpretation of the myth; and any interpretation involves not simply a re-telling of the same myth but rather the expression of a new one, because each performance is the immediate source of meaning.

Myths thus provide meaning or order in experience and unify a community only insofar as they are repeated in rigidly identical expressions. But this is impossible in environments in which new poetic expressions are constantly emerging, because new myths affect the intertextual network by which all myths are understood. Furthermore, variations (updatings) of myths effectively introduce new meaning-formats into experience. This is what happens when the poet's grammatical violations are not seen simply as mistakes but as novel suggestions for meaning. As a result, it becomes impossible to distinguish between a novel meaning and a simple mistake in the expression. Or more precisely put, all errors in mythic expression indicate proposed realignments of reality, which only subsequently will be determined as effective or not. In this sense myths might be understood as imaginative accounts, cautionary tales, fables, or even philosophic systems—any of which might become the basis

9. See Gould, *Mythical Intentions*, 67. Cf. Rodolphe Gasché, "Of Aesthetic and Historical Determination," in *Post-structuralism and the Question of History*, ed. Derek Attridge, Geoff Bennington, and Robert Young (Cambridge: Cambridge University Press, 1987), 139–61.

for determining what is true in virtue of its narrative ability to explain something in ways that unite a community.

Myths become effective, then, for the same reason that they fail to remain myths: Insofar as they provide the basis for organizing experience, they become incorporated into the discursive practices of a community and thus no longer are viewed as source expressions of meaning. To lose sight of this originative function of myth is also to lose sight of the immediacy of discursive practices. In this way we simply forget that variations in expressions define the grammar by which we know the world. Just as startling juxtapositions of terms in imaginative metaphors become dead metaphors and, eventually, literal expressions with few indications of their heritage, so also the heritage of mythic expressions is forgotten in the unfounded assumption that behind myth is some truth to which myth darkly points. Indeed, myth confounds the impulse to discover a rationale behind the performance because, in myth, the performance is what establishes rationality.

Kafka provides us with an example of just such a point: "Leopards break into the temple and drink to the dregs what is in the sacrificial pitchers; this is repeated over and over again; finally it can be calculated in advance, and it becomes part of the ceremony." Here is myth in operation, revealing the performative origins of meaning, the ceremonial redundancy that defines what subsequently becomes the effective, the dependable. But at the moment the poetic violation of the temple of prior grammars occurs, no justification can be given. Myth thus exposes the fragile, haphazard, and even violent source of common discourse. And it is only in those forms of expression identified as myth or in those authors recognized as sensitive to myth that we still find the possibility of recapturing the spirit of genesis within our own daily expressions.

Just as myths define and express the frameworks by which discourse in general becomes common and communal, so particular, even accidental, daily expressions produce shifts in linguistic (and thus social) commitments. Operative within the discursive formation identified by a myth, and challenging the reign of the mythically organized structure itself, are metaphors, myths-in-miniature. Because the meanings contained within and made determinate by myth are functions of recounting the myth, variations within each recounting literally introduce new and ingenious possibilities for future communicative significance.

This is exactly what metaphors do insofar as they invite reinterpretation of not only the myths in which they are embedded but also those grammars of common discourse that have lost touch with the generative character of expression. Within myth, metaphors reassert the essential unity between linguistic expression and ontological status in the very act of restipulating the relations of determinacy. Once such relations are made determinate within myth, the presence of metaphor serves only to remind us of the ineradicably generative character of the mythic expression in each of its re-presentations.

The discursive innovations provided within myth by metaphors give no special privilege to the speaker or writer of expressions, because it is not the speaker or writer who determines meaning-fulness.[10] Instead, it is the functioning of the metaphoric expression within the larger myth that determines meaningfulness. No individual genius or author of novelty lurks behind discourse waiting to disrupt the determinacy of myth with startling metaphors that better describe the world itself or the world as the author sees it. Rather, the "author" is the name given to the introducibility of novel expression, the possibility of mythic renovation, the metaphoricity of discourse. In recognizing the enunciation of expression as ungrounded in anything other than itself and aboriginally novel (autochthonous), the mythic mind stands in awe of that ability of genius within discourse to deviate from the mythic activity of providing expressive determinacy.

However this attitude may recharacterize the role of the enunciator as that impulse of novelty within discourse, it does not set up an opposition between discourse, the world to which discourse supposedly refers, and the speaker or writer of such discourse. In contrast, grammars of discourse that have lost touch with their generative heritage ignore the origins of the formalized structures of literal (as opposed to metaphorical) discourses. As such, the metaphorical basis of literal expression is lost; the enunciation of novel meaning is replaced by an authorial intention struggling with words; and metaphor itself is reduced to a collapsed simile, parasitic to, instead of foundational for, literal discourse.

Recognition of the centrality of figural immediacy to a proper understanding of metaphors cautions against associating metaphors

---

10. Cf. Reiss, *Discourse of Modernism*, 30–32, 41–42.

and similes. For even though similes draw from elements linked in now-dead metaphors, they do not permit literal realignment of the elements related in dead metaphors. Similes presume the comparability of the terms they relate only insofar as those components are no longer open to redefinition by virtue of the comparison. As such, the language of metaphor appeals much more to the presuppositions underlying myths than to those underlying similes.

As Lucretian "swerves" performed by atoms of discourse, or as Diderotian "letters" that rain down as a cataract, blinding and renovating in their fall from mythic integrity into mythic innovation, metaphors serve as the elements of change within myth. The propriety of metaphors (in contrast with similes) does not reside in their appeal to a background of a more encompassing myth or discursive formation, but rather lies in their straightforward linguistic juxtaposition of elements. Metaphor's radical individuality of figural expression assumes the very same groundlessness as that of myth: namely, meaning emerges as a result of metaphoric expression just as meaning emerges as a result of the expression of complexes of metaphors that constitute myths.

In general, myth provides the order by which linguistic, social, and moral relationships are made determinate, but this is accomplished only in repeated discursive re-creations (i.e., in rituals of expression). However, because myths are not conceptualized ideals behind or within mythic expressions, they do not control the expressions. To speak ingeniously or metaphorically, then, is to speak with a reverence for the discourse in which one speaks—humbled, intimidated, and at times terrified by the implications of each re-creation of the discourse. To lose this mythic sensitivity—for example, by means of asserting one's own authorial intention behind the discourse—is to fall into powerlessness before the word and ineffectiveness as a potential contributor of meaning.

METAPHOR IN THE HISTORIOGRAPHY OF PHILOSOPHY

The preceding description of the presuppositions of myth provides a context for the identification of mythic elements in the writings of the classical modern philosophers who serve as the focal sources of this book. As sources, they have suggested some of the points contained in this description of myth.

Accordingly, the dialogue between the historian confronting source thinkers and the texts themselves continually refines the sense of what constitutes myth and continually reclassifies authors and texts in terms of their sensitivity to topics such as creativity, the origins of language, and the genesis of meaning.

I make note of this not in order to refute the apparent circularity of using a description of myth to include the very authors who provide insights into the definition, but rather to affirm that circularity in the broader context of historiographic practices in general. For I recognize a need to identify at the outset what I mean by myth. At the same time, I hope to point to how this sense of myth emerges concurrently in the increasing sensitivity to the interpretive procedures of doing the history of philosophy. It is the genetic character of how interpretation comes about that is central to the task of such a program; and it is for this reason that the mythic focus on the genesis of meaning—here, the meaning of philosophic texts—highlights the necessarily circular nature of such a hermeneutic. For this hermeneutic circle can best be identified by simply acknowledging that texts invite the generation of meaning within their interpretation and that this can be made explicit by treating texts as metaphors. In this sense, metaphor plays the same generative role as myth in the constitution of meaning in interpretation, but myth identifies the project in perhaps a more expansive way than does metaphor.

To give an account of the history of philosophy always assumes certain interpretations about what source thinkers meant in their texts. What the source thinker meant, however, is available only in terms of the text, the meanings of which we can know only in the context of our interpretations of other texts and practices of the period. Even these pre-texts emerge, to use Richard Rorty's term, in our "conversations" with source thinkers who are "creatures of our own phantasy rather than . . . historical personages."[11] But we can push it even further than that: Historical personages themselves are accessible in and through texts to such a degree that the only difference between, say, the "historical" Descartes and the author of the *Meditations* lies in

11. Richard Rorty, "The Historiography of Philosophy: Four Genres," in *Philosophy in History: Essays on the Historiography of Philosophy*, ed. Richard Rorty, Jerome B. Schneewind, and Quentin Skinner (Cambridge: Cambridge University Press, 1984), 71.

which texts (correspondence, early biographies, diaries, school records, manuscripts, published work) we attend to. As such, to change interpretations of texts means to change our understanding of the problems or approaches adopted by source thinkers, which, in turn, means to change our understanding of the history of philosophy.

How change in interpretations affects the historiography of philosophy is my primary concern at this point, though much of what I will argue can be applied to literature and history as well. Specifically, my purpose is to point out how different notions of metaphor function within historiographic attempts to explain change in interpretations, because just such a change in interpretation is what is required in my treatment of modern philosophers in terms of myth. Not only do source thinkers often couch their remarks in metaphoric terms in order to allow for diachronic rereadings of their texts (i.e., rereadings that are sensitive to the historicity of texts and changes in linguistic systems from one age to another); historians of philosophy as well employ assumptions about metaphor that attempt to account for and permit change in interpretations. The hermeneutics of Paul Ricoeur, the deconstructionism of Jacques Derrida, and the semiotics of Geoffrey Hartman (with complementary expansions by Maria Corti and Umberto Eco) recognize the need to accommodate the fact of change in interpretations within structures of meaning. But only a poststructuralist account of interpretative change (such as the one provided by Michel Foucault) properly identifies the metaphorical presuppositions within historical interpretation.

Insofar as metaphor introduces a dynamic tension into the meaning of a text, it permits change in the interpretation of the text. The presence of metaphor within the text or, more important, within the interpretation of the text ensures that the text has a history insofar as the meaning of the questions addressed in the text change. As Rorty, Jerome B. Schneewind, and Quentin Skinner have recently argued, the history of philosophy (or literature or science, for that matter) is precisely history because of the rise and fall of the questions addressed.[12] To ignore this character of change and to treat source thinkers as if

12. See their introduction to *Philosophy in History*, 11.

they address the same questions and use the same language we do is to treat them ahistorically, synchronically. Such a move has the effect, simply, of denying philosophy a history.

However, because texts require interpretation, changes in interpretation indicate how texts are, in fact, historical entities. Insofar as the meanings of texts are understood as open to interpretative change, they have a history without which it is difficult to understand the issues with which the text is concerned. To the extent that historical understanding requires interpretation, historical interpretation likewise requires the possibility of change in interpretations. Rather than being an embarrassment for the study of the history of philosophy, then, the fact of ongoing reinterpretations of texts thus reaffirms the central place of interpretative change not only in the historiography of philosophy but in the history of philosophy as well. In fact, it points to a merging of history and historiography as a response to the metaphorical character of texts insofar as texts both require interpretation and have a history of changing interpretations.

It is obvious that, though these remarks are concerned directly with philosophical historiography, they are not limited to it. Change in interpretation in literature, history, and other areas of study likewise relies on the recognition of the irreducibly metaphoric character of language and texts; that is, it relies on the supposition that language and texts are inevitably open to interpretation in changing (historical) ways. But within philosophic texts the appeal to the language of metaphor or myth appears all the more striking because philosophic discourse supposedly describes truth devoid of figuration, rhetorical flourish, and "irrelevant" religious, literary, political, and ideological concerns.[13]

To treat a philosophic text metaphorically might appear to many as a perversion of the philosophic enterprise. Furthermore, references by source thinkers to the metaphoric or mythic character of their own language or works (some might argue) should be dismissed solely as prudential strategies for handling extraphilosophic problems. The fact of change in interpretation of source works is, from this viewpoint, at best a humbling

13. For how such a supposition characterizes history of philosophy based on what they call analytic philosophy, see *ibid.*

reminder of the need for further research and at worst a continued scholarly disappointment.

To posit metaphor as a basic principle of historical understanding challenges the assumptions of this literalist historiography of philosophy, this "dream" of the history of philosophy, by frustrating the tendency toward closure of interpretation. It also raises the issue of how the structures of meaning emerge in the first place—an issue with which various contemporary subdisciplines have been concerned. For example, hermeneutics as the science of interpretation explains how meaning emerges within the context of limited ambiguity or plurivocity in language.[14] Deconstructionism highlights the unlimited plurivocity of meaning by showing how the linguistic attempt to make meaning determinate by making it public (in "writing") actually provides for meaning without restrictions on reference. Semiotics indicates how language is developed and understood by users employing a system of signs whose meaningfulness emerges in the sender-addressee dynamic as many-layered (often contradictory) codifications.[15]

For these three approaches, however, change is a derivative concept. Because meaning is defined in terms of a structure, change is either explained in terms of the structure—as in the resolution of structural tensions or in the structure's internal tendency to become destructured—or is not explained at all insofar as (as is sometimes proposed) change is proto-structural.

To move beyond a structural account of change in interpretation, as Foucault's poststructuralist position does, is to identify change as irreducible to structure: change or historicity is precisely the irresolvably novel or creative character of the structure. Rather than denying that there is any real structural change and thus keeping the structural basis of the meaning of the explanation intact, the poststructuralist account answers the question "How is real structural change (e.g., change in interpretation) possible?" by positing the a priori character of creativity or radical discontinuity.

14. See Paul Ricoeur, "Creativity in Language: Word, Polysemy, Metaphor," in *The Philosophy of Paul Ricoeur*, ed. Charles E. Reagan and David Stewart (Boston: Beacon Press, 1978), 127, 129–33; and, also in this collection, Ricoeur, "Metaphor and the Main Problem of Hermeneutics," originally in *New Literary History* 6 (1974–75): 110.

15. See Terence Hawkes, *Structuralism and Semiotics* (Berkeley: University of California Press, 1977), 141.

Foucault admits that within any particular culture's "episteme" or "discursive formation," structures determine meaning. But this does not exclude the possibility that, like change in philosophical, literary, or historical interpretations, the emergence of new discursive formations or the coexistence of simultaneously contradictory elements within a discursive formation is also meaningful. Once incorporated into a structure (what Foucault sometimes calls an "archive"), even the change from previous structures or interpretations appears meaningful in structural terms. But such a move ignores the apparent meaninglessness of the creative origin of the structure itself at the time of its emergence.[16] It is precisely Foucault's insistence on the possibility of the meaningfulness of discontinuities of structure that identifies changes in interpretations as part of the very nature of what makes a text historically meaningful. Any allusion to the contradictory character of metaphorical writing in philosophy (as "literally" false but still true in some suggestive or creative way) thus indicates either an author's awareness of such creative possibilities in interpreting his or her text or the text's availability for creative reinterpretation. Either way, it is the metaphorical character that permits the historicity of the text to become exhibited in the fact of change in interpretations.

Much of the traditional way of studying the history of philosophy is based on the presupposition that the interpreter's task is to discover the true intent of the author behind his or her text. Change in interpretations in this view amounts to implying that other interpretations, to some degree, misinterpret the true intent of the author.

In contrast to this traditional approach, recent historiography replaces the charge of successive misinterpretations with the suggestion that philosophic texts have meaning only in the context of some reading or interpretation: that is, texts are understood metaphorically rather than literally. This means, in effect, that the historian of philosophy cannot approach a text as if it contained a set of already determinate and literal meanings—meanings that bracket the presence of the historical reader.

16. See Michel Foucault, *The Archaeology of Knowledge*, tr. A. M. Sheridan Smith (New York: Harper and Row, 1972), 145–46.

From this newer perspective, the meaning of the text does not lie in the discovery of some intent of the author that somehow, it is hoped, is perceivable in spite of the interpretive activity of the reader.[17] To treat a text as literally meaningful assumes that the meaning of the text in no way requires the presence of a reader: Its meaning rests in the text itself or in the intent of the author, and any reading or interpretation of the text attempts simply to identify that meaning.

To treat a text metaphorically, on the other hand, means to treat the text as a locus for the emergence of meaning.[18] To observe, as Derrida does, that "metaphor is the characteristic that relates language to its origin" does not imply the existence of an extralinguistic referent for which metaphor substitutes.[19] Rather it undermines the hidden presumption of substitutability—a characteristic of analogy, not metaphor—in presenting language as an origin. Texts as metaphors establish the syntax for emerging meanings, thus eliminating the need to identify alternative interpretations as misinterpretations; to treat texts as metaphors also avoids portraying the study of the history of philosophy as a history of misinterpretations. To assume that a text has one proper literal meaning (the meaning intended by the author) creates the condition for the emergence of rampant misinterpretation. But to assume that a text is originally metaphoric means that it becomes literally meaningful within the context of interpretations, none of which necessarily have to be identified as misinterpretations simply because they differ from one another.

Insofar as the study of the history of philosophy reveals a fascination for change in the interpretations of classical texts, it betrays its refusal to structure the emergence of meaning in literal ways. In other words, the fact of the continual reinterpretation of the history of philosophy indicates a widespread, though perhaps seldom acknowledged, belief either that all previous interpretations are literally inaccurate as representations of the

17. For example, see Ricoeur, "The Model of the Text: Meaningful Action Considered as a Text," *New Literary History* 5 (1973–74): 95; and Charles E. Reagan, "Hermeneutics and the Semantics of Action," *Pre/Text* 4 (1983): 243–45.

18. See Derrida, *Writing and Difference*, tr. Alan Bass (Chicago: University of Chicago Press, 1978), 27; and Mark Krupnick's introduction to *Displacement: Derrida and After* (Bloomington: Indiana University Press, 1983), 4–5, 23.

19. *Of Grammatology*, tr. Gayatri C. Spivak (Baltimore, Md.: Johns Hopkins University Press, 1976), 271.

mind of the author, or (as I think is more likely) that no text is literally meaningful apart from its emergence as a text made meaningful within an interpretation. It is not the task of the historical study of philosophy simply to construct a museumlike taxonomy of literal (structurally determinate) philosophies consisting of dead metaphors. Rather it is precisely the presumption of the metaphoric or mythic character of philosophic texts that explains how historians of philosophy can allow new interpretations to emerge. Source philosophers who identify the mythic or metaphoric character of their own texts, then, not only recognize how sign systems within languages or discursive practices, and not their own intent, restrict interpretation; but they also insure their work against the petrifying effect of literal historical interpretation.

Insofar as historians of philosophy treat the language of a text literally, they assume that the source thinker shares their concerns and uses their language literally to express his or her ideas. It comes as no surprise that major thinkers are often made to appear, in this most ahistorical way of doing history, as misdirected or simply wrong in their treatments. To treat texts metaphorically, on the other hand, means that the historian must assume that the source philosopher does not share a language literally identical to his or her own. In this way the history of philosophy becomes less a record of literally erroneous approaches and more an account of the metaphorical origins of meaning. To treat texts literally takes them out of any truly historical context; indeed, it challenges the very possibility of a history of philosophy. Emphasis on the study of the history of philosophy, accordingly, suffers when classical philosophic texts are studied only in literal (nonmetaphorical) ways.

Four overlapping themes thus guide the historiographic study of philosophy. (1) Insofar as discourse is recognized as open to change in interpretation, it contains an irreducibly metaphoric or mythic character. (2) The metaphoric character of philosophy itself does not threaten meaning but rather provides for the possibility of the emergence of meaning within discourse. (3) This turn to the generative context of meaning highlights that function of metaphor and myth which classical modern thinkers such as Descartes or Vico assert is tied to the activity of *ingenium,* creative and natural ingenuity. (4) Interpretations of classical modern discussions of metaphor and myth reveal themselves as mythopoetically sensitive to the extent that they recognize their own "ingenious" (i.e., genetic) activity as collaborations with source thinkers in a text out of which meaning emerges. In short, the historiography of philosophy (especially modern philosophy) reveals its own history of creating new interpretations by creating anew texts that permit such re-creation insofar as the texts themselves have meaning because of their metaphoric/mythic character.

Rather than attempt to highlight Descartes' association of creative ingenuity and myth, Mandeville's or Vico's fascination with the origins of language within a mythic context, or Berkeley's or Leibniz's study of the origins of meaning within a system of signs, I am here more concerned with the implications of the use of metaphor for the historical study of philosophers. (I will, however, address such topics in the chapters to follow.) Obviously we would not have to limit ourselves to classical modern philosophers for whom metaphor and myth have a role in explaining the genesis of meaning, for such concerns permeate the work of many others, such as Nietzsche, Heidegger, and Cassirer. What is important to note is the recurrence in the historiography of philosophy of the association of metaphor and myth with accounts of the historical character of the genesis of meaning. Hermeneutics, deconstructionism, semiotics, and post-structuralism return to this same enterprise of explicating the texts of a Descartes, Berkeley, or Condillac and making the explicator self-conscious in his or her own metaphors of explication.

Insofar as metaphor inhabits the boundary region of a philosopher's attempt to impose order on experience, so metaphor also infects the historian's explication. What this means is that as historians of philosophy recognize the metaphoric character of their own thought, they become more sensitive to the metaphoric expressions of their subjects. Accordingly it becomes more difficult to ignore or dismiss a source thinker's awareness of the metaphoric basis of philosophizing as expressed in the appeal to fable or myth (as in Descartes or Vico) or in the use of metaphor as a self-reflexive indication of the creative or genetic aspect of a philosophy (as in Berkeley). Whether major philosophers of the seventeenth and eighteenth centuries, for example, were explicitly aware of the metaphoric character of their expressions is not at issue—some, no doubt, were not. What is at issue is the degree to which the historian's understanding of their remarks depends on a recognition of the metaphoric contexts within which their teachings are seen as acts of ingenuity, creativity, or genius.

As the language of genius—and conversely, as the genesis of language—metaphoric expression reveals the original contexts or backgrounds out of which emerge the meanings that are intelligible to the historian. That is, the historian is able to distinguish literal usage from metaphorical usage in a philosopher's text only by assuming that the historian and the source thinker both share the same pattern for distinguishing them. The more the historian becomes aware of the metaphoric character of historical thought, the more he or she understands why philosophers use the metaphors they use or why they make explicit reference to the prephilosophic function of metaphor. From modern philosophers who treat explicitly of metaphor and myth (e.g., Vico), the historian in turn learns how to understand the methodological implications of metaphor for any particular reading of those and other philosophers. As such, contemporary analyses of metaphor refocus attention on thinkers for whom the topic is important. Likewise, to highlight topics associated by classical modern thinkers with metaphor—such as myth, ingenuity, and the origins of meaning and language—reflexively recharacterizes the contemporary analyses.

This methodic "conversation" between contemporary analyses of metaphor and the classical treatments of metaphor calls for an acknowledgment of the metaphoric character of the historiography of philosophy. Starting with a philosophic understanding of metaphor (for example, in terms of hermeneutic or semiotic approaches), the historian of philosophy examines sources to determine the extent to which metaphor is used and is recognized as providing the context out of which meaning and philosophic determinateness develop. But the more the historian is able to provide a determinate interpretation of source thinkers' doctrines of metaphor, the more obviously such interpretations can stand as indictments of the historian's inability to recognize the metaphoric character of his or her own interpretations. The meaning of the interpretations is grounded in and presupposes a generative context in which metaphor and myth function. In recognizing the classical modern insistence that metaphor and myth must be tied to ingenuity and origins of language, historiography of philosophy is forced to acknowledge the mythopoetic generation of the meaningfulness of its interpretations. Just as philosophy and rational thought in general presuppose a context of meaning generated through metaphor and myth, so also history of philosophy presupposes metaphoric and mythic contexts in which interpretation is made possible.

The question could easily arise as to why such observations should be considered significant or helpful in further understanding the historiography of philosophy. Years ago we learned from Collingwood that, when historians make judgments about what counts as a past event, they reveal as much of their presuppositions about what is meaningful and real as they reveal about the past. Now, when students of Descartes identify their use of hermeneutical or deconstructive techniques, or when students of Berkeley recognize their strategies as semiological, they make clear their sensitivity to methodology.

What is not so clear, however, is how such structuralist or taxonomic analyses undercut the diachronic and generative character of metaphor. They portray metaphor and myth as fixed contexts, a horizon of undefined relationships that become determinate once they are formalized into a syntactic and semantic complex of dead metaphors. Vico, though, challenges such a move. He insists that myths and metaphors (which he calls abbreviated myths) are activities of ingenuity (ingenium), creativity, emerging novelty. Characterized first and foremost by their generative abilities, their genius lies in genesis.

Any treatment of metaphor other than in terms of a genetic account indicts such an account as a structuralist attempt to explain the procedures by which structures of interpretation change without any real need to appeal to metaphor in the first place. Certainly within a structuralist account there is no need to explain radical novelty or ingenuity, since the motive force behind the change is contained implicitly within the stresses and strains on the structure in the form of syntactic or semantic incompatibilities. In the course of studying the function of myth and metaphor in classical modern philosophy—especially in terms of the often mentioned connection between metaphor and ingenium—the historian of philosophy thus has to acknowledge how the metaphorical structure of a sign system or of a theory of interpretation employing notions of field or ground cannot accommodate the genetic character of metaphor.

Foucault's poststructuralist account of both metaphor and the metaphoric character of the historiography of philosophy challenges the historian of philosophy to reveal the activity of metaphor and myth within classical philosophies insofar as those philosophies can be identified as expressing creative ingenuity.

This has the reflexive impact of emphasizing how ingenious historiography of philosophy is fundamentally metaphoric and mythic. Instead of being simply a vehicle of interpretation, the metaphor or myth thus becomes the basis for the emergence of a text to be interpreted. Though structuralism uses metaphor or myth as an interpretative device essential for distinguishing the determinate from the indeterminate in the text, poststructuralism reveals how the text emerges as a mythopoetic act in which interpretation is tantamount to the self-constitution of the historian. The emergence of the text is thus the act of genesis; it coincides with the creation of the historian of philosophy as historian in virtue of his or her becoming related to an object of study.

The current interest in metaphor, accordingly, has created somewhat of a dilemma for philosophy.[20] On the one hand, insofar as metaphor is to be treated philosophically, it is to be described (if possible) in nonmetaphoric terms: A philosophy of metaphor, it is sometimes thought, need not be a metaphoric philosophy. This means that a philosophic treatment of metaphor must reduce metaphor to the status of a collapsed simile or analogy, a figure of speech in part literally true and in part literally false. If, as Richard Kuhns suggests, the general tendency in most philosophic circles has been to restrict the appeal to metaphor, then philosophy will fail to describe the essentially creative and genetic character of metaphor.[21] The conceptual restriction of a so-called philosophic treatment would demand that the language of the philosophic description itself be understood as literal and not intended to generate new meanings. Even if an attempt were made to describe metaphor literally in terms of determinate categories of creativity or ingenuity, the categories themselves would fail to capture the import of metaphoric activity insofar as they could not be used to explain the genesis of the categorial scheme itself, which makes the literal discussion possible. The philosophical effort to depict metaphor in literal terms thus rests on the unjustifiable assumptions, first, that literal meanings are independent of their genetic heritage and, second, that conceptual rigor is possible

20. Recent collections of studies include *On Metaphor*, ed. Sheldon Sacks (Chicago: University of Chicago Press, 1979), and *Philosophical Perspectives on Metaphor*, ed. Mark Johnson (Minneapolis: University of Minnesota Press, 1981).
21. See Richard Kuhns, "Metaphor as Plausible Inference in Poetry and Philosophy," *Philosophy and Literature* 3 (1979): 237.

only when philosophic discourse is understood as meaningful in terms of a synchronic context.

On the other hand, if philosophy recognizes the genetic character of metaphor—that is, if philosophy recognizes how metaphor generates diachronically the syntactical relationships that are formalized (as dead metaphors) in literal discourse—it reveals its own presuppositions as metaphoric. To try to describe these presuppositions ("metaphors of philosophy," Kuhns called them) in literal terms begs the question about the sources of meaning of the so-called literal discourse used in the description. Regardless of whether the attempt is made to identify the sign system or hermeneutic context of particular emerging meanings (as in the case of metaphors) or whether the attempt is made to explain the emergence of whole networks of discourse (as in the case of myths), the implications for philosophy, especially history of philosophy, are the same: namely, philosophic (literally "true") explanations of metaphor and myth serve only to highlight the metaphoric and mythic contexts out of which literal meaning and the capacity for truth-claims have emerged.

Such contexts have been described in two ways. First, as historically prior to literal usage, myth can be understood to precede philosophy, and metaphoric uses of terms can be said to precede their adoption as literal usages. Second, as conceptually prior, myth and metaphor are portrayed in hermeneutical analyses as the horizon of meaning by which interpretations in literal usage are made possible;[22] in semiological analyses metaphor and myth are depicted as characters establishing the intelligibility of sign systems.[23]

However, both historical and conceptual ways of describing the contexts provided within the functioning of metaphor and myth easily can be misunderstood to imply that metaphor and myth are transcended once they have been incorporated into an account that lays claim to philosophic truth. The only caution against falling into methodological self-deception—that is, the deception of thinking that the methodology of mythopoetic

22. See Joseph J. Kockelmans, "On Myth and Its Relationship to Hermeneutics," *Cultural Hermeneutics* 1 (1973): 69; and Paul Ricoeur, "The Metaphorical Process as Cognition, Imagination, and Feeling," in *On Metaphor*, 151–52.

23. See David C. Pierce, "Claude Lévi-Strauss: The Problematic Self and Myth," *International Philosophical Quarterly* 19 (1979): 389.

etymology, hermeneutics, or semiotics exempts philosophy from having mythic and metaphoric principles—lies in recognizing, from a poststructuralist perspective, the taxonomic and synchronic character of such analyses. From within such analyses, the caution can be recognized by explicit reference to the metaphoric nature of the approach itself. In such a way philosophy as literal discourse identifies its mythic and metaphoric roots, which it is ultimately unable to transcend. For to transcend its metaphorical genesis would mean that discourse is no longer historical, that is, open to change in meaning, and therefore is no longer in need of interpretation.

To remove interpretation from discourse is to ignore the constitutive collaboration of author and reader in the discursive enterprise, to ignore the historicity of discourse by ignoring the *discursus* within discourse, the *litteratus* within the literal. As such, the appeal to metaphor and myth explicitly marks, for both source thinker and historian, the text as a historical creation of collaborative human interests. When Descartes, for example, begins his description of the world in *Le Monde* by saying that he is going to present his physics in the form of an entertaining myth (*fable*), he acknowledges the presence of and the need for interpretive readers within discourse. The literal (*litteratus*) thus invites its own continual erasure (*litura*). For it not to do so would be both to blot out the temporary and temporal resolution of meaning contained within the literal and to pretend that etymology and rhetoric are accidental to philosophic understanding.

FOUR METAPHORIC METHODOLOGIES

A survey of the current situation regarding metaphor/myth and the historiography of philosophy thus points to the following four considerations.

First, to attempt to describe metaphor literally is to appeal to structures that value stability over change—when the genesis of change by means of metaphor is precisely what needs to be explained. As part of a hermeneutical reply to this, Ricoeur explains metaphor as an attempt to abolish literal sense while at the same time preserving it, suspending ordinary descriptive reference in order to project new possibilities of redescribing the

world.[24]   To portray metaphor in this way is to highlight the
"ambiguity in reference" of ordinary language, the multiplicity of
specific but as yet unrecognized meanings of a usage.   The
structure of determinate relationships is assumed; all we need to
find out is how it may be fleshed in.

What Ricoeur's account fails to do, however, is precisely what
makes the association of metaphor with inventive genius so
crucial.   It does not examine the structure itself and, as such, is
unable to account for change in usage other than in terms of
linguistic recommitments within the structure.   The permanent,
determinate, and specific meanings of literal usage within a
syntactic structure are replaced only by variant, ambiguous
meanings within the structure.   No attempt, though, is made to
explain the genesis of the structure or to allow for change of the
structure itself.   Such change, after all, could not be explained in
any literally meaningful way.

In terms of the history of philosophy, this first approach allows
for differing interpretations of philosophic texts only if the
syntactic structure of the text permits realignments of linguistic
commitments.   This, of course, means that the structure shared
by the source philosopher and the historian must be the same,
and changes in philosophic outlook from one to the other must
be explainable in terms of the structure.

It is not enough to point out, as Ricoeur does, that "what the
text says now matters more than what the author meant to say,
and every exegesis unfolds its procedures within the circum-
ference of a meaning that has broken its moorings to the
psychology of its author."[25]   True, concentration on the written
text elevates the discussion of the author's intention beyond what
the author may have meant.   But by saying that this does not
apply equally to the spoken word, since the word is identified
with the meaning or intention of the author, Ricoeur ignores the
possibility of metaphor as origin of polysemy within speech, a

---

24. See Ricoeur, "Discussion of Nelson Goodman's *Ways of Worldmaking*,"
Philosophy and Literature 4 (1980): 110–18; and "Metaphorical Process," 151–52.

25. Ricoeur, "Model of the Text," 95; cf. Charles E. Reagan, "Psychoanalysis as
Hermeneutics," in *Studies in the Philosophy of Paul Ricoeur*, ed. Charles E. Reagan
(Athens: Ohio University Press, 1979), 156–58.   For semiotic parallels to this, see
Hawkes, *Structuralism and Semiotics*, 142.

role that is not transcended by appeal to the psychology of the author.[26]

Second, the understanding of metaphor as "ambiguity in reference" might be pursued further. Derrida suggests, for example, that metaphor highlights the deviations of syntax, the lack of specific and determinate meanings necessary for claims of truth. The *mythos* or universal syntactical structure (reason, *logos*) which could provide the "true" metaphor (and thus no real *metaphor*)—what Derrida calls "the dream at the base of philosophy"—is actually hindered by the presence of metaphors.[27] As each metaphor expands the syntactical deviations of meaning usage, "obliterating itself, endlessly constructing its own destruction," so the proliferation of metaphors within ordinary language threatens the possibility of attaining truth. Metaphor, as "the moment of detour in which truth can still be lost," creates an inexhaustible text, a text whose open-endedness of possible meanings permits no hope of arriving at a determinate understanding of the text. Since the invention of metaphors is "an innate, natural, congenial gift, a mark of genius," it stands only as a mocking testimony to the inadequacy of the structuralist interpretation of knowledge and truth.[28]

Derrida's position on how we can approach any philosophic text can be understood in two ways. On the one hand, Derrida argues, if we assume (as in hermeneutics or semiotics) that a philosopher's written or spoken remarks are to be understood literally, we have to assume that the remarks are accessible as literal either (1) as part of a system of signs or as a system of discourse independent of any intention of the author, or (2) as part of a system or as a system of discourse in which the intention of the author itself is understandable in terms of the system of signs or system of discourse. Either way, the problem of private language is avoided by subsuming the self into the interplay of readings or systems of figurative discourse that Derrida designates by the term *writing*. In this way "writing is the forgetting of the self" insofar as there is no specific author

26. See Ricoeur, *Hermeneutics and the Human Sciences*, ed. and tr. John P. Thompson (Cambridge: Cambridge University Press, 1981), 201, 217; and Reagan, "Hermeneutics and the Semantics of Action," 243.

27. See Derrida, "White Mythology: Metaphor in the Text of Philosophy," tr. F. C. T. Moore, *New Literary History* 6 (1974–75), 11, 70–71.

28. *Ibid.*, 42, 45.

of any text, since literal meaningfulness is possible only by
making that which is present (the figuration of the text) the
basis for literal or "proper" meaning. "A precise and exact
language," Derrida claims, "should be absolutely univocal and
literal [*propre*], nonmetaphorical."[29] Any expression that points
beyond itself as part of a system of public discourse lapses into
myth or metaphor: it points to that which is absent literally, a
meaning or a self that is not literally present either within or
behind the expression itself.

   To get to the literal meaning of the text, then, is to engage in
the forgetting of a self as accessible and meaningful. The very
possibility of literal meaning requires repression of the self. For
Derrida, "This concept of repression is thus, at least as much as
that of forgetting, the product of a philosophy (of meaning)."[30]
It is this repressing or active forgetting of the self that occupies
most of the energies of not only philosophy as a search for
literal meaningfulness but also the history of philosophy as a
search for literal or true interpretations of the ideas of source
thinkers.

   On the other hand, we can adopt a different deconstructive
tactic, one in which we accept the mythic and metonymic nature
of philosophic discourse. But even here metaphor becomes
suspect. "Metaphor," Derrida notes, "is never innocent. It
orients research and fixes results."[31] Metaphor fixes meanings in
time and establishes syntaxes that provide grounds for literal
metaphysics. In fact, literal metaphysics is a memorial composed
of dead metaphors, the history of what Derrida calls "the
submission of Being to the existent," the repressing of discourse
in order that there be *historia*.[32] In an ironic reversal of roles,
metaphor (which provides the apparatus for change in linguistic

---

29. Derrida, *Of Grammatology*, 24, 271. On the relationships between authorial
intention, contexts, and text, especially in light of Derrida's analysis, see Dominick
LaCapra, "Rethinking Intellectual History and Reading Texts," in *Modern European
Intellectual History: Reappraisals and New Perspectives*, ed. Dominick LaCapra and
Steven L. Kaplan (Ithaca, N.Y.: Cornell University Press, 1982), 57–67, 73–78.
30. Derrida, *Of Grammatology*, 286; also see Derrida, "Plato's Pharmacy," in
Dissemination, tr. Barbara Johnson (Chicago: University of Chicago Press, 1981),
109.
31. Derrida, *Writing and Difference*, 17. See Gregory Ulmer, "*Op Writing*:
Derrida's Solicitation of *Theoria*," in *Displacement: Derrida and After*, ed. Mark
Krupnick (Bloomington: Indiana University Press, 1983), 29; and Krupnick's introduction, 4–5.
32. Derrida, *Writing and Difference*, 27.

disruption) must be repressed in literal discourse so that a past, a "history," can become determinate. A dead metaphor thus provides access to historical texts only insofar as they are closed to the conversation of further interpretation. But while they are live, metaphors challenge the literal in ways of metonymy and myth. As such, metaphor as originative threatens syntax by setting out in syntax its deviations.

In terms of the history of philosophy, deconstructionism, like Ricoeur's hermeneutics, notes that the source philosopher and the historian share the same syntactic structure. With Derrida, though, the syntax becomes so encumbered by metaphoric expansion that any and all interpretations of the source thinker's text are permitted and are equally justified. This is language turned against itself, syntax made nonsyntactical—a condition that Derrida suggests can be corrected only by appealing to the "good metaphysics," which he quotes Condillac as saying began before language.[33] Philosophy structured by means of linguistic syntax can only yield to the metaphoric advances of genius and, impregnated with deviations in usage out of control, destroys itself from within because of its inability to explain change in other than structural terms.

Third, in order to introduce the fundamental (creative, aboriginal) character of metaphor and myth into this discussion, Geoffrey Hartman proposes that we should understand all discourse as indeterminate.[34] Following Coleridge's suggestion that genius operates under laws of its own making, Hartman notes that an attempt to be understood and to communicate genius imposes on itself conditions of closure that remove the indeterminacy of meaning in the emergence of a text. With the emergence of the text, knowledge and understanding are made possible ("all knowledge remains knowledge of a text"). As such, knowledge relies again upon the emergence of a structure, this time (it is true) one of genius's own making. But since knowledge requires the closure of meaning within a text, how

33. Derrida, "White Mythology," 73. For a comparison of Derrida and Ricoeur on metaphor, see Dominick LaCapra, "Who Rules Metaphor? Paul Ricoeur's Theory of Discourse," in LaCapra, *Rethinking Intellectual History: Texts, Contexts, Language* (Ithaca, N.Y.: Cornell University Press, 1983), 118–44.

34. See Geoffrey H. Hartman, *Criticism in the Wilderness* (New Haven, Conn.: Yale University Press, 1980), 269–72.

such a structure emerges cannot itself be known. The principles of change and inventive genius themselves cannot be explained without the emergence of a text by which creativity in metaphoric thought petrifies in dead metaphors. Masterpieces or works of genius serve to codify such principles of closure and, as such, are central in any semiotic account of literary discourse.

In more explicitly semiotic terms, this means that all literature acts as an information system employed for communicative ends, thus binding senders (authors) to receivers (reading publics) by way of messages codified in functional rules.[35] Such rules are shaped not only by forces internal to the system of literature but also by "social facts" that affect the addressees' understanding of and receptivity to literary messages. The text is thus properly understood as a "literary fact," a communication of meaning in different sign-system contexts.[36] Such contexts, most often codified within genres through the work of minor authors, provide readers with the structures of meaning (or, as Maria Corti calls them, "grammars of language") necessary for decoding sign functions of literary works, including masterpieces.

Yet, it is in understanding how masterpieces (e.g., central or classical philosophic texts) function in numerous sign contexts and in numerous times that we find the semiotic account of the emergence of new codes, sets of rules, and syntactical strategies. For semioticians like Corti and for theorists like Hartman, a programmatic overreliance on constructs like "masterpieces," "great writers," "genius," and "literature at its highest level" pinpoints the need to distinguish our "grammar of vision" (the ordinary associations and codes involved in perceiving the world) from our grammar of language codified most obviously in genres or in other strategies emphasizing continuity.[37] Masterpieces transform our grammar of vision by showing how our grammar of language contains fruitful possibilities. Works of genius prod the collective consciousness, disrupting and rearranging syntax (the hierarchy of cultural codifications).

35. See Maria Corti, *An Introduction to Literary Semiotics*, tr. Margherita Bogat and Allen Mandelbaum (Bloomington: Indiana University Press, 1978), 144; and Hawkes, *Structuralism and Semiotics*, 141.

36. See Corti, *Literary Semiotics*, 15–16; and Umberto Eco, *A Theory of Semiotics* (Bloomington: Indiana University Press, 1976), 261–76; 314–18.

37. See Gerald Prince's review of Corti's *Introduction to Literary Semiotics* in *Modern Language Notes* 94 (1979): 868–69.

The masterpiece, however, is designated as such only in virtue of its public resonance; it is originally, Corti notes, an artistic wager.[38] There is no grammar of genius per se; that is, to use Hartman's phrase, no structure mediates the masterpiece aboriginally, since it becomes meaningful, even as disruptive, only within the sign systems of the grammar of language. An unmediated grammar of vision is impossible because its very systematic (grammatical) character ensures its ability to provide meaning in the first place. However original his or her work, the writer is also a reader, a collaborator in the mediation of the generative structure of the text.[39]

In terms of the history of philosophy this third approach allows the historian to acknowledge that his or her interpretation of a source thinker is intended to create a text from which meaning emerges. Unlike in the Derridean historiography, in which no interpretation is necessarily meaningless because the one structure permits all syntactical deviations, in Hartman's case an interpretation is possible only within a "text" or literary fact, a determinate syntactical structure or myth (to use Derrida's expression) mediated by the sign-system collaboration of source thinker and creative historian. A "true" interpretation would rely on the historian's creative, mythic claim to be sharing the same myth (or "unmediated vision") with the source thinker. Changes in interpretations could be accounted for from within a structure; for example, a historian could decide to revise his or her interpretation of Descartes' physics to make it consistent with the historian's understanding of Descartes' remarks on ethics. In such a case, however, the problems mentioned in regard to Ricoeur and Derrida would again come into play.

On the other hand, changes in interpretation could also be accounted for as proto-structural. That is, such change would receive a retroactive designation as a change. No account could be given, however, as to the rationale for the changes, since no syntactical sign system or structure mediates the account of its origins. This lack of an explanation does not argue against this approach to the historiography of philosophy as much as it high-

---

38. See Corti, *Literary Semiotics*, 19, 73–74, 137, 145.
39. See Hartman, "Words, Wish, Worth: Wordsworth," in *Deconstruction and Criticism* (New York: Seabury Press, 1979), 187; and Hartman, *The Unmediated Vision* (New Haven, Conn.: Yale University Press, 1954). Cf. Foucault, *Archaeology of Knowledge*, 112.

lights how the approach argues against any unmediated account of the emergence of interpretive structures. This much, though, can be said: The ways in which a source thinker comes to have novel insights (as unexplicated as they are in this view) are the same as the ways in which a historian comes to interpret a source text in a novel manner, because the interpretation as novel recaptures the disruptive yet intentionally communicative character of the source thinker's activity.

Fourth, the poststructuralist criticism of these three approaches to metaphor and myth could be summarized by pointing out how all three try to explain change in terms of a structure when the emergence of the structure itself is the question at issue. Rather than trying to resolve this question by developing simply another structure containing a category for change, Foucault's negative criticism of structuralist approaches suggests simply not trying to explain change in terms of continuities. "Our reason," he says, "is the difference of discourses, our history the differences of times, our selves the difference of masks. That difference, far from being the forgotten and recovered origin, is this dispersion that we are and make."[40] To treat history as a temporal continuum in which change is explained away in a reduction to perfect continuity exhibits the "transcendental narcissism" of structuralist thinking.[41] Reason and history are, at their core, based on displacement, change, *dis-cursus*. No transcendental phenomenology captures history as a formal category entitled the historical: indeed, the aim of Foucault's archaeology is "to free history from the grip of phenomenology."[42] No proto-time is to be recovered, no interior thought revealed behind the exterior text or practice, no original self to be discovered that will make sense of the temporal flux in terms of structural eternity.

That which is "prediscursive" is not prior to discourse but is rather "an immense density of systematicities, a tight group of multiple relations" within the dimension of discourse.[43] It is the density of such relations, rather than their structured or systematic

40. Foucault, *Archaeology of Knowledge*, 131. For contrasts between Foucault and Derrida, see E. M. Henning, "Archaeology, Deconstruction, and Intellectual History," in *Modern European Intellectual History*, 153–96.

41. Foucault, *Archaeology of Knowledge*, 171, 203. See Mark Poster, "The Future According to Foucault: *The Archaeology of Knowledge* and Intellectual History," in *Modern European Intellectual History*, 140–52.

42. Foucault, *Archaeology of Knowledge*, 117, 122, 203.

43. *Ibid.*, 76.

character, that frustrates the attempt to uncover an interpretation or to decide on a rationality. Rather than resolving irregularities, such a density highlights the multiplicity of contradictions within a "positivity" that retains oppositions within discursive formations.[44] Indeed, the very historicity of discourse depends upon ongoing disruptive escapes from the continuity of discourse: "Contradiction," Foucault notes, "functions throughout discourse as the principle of its historicity."[45] In contrast to the history of ideas, Foucault's archaeological analysis refuses either to reabsorb contradiction within the dialectical unity of discourse itself or to trace the origin of discourse back to extradiscursive (and thus extrahistorical) contradictions. Discourse is thus accessible as history only in terms of internally contradictory strategies.

This enunciative function of disrupting semantical structures without resolving contradictions is what I have, throughout my discussion, referred to as the metaphorical character of language and texts. Metaphor expresses the emergence of novelty, creativity, genesis/genius only by permitting the comparison of discursive practices to retain a historical character. Though Foucault insists that the archaeological analysis of discursive practices does not distinguish acts of genius or creativity from imitative or "regular" practices, such an analysis identifies different discursive formations as historical from within an enunciative field (or "archive").[46] But to say that they are historical (i.e., different, contradictory) is to highlight their novelty or genius from within the same enunciative field. That is, the identification of contradictory discursive practices is itself historical insofar as it embodies the contradictory (historical, generative) character of metaphoric expression. As such, metaphor and myth are not elements within a pattern; they are the indicators of the aboriginal character of a pattern of thought. The radical discontinuities revealed in an archaeology of knowledge display the emergence of new metaphors and myths, philosophies and systems. To refer to them as metaphoric or mythic is simply to point out their irresolvably creative character.

In terms of the history of philosophy, this poststructuralist approach reveals the fact that different interpretations of classical texts arise not in any particular order or based on any particular

---

44. *Ibid.*, 125, 148, 155–56.
45. *Ibid.*, 151.
46. *Ibid.*, 128–30, 143–45.

rationale. Insofar as philosophers or historians of philosophy are
self-consciously aware of themselves as doing something ingenious
or creative, they will generally indicate it by appealing to the
language of myth and metaphor. They do this not because they
use myth and metaphor as ways of making the intelligible easier
to understand, but because myth and metaphor are the ways by
which meaning as accessible in history is established in the first
place. In spite of the tendency to depict nature and the world
of human experience in terms of a determinate structure, a system
of signs, or a taxonomy of classifications, both source thinkers and
historians express (again, sometimes consciously and sometimes
not) the novelty of their insights by turning to metaphor. When
such individuals portray nature as a temple, a labyrinth, a labora-
tory, a language both mathematical and poetic, or a machine,
they display the creative impulse at work.[47] Genius, in short, will
not be denied its appeal to metaphor and myth. Try as they
may, historians of philosophy cannot ignore the predominance of
metaphors in any age aware of the novelty of its genius and the
need to re-create languages to express such insights.

This is not to say that there is no way to understand thinkers
of creative insight apart from their use of specific metaphors.
What it does imply is that their appeal to the vocabulary of metaphor and myth signals structural disruptions of literal discourse.
Insofar as the historian's work is likewise ingenious, he or she
views the writings of source thinkers metaphorically, disrupting
the literal meaning of the text in again making it creative, a new
text. Ingenious interpretation, then, is literal misinterpretation
because ingenuity requires the metaphoric re-constitution of
meanings. Such misinterpretation is not to be avoided, however,
for it is a requirement of the metaphoric character of genius.

In summary, then, the techniques developed by Ricoeur,
Derrida, Hartman, and Foucault reveal not only the metaphoric
character of language but also the implicitly metaphoric character
of the interpretive process by which philosophic texts introduce
novel meanings into philosophic discourse. Specifically, the
historiographer of philosophy can best explain change in interpretations by highlighting the creative (metaphoric, mythic)
character of the reading of any text.

47. See Foucault, *The Order of Things* (New York: Random House, 1970), 57; and
Elizabeth Sewell, *The Human Metaphor* (Notre Dame, Ind.: University of Notre
Dame Press, 1964), 60–71.

The adoption of a poststructuralist approach challenges the assumption that the text has a syntactic structure prior to and apart from its interpretation. The interpretation contributes a structure to the text, actually constituting it as an accessible and meaningful text. Once so constituted within the structure of an interpretation, the text takes on the character of literal discourse: it claims to represent the intent of the author (which intent becomes meaningful only in the interpretation); and alternative interpretations are presented as misinterpretations, since they claim a conflicting literal intent of the author. As long as texts permit contradictory interpretations, though, they contribute to the emergence of meaning as historical. But when texts are permitted only one (literal) interpretation, with all others being misinterpretations, they lose their metaphoric and mythic character. Such a loss undermines the possibility for recapturing a sense of historicity within philosophic historiography.

POSTMODERN HISTORIOGRAPHY AND THE CANON

Recent developments in historiography, particularly in the historiography of philosophy, indicate how both the study of the history of philosophy and the evaluation of the significance of individual thinkers have predominantly reflected the biases of what Foucault calls the Classical Age. Within such a view, and characteristic of much of seventeenth-century philosophic attitudes toward the history of thought, the importance of movements and particular philosophers is judged according to a standard that presumes that philosophy and inquiry in general attempt to represent the world. Furthermore, the classical conceptual framework or episteme considers the history of philosophy as an ongoing attempt to provide an ever-clearer picture or mirror of that reality.[48] Continuity is essential in such a model: Thinkers and movements are judged according to how they refine, respond to, or react against their antecedents.

This classical assumption of the ideal meaning sought in all philosophy ignores or treats as unfortunate encumbrances the rhetorical features of philosophy, such as style and genre.

48. See Foucault, *Order of Things*, 50–71, 303–12; and Richard Rorty, *Philosophy and the Mirror of Nature* (Princeton, N.J.: Princeton University Press, 1979), especially 3, 12, 131–38.

Likewise, it regards movements and individuals who do not fit
into this momentum toward the ideal explanation as peripheral
or unimportant. Thus, insofar as Renaissance philosophy treats
rhetoric itself as prior to and constitutive of logic, it does not
presume an ideal structure behind speech; and so it is treated in
most (i.e., classical) historiography as expendable in the study of
the history of philosophy. The same is true of thinkers who,
either by their writing styles or by their emphasis on proto-
philosophic (mythic, poetic) themes, challenge the assumption
that the task of philosophy is to discover "the truth" behind,
and in spite of, metaphors, aphorisms, dialogic forms, and myths.

To challenge this classical assumption is to challenge the canons
of philosophy by focusing attention on the presuppositions that
elevate Descartes, Leibniz, Locke-Berkeley-Hume, Kant, and Hegel
to a higher status than Pascal, Condillac, Vico, Herder, and
Lessing. Foucault's many references to little-known thinkers
embodies just such a challenge. To presume a thinker unimportant because he or she does not contribute to a certain movement
(for example, to think that Shaftesbury can conveniently be
ignored or should be considered a minor figure because he does
not fit neatly into the "from Locke to Hume" sequence) or to
designate a thinker's work as unphilosophic because of its topic
(for example, Bacon's treatise on mythology *On the Wisdom of the
Ancients* or Hume's *History of England*) uncritically assumes the
propriety of the classical model.

In what follows I would like to indicate not only how this
classical model determines who or what is included in the canons
of philosophy. But I would like also to indicate how shifts away
from such a model would change how we study and appreciate
figures (both "major" and "minor") and movements in the
history of philosophy. The shift in historiographic emphasis from
the classical model to what I will later identify as Romanticist
historiography finds its roots admittedly in the self-critiques of
some of the late-eighteenth- and early-nineteenth-century thinkers
with whom I end this book. The full significance of this transformation, however, appears only gradually, culminating perhaps
in poststructuralist or postmodernist analyses.

Particularly in *The Order of Things* and *The Archaeology of
Knowledge*, Foucault has provided us with hints as to how this
shift might be understood by means of his descriptions of the
epistemes of postclassical (late eighteenth century and later)
thought. Just as Foucault identifies the immediate successor to

representationist thought as ideological thought, so also I would argue that classical historiography is succeeded by the claim that all historiography is ideological. This second stage is characterized, for example, by neo-Kantian or Hegelian ways of determining the canon.

This second approach is followed, in turn, by modernist moves to respect the historicity or facticity of expression as constitutive of meaning. Rhetorical expression becomes the historically significant determinant in showing how meaning is made possible prior to any discussion about truth. Within that kind of historiographic perspective, definite shifts in the canon take place: the Stoics rise to prominence, the Cambridge Platonists eclipse the Cartesians, Coleridge is welcomed into the philosophic fold, and Cassirer's and Heidegger's work on myth and poetry replace analytic philosophy.

As is apparent from the beginning, representation is central to the study of the philosophic canon, for our knowledge of the history of philosophy hinges on how we assume that the recurring reinterpretations of texts attempt to provide supposedly more accurate representations either of the thought of the writer or of the nature of reality. *If* representation is the goal of philosophy, then the history of philosophy is the story of false starts, abortive attempts, and temporary or localized successes in dealing with specific difficulties that remain conceptually the same today.

According to classical or traditional history of philosophy, the mind-body problem or the question of God's existence is the same for Plato, Anselm, Descartes, James, Wittgenstein, or Heidegger. The fact that they write at different times explains why their approaches differ; but (the argument goes) that does not affect the ahistorical character of the issues with which they are concerned. Anthologies with selections on such topics, imaginary conversations among thinkers separated by centuries, and appeals to the history of philosophy to shed light on contemporary philosophic disputes undermine the historical character of philosophy insofar as the problems themselves are not presented as changing, but only their answers.

From the perspective of this representationist form of doing history, changes in philosophic approaches or in interpretations of texts indicate corrections of previous views. The history of philosophy is accordingly defined in terms of possible ways in which topics can be ordered in a taxonomy of identities and differences that specify the character of succession beforehand.

Historical succession appears under the guise of permutations, amplifications, or "logical extensions" of concepts deductively ordered and conveniently proposed by followers, apologists, and adversaries. The emergence of new ideas is explained in terms of structural stresses in prior conceptual frameworks, and philosophies and works that cannot be incorporated into this classical representationist model disappear from the canon or are relegated to antiquarians. In such a view, the work of medieval logicians or Giordano Bruno, for example, can be resurrected only by showing how the problems with which these philosophers are concerned are the same problems with which we currently struggle; it is only unfortunate that these earlier writers speak in ways that confuse or cloud what they want to say about issues we can discuss more perspicuously.

Classical historiography of philosophy, based as it is on the representationist epistemology particularly of seventeenth- and eighteenth-century thinkers, has the ironic effect of excluding from serious philosophic study or curricular attention not only most post-Aristotelian ancient philosophy and almost all medieval philosophy, but also much of early modern philosophy itself. To reinstate medieval philosophy to any significant historical importance within the philosophic canon with the excuse that medieval thinkers had some good ideas on God, evil, logic, or political organization reduces such philosophies to half-baked anticipations of more mature developments. Likewise, works such as the early drafts of Locke's *Essay Concerning Human Understanding* or his *Essays on the Laws of Nature*, Spinoza's *Metaphysical Thoughts*, or the essays, letters, textbooks, and polemical discussions of Montaigne, Suarez and the other Catholic or Protestant scholastics, the Deists, and the whole museum of French and German thinkers from Bayle to the Encyclopaedists—all become peripheral to the central story of rationalism and empiricism struggling toward Kant. Poor Malebranche is thus condemned to be a footnote to Descartes or perhaps an inspiration for Berkeley. But happy is Berkeley's fate, blessed as he is to be the stepping-stone from Locke to Hume, his place in the history of philosophy ensured by the deductive necessity of the representationist structure. Fortunately for him, he committed his youthful thoughts on epistemology to paper in the *Principles of Human Knowledge* and the *Dialogues Between Hylas and Philonous* before he strayed from the truth onto the path of divine semiotics in *Siris*.

Leibniz, though, has always presented a problem for this way of handling the canon. Within his monadology we begin to see the metaphysical and epistemological framework that permits the emergence of reason or meaning as a historical process guided by laws of its own making. For Shaftesbury as well, implicit within understanding both the world and the philosophic mind as dynamic processes are the wealth of associations by which the representor becomes a representor in the first place. In such a view, a proper historian of philosophy recognizes the propriety of his or her selections for the canon in terms of a sympathy or harmony between the passional development of one's own mind and the unpacking of implicit connections among philosophers or their writings. With Leibniz, Shaftesbury, and Burke, the experience of such harmony is the experience of beauty in an act of genius.[49] For the genius of the artist–historian emerges precisely when he or she is able to synchronize the genetic pattern of associations implicit within his or her own monadic constitution with the pattern of genesis expressed in connections in the world (including the world of source thinkers' texts).

After Leibniz the task of much of eighteenth-century philosophy is not so much to describe an external, geometrically ordered world as to reveal the agency of constructive reason as internally teleological. As Foucault has pointed out, this shift from representationist structures to eighteenth-century emphases on anthropological and critical approaches to knowledge transforms the question of the progress of rationality (and thus of history also) into a question of the ideological character of knowledge.[50] That is, for much of the century, meaning can be said to have a history only because history (as knowledge) is representation. For Bayle and Condillac, Voltaire and Diderot, Rousseau and Hume, human interests or passions determine the world as perceived (i.e., they determine "facts"), and knowledge of the world reveals less about an external world than about the biological, psychological, or anthropological character of the representor.[51] Kant's move to stabilize this anthropological tendency only points

49. See Ernst Cassirer, *The Philosophy of the Enlightenment* (1951), tr. Fritz C. A. Koelln and James P. Pettegrove (Princeton, N.J.: Princeton University Press, 1979), 80–89, 121–22, 313–18, 325–31.

50. See especially Foucault, *Order of Things*, ch. 7, "The Limits of Representation."

51. See Cassirer, *Philosophy of the Enlightenment*, 18, 101–7, 220–28.

up all the more how the need to impose order on experiences displaces the world in favor of structural organization. And in our own century Collingwood's claim that historical facts are primarily products of the interests of the historian reappropriates this ideological concentration within a historical a priori.[52]

In Kant and Hegel designation and articulation themselves are represented. That is, the representations are themselves represented in the recognition of the emergence of a literature as such. In this way all representation becomes identified as ideological, and all history of representation (as the history of philosophy) likewise becomes ideological. Since all knowledge (including historical knowledge) is ideological, all designation and articulation can properly be accounted for only in terms of origins (i.e., anthropologically) or in terms of the possibilities of knowledge (i.e., in terms of critical philosophy). This move questions whether metaphysics can any longer represent the world and whether doing history can properly represent the past, for the metaphysical and historical structures of ideology define the positivities that make knowledge possible.

In short, the classical model of historiographic explication attempts to represent eternal structures. The Leibnizian variation on that classical model identifies historiographic genius in the harmony of one's own progression of ideas with the dynamic development of philosophic speculation in order to identify what is truly historical. In the move to ideology and critical philosophy, however, the history of representation is displaced by the representation of history because history as representation has no transcendental grounding apart from designation and articulation. Kantian or Hegelian histories of philosophy thus recount the history of mind because nothing else can have a history. And philosophies or works that do not contribute to that end are accordingly excluded from the canon.

The discursive formation in which historiography becomes ideological itself is succeeded (in Foucault's term) by that of the so-called modern age. The episteme of the modern age reasserts the possibility of a viable metaphysics by redefining metaphysics in terms of the memory of places: What has happened is what is remembered or what is uncovered to perception. No teleology

52. See Robin G. Collingwood, *The Idea of History*, ed. T. M. Knox (Oxford: Oxford University Press, 1956).

restricts the possibilities for discontinuity; only the facticity of the text defines the historical. The organization or internal architecture of language as speech is not representative of something beyond itself, nor is it meaningful as a revelation of the transcendental structures of possible experience. In the modern age the text becomes the historical antecedent of meaning because the juxtaposition of words in language, or of sounds in music, defines history in terms of progressions that only subsequently become meaningful as history.

In revising the canon of the history of philosophy, this modern episteme refocuses attention on the rhetorical and linguistic concerns of philosophic writers and elevates to prominence thinkers and works for whom the metaphoric rather than the literal, the aural rather than the visual, holds sway. Even at the beginning of the eighteenth century, this sensitivity to the figural immediacy of metaphor attracts attention from thinkers who, in classical historiography, work outside the mainstream of empiricism and rationalism. Early on, Vico had identified the etymological surface of language as the locus of meaning. For him the meaning of language resides not in its referential character but in its grammatical structuring of the world along the lines of a grammar of myth and metaphor. Both Herder and Lessing later return to the theme in arguing that meaning and reason emerge in the historical or temporal presentation that is the sensory experience of change itself.[53] And aesthetics, according to both Baumgarten and Goethe, need not go beyond sensory experience for its laws, for aesthetic experience points to nothing beyond or beneath the phenomena.

Just as Herder, Schelling, and Blake turn with fascination to the mythic origins of language as speech and sound, so also Haydn and Mozart attempt to create progressions that only subsequently become systematized or structural. It is the awareness of the boundlessness and the terror associated with not having the guidance of structures within the world or as represented in the mind itself that Burke and Kant identify in terms of the sublime and that Mozart makes explicit in *Don Giovanni* and his *Requiem* Mass. The immediacy of the word or music thus epitomizes the temporal character of the experience in a way that prevents the distancing implicit within the temporal self's contact with painting,

53. See Cassirer, *Philosophy of the Enlightenment*, 230–33, 338–60.

sculpture, or architecture. However, in the process of being caught up in this immediacy of contact, the individual self is displaced by the text, the narration, or the composition, because the verbal or aural no longer needs a self behind the performance in order to give it meaning; its meaning is intertextual.

This loss of the individual self within music and literature also means the loss of access to any authorial intention behind the philosophic text as well as loss of the presence of the self of the historian reading the text. It is this loss of the personality of a preferred historical perspective that lies behind Burke's, Kant's, and Mozart's sense of terror when confronted with the sublime, the mythic, or the proto-philosophic context out of which reason and the canon emerge. The figuration of originative myth in sound (as language and as music)—only hinted at in the sketches of Blake, Goya, Fuseli, and Piranesi—thus replaces both the seventeenth-century model of a deductive and static visual structure and the early-eighteenth-century model of an anthropological teleology of structural representation.

In making these allusions to art in the context of recent historiographic developments, I hope to point out how the canon is likewise affected. The archaeology of the modernist historian of philosophy is no longer guided by preconceptions of limits of philosophic interest. Or more properly stated, the rules of what philosophy is are determined only in the juxtaposition of expressions that attempt to present what is unpresentable prior to the presentation. In Lyotard's words, this amounts to working "without rules in order to formulate the rules of what *will have been done.*"[54] Just as in the case of Shaftesburian or Burkean historiography, in which we might be able to imagine beauty in doing history of philosophy, so in modern historiography we must imagine a sublime history, a history with no teleological, continuous, or imposed movement, no internal dynamism of a constituent consciousness, no narrative structure justifying the juxtaposition either of thinkers arranged in the canon or of works selected for emphasis. Like Bayle in compiling the *Dictionary,* we are free to juxtapose the well known with the obscure, for it is in such ordering that a sense of the historical and of the philosophic emerges upon which the canon is based.

54. Jean-François Lyotard, "Answering the Question: What is Postmodernism?" in *Innovation/Renovation*, ed. Ihab Hassan and Sally Hassan (Madison: University of Wisconsin Press, 1983), 340–41.

My later discussion of Aesopic fables in England embodies just this point. Although it can be characterized as a typical study in literary history, its inclusion in the context of myth and philosophy challenges historiographic strategies that exclude fables from philosophic consideration. But in order to justify their inclusion here in the discussion of myth, I also point out how early modern theorists associate Aesopic fables with classical myths; for the modern revision of the canon depends as much on the persuasive power inherent in the introduction of new candidates as it depends on the provocative character of such suggestions.

Modern historiography invites an explosion of texts, translations, and publication of working drafts (complete with the identification of where erasures, deletions, and reworkings occur), for no preconceived model of what is historically significant or philosophically appropriate exists. Critical editions of texts proliferate in such a climate, not because of a historical interest in determining the mind of the author or the "true" text but because of a recognition that the story of the text shows the history of meaning emerging through historiographic examination.

In the modern age, there is no history of philosophy, only historiography. Thinkers who write as if the text were expendable—preferring to get to the idea or meaning behind the words—now are transformed by their very act of writing in an intertextual network. Descartes' *Meditations* is rescued from its solipsistic context by a reappreciation of the dialogic character of the *Replies and Objections.* Nietzsche's doctrines on playfulness become the editorial principles for deciding whether a remark about forgetting his umbrella is part of the Nietzschean corpus. Wittgenstein's cautions about saying anything regarding the mystical ground metaphorical strategies for reading him and other thinkers. In fact, diaries, interviews, correspondence, stories, jokes, and even laundry lists threaten to violate the pristine isolation of the ahistorical philosophic mind.

These last few remarks about modern historiography of philosophy raise the issue of how "postmodern" historiography is possible. Furthermore, considering my references to Foucault, one might think that my account should conclude on a "poststructural" rather than a "postmodern" note. Even though such a distinction today invites more questions than any simple answer can address, certain themes do emerge in comparing poststructural and postmodern stances.

For example, for the poststructuralist, literary and political activities—because they are self-consciously changing and historical—displace structures of scientific knowledge as bases for discursive determinacy. This emphasis on *praxis* reasserts the aesthetic (specifically visual) sense of *theoria* and thus undermines the divisive polarities of philosophy/literature, truth/poetry, science/rhetoric.[55] While the postmodernist (e.g., Lyotard) cautions against preferring any metanarrative or metadiscourse as the basis of legitimation for knowledge-claims, the poststructuralist (e.g., the later Barthes, the later Foucault, or Baudrillard) identifies, in a marriage of *praxis* and *poesis*, political and literary strategies whereby closure of meaning is temporarily achieved.[56]

Through the appeal to such strategies, poststructuralism highlights those characteristics of metanarrative that permit continued discourse without introducing a metadiscourse to be used to legitimate closures of meaning in terms of some ultimate ground. Poststructuralism overcomes the ahistorical structures of meaning-grounding and legitimation by means of a social, political, and linguistic critique of the foundationalist addiction to patterns of legitimation. The postmodernist goes even further in extending the critique of legitimation back into poststructural invitations to attain some closure within changing, historical patterns.

By choosing to refer to my analysis or overview as postmodern I seek to imply three things:

(1) Historiography of philosophy in the late twentieth century acknowledges its intertextual dependence on classical "modern" (seventeenth- through nineteenth-century) philosophy while recognizing the ruptures in epistemes that are essential to history itself.

(2) Postmodernism identifies a *literature* more readily than does poststructuralism; and it is precisely the literary and rhetorical character of philosophy that is elevated in this reaction to

---

55. Cf. Richard Harland, *Superstructuralism* (New York: Methuen, 1987), 3; and John R. R. Christie, "Introduction: Rhetoric and Writing in Early Modern Philosophy and Science," in *The Figural and the Literal: Problems of Language in the History of Science and Philosophy, 1630–1800*, ed. Andrew E. Benjamin, Geoffrey N. Cantor, and John R. R. Christie (Manchester, Eng.: Manchester University Press, 1987), 2.

56. Cf. Jean-François Lyotard, *The Postmodern Condition*, tr. Geoff Bennington and Brian Massumi (Minneapolis: University of Minnesota Press, 1984), xxii–xxv, 65–67; and James Bohman's introductions to Lyotard and Foucault in *After Philosophy: End or Transformation?* ed. Kenneth Baynes, James Bohman, and Thomas McCarthy (Cambridge: MIT Press, 1985), 67–71, 95–98.

histories of philosophy that regret that philosophers must bury their messages in literary forms such as aphorisms, meditations, dialogues, *summae*, or *quaestiones*. But because poststructuralism treats literary history as a product of literary theory, for purposes of discussing the philosophic canon poststructuralism and postmodernism amount to much the same thing.

(3) Among those "modern" philosophers for whom language and literature are central, the loss of a structure or of a self whose presence could otherwise ameliorate the arbitrary juxtaposition of experiences and texts creates a condition of anguished alienation, in which the loss of the self means the loss of the possibility of history in an anarchic profusion of texts. But in postmodernism there is no anguish because there never was a self to lose or from which to become alienated apart from that found in and as the text.

To put this last point differently, the modern historian of philosophy hopes that his or her account might be recognized as a plausible explanation of the doctrine of the source thinker; the postmodern historian knows there is no source thinker behind the text, only the one who emerges in the reading. In this way Freud, Marx, and Nietzsche (to appropriate Foucault's trio) attempt to escape from being objects of the historian's study by pointing out the self-effacing character of their own works.[57]

In this way as well, the historiography of philosophy displaces the history of philosophy by questioning whether there is anything philosophical to be represented historically apart from that revealed in historiography. For to treat Freud, Marx, or Nietzsche simply as objects of historical study is to ignore their indictments of historical thinking as aboriginally unself-conscious. The beauty—or rather, the sublimity—of postmodern historiography is that it revels in the thought that disagreements, false starts, dead ends, and condemnations to the oblivion of occasional footnote references are precisely the acts of erasure that make possible the development of a canon in the first place. And it is this escape from the anxiety of the historical to the immediacy of mythic, metaphoric, or poetic recharacterizations of the canon that permits the postmodern historiographer to feel blameless in the midst of his or her transgressions.

57. Cf. Foucault, "Nietzsche, Freud, Marx," quoted in Pamela Major-Poetzl, *Michel Foucault's Archaeology of Western Culture* (Chapel Hill: University of North Carolina Press, 1983), 32–35.

CHAPTER ONE

Myth and the Grammar of Discovery in Francis Bacon

BY MEANS OF HIS DOCTRINE of "literate experience"—that is, the experience appropriate for the investigation of nature as a language—Bacon suggests that the appeal to mythic thought contains the key for developing a theory of discovery or a logic of problem solving. His depiction of nature as a book or language involves more than simply an appeal to a suggestive model for interpreting nature. More important, his description of nature as a language regulated by what he calls a "philosophical grammar" (*grammatica philosophica*) is intended to point out how procedures of discovery can be developed by treating nature as a poetic and metaphoric language instead of as a logical, mathematical, or rationally regulated language.[1] Mythic thought provides the context for specifying the prerational and prephilosophic structures upon which a theory of discovery can be based. But in Bacon's view, the success of such a theory depends on a proper understanding both of the kind of poetic language in which nature is written, and of the metaphysical and epistemological features of a mythic approach to nature.

Relying primarily on his *Novum Organum* (1620), *De Augmentis Scientiarum* (1623), and *On the Wisdom of the Ancients* (1609), my remarks highlight three themes in Bacon's treatment of the philosophic function of myth and metaphor. First, the procedure of discovery for Bacon relies on the literary character of both nature and our experience of it: In this sense, Bacon's view parallels claims of Derrida and Ricoeur that metaphors construct the text of the world.[2] Second, mythic and metaphoric writings are especially appropriate for the description of the world as created and yet still resistant to closure of meaning. That is, to

1. On Bacon's reference to this "philosophical grammar," see *De Augmentis Scientiarum* (1623), in *The Works of Francis Bacon*, ed. J. Spedding et al., 7 vols. (London: Longman and Co., 1857–59), 4: 441.
2. See Jacques Derrida, "White Mythology: Metaphor in the Text of Philosophy," tr. F. C. T. Moore, *New Literary History* 6 (1974–75): 70–71; and Paul Ricoeur, "Creativity in Language: Word, Polysemy, Metaphor," *Philosophy Today* 17 (1973): 110–11.

describe the world in mythic terms reveals how the referential meaning or representational claims of any account of the world must remain indeterminate: Closure of meaning is possible only within the domain of the signifying-signified.[3] Third, the linguistic presuppositions that regulate epistemological development and the procedure of discovery are the presuppositions that operate on the prerational level of myth.[4] It is this level to which Bacon's theory of inventive genius and discovery points.

THE LITERARY CHARACTER OF NATURE AND EXPERIENCE

As Michael Polanyi's discussions about the nature of discovery have made clear, at least part (if not all) of an explanation of discovery focuses on the psychological, paraphilosophical, or prephilosophical nature of inventive genius.[5] Bacon recognizes this fact but insists on the possibility of developing a method of discovery more accessible than that permitted by an uninformative appeal simply to the acuteness and strength of what he calls individuals' wits (*ingenia*).[6] His own theory, he notes, provides a method that can guide all intellects and wits in a procedure of inquiry in which discovery in the arts and sciences is raised to the level of a methodic art rather than left to chance.[7]

However, while Bacon does not want to propose an idiosyncratic psychology of discovery, neither does he want to suggest that a deductive approach holds promise for a "logic of discovery."[8] Intent on providing an alternative to the Ramist doctrine that

3. See Geoffrey H. Hartman, *The Fate of Reading* (Chicago: University of Chicago Press, 1975), 226–27; and Hartman, *Criticism in the Wilderness* (New Haven, Conn.: Yale University Press, 1980), 269–71. Also see Michael Polanyi and Harry Prosch, *Meaning* (Chicago: University of Chicago Press, 1975), 61.

4. See Elizabeth Sewell, *The Orphic Voice: Poetry and Natural History* (New York: Harper and Row, 1971), 20.

5. See Michael Polanyi, *Personal Knowledge* (Chicago: University of Chicago Press, 1958); and Richard J. Blackwell, "Scientific Discovery and the Laws of Logic," *New Scholasticism* 50 (1976): 333–44.

6. See *Novum Organum* (1620), in *Works*, 4: 19, 62–63.

7. *Ibid.*, 109; and *De Augmentis*, in *Works*, 4: 408–10.

8. Karl Wallace, *Francis Bacon on the Nature of Man* (Urbana: University of Illinois Press, 1967), 6, and James Stephens, *Francis Bacon and the Style of Science* (Chicago: University of Chicago Press, 1975), 56, speak of Bacon's "psychology of discovery"; Lisa Jardine, *Francis Bacon: Discovery and the Art of Discourse* (Cambridge: Cambridge University Press, 1974), 3, refers to Bacon's "logic of scientific discovery."

inventive discovery is simply a rhetorical method of recalling already received or agreed-upon assumptions, Bacon argues that true discovery or invention (*inventio*) provides new knowledge and that his method indicates the order of such inventive investigation.[9]

This method, which Bacon calls the "anticipation of the mind" (*anticipatio mentis*), employs models of inquiry, not as illustrations or exemplifications of some truth already known, but as the specific guides for the expansion of knowledge itself.[10] These models are "the actual types and structures [*plasmata*], by which the entire process of the mind and the whole fabric and order of invention from the beginning to the end, in certain subjects, and those various and remarkable, should be set as it were before the eyes."[11] Such models anticipate the process of the mind's discovery of new things by laying out the specific order or structure, not of nature per se, but of the movement of thought specifically appropriate for invention.

Logical derivations, continued research and meditation, and agitation of the mind to produce inspiration all are ineffective ways of discovery. What we need, Bacon suggests, is a "thread through the labyrinth" (*filum labyrinthi*) of nature by which we guide our experience using clues to regulate our tracking of the "footsteps or little signs of nature" (*naturae vestigia aut signacula*).[12] In our attempt to understand the totality of things—that is, in our "hunt of Pan, or Nature"—we *read* the signs in nature and detect the footprints of the things of nature in language.[13] These signs serve as the clues that point to, but are not identical with, the axioms by which nature is to be interpreted and ordered in his New Organon. Once we have the axioms from which we can deduce particular experiments, we will be able (in Bacon's view) to discover new things about nature. Bacon, though, does not foresee any quick completion of the project of generating axioms. He suggests that, even when

9. *Novum Organum*, in *Works*, 4: 24, 31, 42, 80.
10. *Ibid.*, 42.
11. *Ibid.*, 31.
12. *Thoughts and Conclusions* (1607–9), cited in Benjamin Farrington, *The Philosophy of Francis Bacon: An Essay on Its Development from 1603 to 1609* (Liverpool, Eng.: Liverpool University Press, 1964), 73, 90–92, 97, 101; see *Works*, 3: 591, 608–10, 615, 620. Also see *De Augmentis*, in *Works*, 4: 339; and *Novum Organum*, in *Works*, 4: 63–64.
13. See *De Augmentis*, in *Works*, 4: 413, 441; *On The Wisdom of the Ancients* (1609), in *Works*, 6: 711; and the *Advancement of Learning* (1605), in *Works*, 3: 401.

axioms are formulated, the procedure for the inventive discovery of knowledge (even in mathematics) cannot be equated with its method of presentation. Just as the formulation of axioms must be guided by clues that suggest how aspects of experience should be collected and ordered, so the interpretation of nature must be the product of a selection of ways in which even formal deductive structures are to be organized.[14]

For Bacon there are thus three ways of speaking about discovery: first, in terms of rhetorical recall or quick-witted invention (which, according to Bacon, is not really discovery at all because it reveals nothing new); second, in terms of particular revelations deduced from axioms upon which a truly philosophic interpretation of nature is based; and third, in terms of the imaginative extension of experimental knowledge through metaphorical or analogous translation of the knowledge gained in one art or science into another. This third method of discovery, which he calls "literate experience, or the hunt of Pan" (*literata experientia, sive venatio Panis*), is essential both for the discovery of new particulars that are as yet unincorporated into an axiomatic explanation and for the selection of those experiences that guide the formulation of the axioms from which numerous other discoveries will follow.[15] As such, even though literate experience is "ingenious or sagacious" rather than immediately philosophic ("rather a sagacity and a kind of hunting by scent, than a science"), it acts as the basis for legitimate philosophic discoveries (i.e., those discoveries that are based on the axiomatically grounded "interpretation of nature").[16]

Literate Experience must hardly be esteemed an art or a part of philosophy, but rather a kind of sagacity; whence likewise (borrowing the name from the fable) I sometimes call it the Hunt of Pan. Nevertheless just as a man may proceed on his path in three ways: he may grope his way for himself in the dark; he may be led by the hand of another, without himself seeing anything; or lastly, he may get a light, and so direct his steps; in like manner when a man tries all kinds of experimenting, it is as if he were led by the hand; and this is what I mean by Literate Experience. For the light itself, which was the third way, is to be sought from the Interpretation of Nature, or the New Organon. Literate Experience, or the Hunt of Pan, treats of the methods of experimenting. . . . The method of experimenting proceeds

14. *Valerius Terminus* (1603), in *Works*, 3: 248.
15. See *De Augmentis*, in *Works*, 4: 413; *Novum Organum*, in *Works*, 3: 96.
16. *De Augmentis*, in *Works*, 4: 366, 406, 421.

principally either by the Variation, or the Production, or the Translation, or the Inversion, or the Compulsion, or the Application, or the Conjunction, or finally the Chances, of experiment. None of these however extend so far as to the invention of any axiom. For all transition from experiments to axioms, or from axioms to experiments, belongs to that other part, relating to the New Organon.[17]

Literate experience thus indicates which types of questions are fruitful and serves accordingly, in Bacon's eyes, as the "half-knowledge" of prudent or guided interrogation.[18]

By means of his conception of literate experience Bacon is able to show how the imaginative ingenuity and poetic wisdom characteristic of mythic writings embody features of metaphoric thinking essential for a theory of discovery. In order to be able to discover new things by means of literate experience, the mind (Bacon argues) must be able to transfer the knowledge it gains in certain experiences to other types of experience. Such a *translatio* or *meta-phor* is justified only insofar as nature itself exhibits or is seen as exhibiting a structure that is primarily linguistic rather than geometrical or logical. Though a geometrical and deductive method can serve as the model upon which the interpretation of nature is developed, it does not suggest the same fruitful possibilities for communication and shared communal investigation opened up by a linguistic model that permits metaphorical crossovers among rationally distinct categories.

In order to encourage new discoveries and new ways of thinking about our experience, Bacon balances the Galilean move toward a mathematical depiction of nature with an insistence on the literary (especially poetic) character both of our experience of nature and of nature itself. Experience, he notes, must be made literate, for no course of inventive discovery can be satisfactory except insofar as it can be written or expressed in the linguistic forms that characterize that "book of God's works" or "volume of Creation," nature itself.[19] "Hitherto," he complains, "more has been done in the matter of invention from the standpoint of meditation than from that of writing; and experience has not yet been made literate. No new course of invention can be satisfactory unless it be carried on from the standpoint of writing.

17. *Ibid.*, 413.
18. *Ibid.*, 423. See Paolo Rossi, *Francis Bacon: From Magic to Science*, tr. Sacha Rabinovitch (Chicago: University of Chicago Press, 1968), 154.
19. *Advancement*, in *Works*, 3: 268.

But when this is brought into use, better things may be hoped from experience finally made literate."[20] Nature itself is made more accessible to men once it is seen as embodying features of metaphor, which simply do not survive in the attempt to explain nature using a mathematical or purely rational method. According to Bacon, men need to

unroll the volume of Creation, to linger and meditate therein, and with minds washed clean from opinions to study it in purity and integrity. For this is that lecture and language [*sermo et lingua*] which went forth into all lands, and did not incur the confusion of Babel; this should men study to be perfect in, and becoming again as little children condescend to take the alphabet of it into their hands, and spare no pains to search and unravel the interpretation thereof.[21]

To treat nature as a metaphoric language regulated by the "philosophical grammar" of the poet and mythmaker rather than that of the logician and the mathematician opens thinkers up to the possibilities of accounting for discovery in prerational, though epistemologically justifiable, ways. The poet or philosophical grammarian is not limited in his or her movement of thought by a "literary grammar" or "literal grammar" (*grammatica literaria*) whose structure is controlled by an emphasis on the logical relationships (or "analogy") of words to one another. Rather, he or she develops his or her inquiry using that philosophical grammar which treats of "the analogy between words and things, or reason" (*analogiam inter verba et res, sive rationem*).[22] The analogy between spoken or written language and the language of nature is what is meant by reason, and (Bacon points out) it is the task of philosophy to clarify the implications of the analogy upon which this philosophical grammar is based. When the grammar of the poets is eliminated as a proper concern and tool of philosophy (as occurred in classical Greek philosophy and rational science), the discovery of useful works comes to an end.[23] Socrates broke the chain that linked arts and sciences to one another and that permitted the mutually interactive extension

20. *Novum Organum*, in *Works*, 4: 96.
21. *The History of Winds* (1622), in *Works*, 5: 132–33. On the metaphors of nature, see Sewell, *The Human Metaphor* (Notre Dame, Ind.: University of Notre Dame Press, 1964), 60–69; and Margreta de Grazia, "The Secularization of Language in the Seventeenth Century," *Journal of the History of Ideas* 41 (1980): 319–29.
22. See *De Augmentis*, in *Works*, 4: 406, 441; *Advancement*, in *Works*, 3: 401.
23. *Novum Organum*, in *Works*, 4: 83.

of knowledge or "Circle Learning" characteristic of the "universal
Sapience and knowledge both of matter and words" taught by the
poets and by the rhetorically sensitive early Greek thinkers:
"Socrates divorced them [matter and words] and withdrew philosophy and left rhetoric by itself, which by that destitution became
but a barren and unnoble science."[24]

Nevertheless I that hold it for a great impediment towards the
advancement and further invention of knowledge, that particular arts
and sciences have been disincorporated from general knowledge, do not
understand one and the same thing which Cicero's discourse and the
note and conceit of the Grecians in their word *Circle Learning* do intend.
For I mean not that use which one science hath of another or orna-
ment or help in practice, as the orator hath knowledge of affections for
moving, or as military science may have use of geometry for fortifica-
tions: but I mean it directly of that use by way of supply of light and
information which the particulars and instances of one science do yield
and present for the framing and correction of the axioms of another
science in their very truth and notion.[25]

The relationships of words to things and of rhetoric to philosophy
(best embodied in the mythically responsive thought of the
ancient Greeks) are, in short, not ones of ornamentation, but are
the integral bases for wisdom and for the possibility of discovery.
    Discoveries in nature by means of literate experience are possi-
ble because literate experience begins with the assumption that
the elements of nature, like those of language, are tied to one
another through imagery, analogy, imaginative variation, and
even metaphorical contradictions of logical orders and structures.
In literate experience inventive discoveries still occur through the
use of models that direct inquiry. However, literate experience
succeeds in providing an art of inventive discovery where logic
and rational science do not because literate experience reinstates
that prephilosophic and prerational frame of mind in which
mythic expression reveals some truth, and yet cautions against
limiting the import or application of the revelation as truth.
    Although the classical myths do not properly describe the
structure of nature as finally revealed in the axiomatic account
that Bacon will identify as the "interpretation of nature," they do
serve as the guiding threads or models of inquiry within his
method of discovery. They serve as the models of inquiry in that

    24. *Valerius Terminus*, in *Works*, 3: 228.
    25. *Ibid.*, 228–29.

process whereby we recognize the literary character of nature, the analogy between words and things that defines or establishes the rational (*ratio*). To the extent that "words are the footprints [*vestigia*] of reason," the very names of some mythological characters reveal the conformity of mythic language with the nature of reality and point out the way in which myths identify and make determinate those things they signify.

Due to my being enamored with the reverence of antiquity, or because in some fables, both in their very structure and in the propriety of the names by which the persons or actors in them are distinguished and labeled, I find a conformity and connection with the thing signified, so close and so evident, that one cannot help believing such a signification to have been designed and thought out from the beginning and purposely shadowed out. . . . Metis, Jupiter's wife, plainly means counsel; Typhon, swelling; Pan, the universe; Nemesis, revenge; and the like.[26]

The very language of the myths thus suggests that they be treated as models or guides within a method of discovery, not only because their explicit linguistic ties to the realities they signify alert us to the linguistic procedures that guide the process of discovery in coming to understand nature, but also because myths both appeal widely and are not limited by dictates of rational science or logic in their explanatory abilities.   (As an indication of this wide appeal, I need only note that Bacon's own 1609 collection of mythological interpretations, *On the Wisdom of the Ancients*, went through nine editions in Latin, five in English, two in French, and one in German in the seventeenth century alone—a popularity vastly eclipsing his more commonly recognized philosophic works.)[27]

Essential to Bacon's enterprise of developing a new theory of discovery is the recognition that no insight into nature becomes a discovery until it gains the support of popular or critical acceptance.   It is important that such insights be presented through some form of expression, like myth or metaphor, that appeals to fellow researchers both by explaining features of such insights and by revealing potential avenues of investigation opened up through the use of the poetic language of myth. Such an appeal tests the degree to which an insight is communicable and is able to tap into the resonances between the communicative system needed for communal philosophic or scientific

26. *De Augmentis*, in *Works*, 4: 441; *Wisdom*, in *Works*, 6: 696–97.
27. See Farrington, *Philosophy of Francis Bacon*, 121.

discovery and the linguistic or communicative basis of the order of nature itself.

No course of inventive discovery is thus capable of success except in linguistic terms for two reasons: first, a communal, communicative effort among researchers is essential if Bacon's dream of a New Organon is to be achieved; and second, the key for understanding the book of nature lies in considering it seriously as a metaphor, a language, or a mythic construct, in just such a way that a literate explication becomes the single most promising method permitting discovery. To learn the language of nature in terms of discovery is to open nature up to translation into an axiomatically derivative interpretation (i.e., the "interpretation of nature" of the New Organon). Such a *translatio* of the language of nature is accomplished through the comparative and metaphorical examination of different arts or areas of experience. Myth and metaphor exhibit a language (or more precisely, a grammar) that makes discovery in nature possible because they assume a method of writing or speaking appropriate to the literate experience underlying the procedure of discovery. Literate experience thus implies both a literature (viz., the "book of nature") and a way of speaking and writing appropriate for it (viz., myth).[28]

EPISTEMOLOGICAL REGULATION WITHIN MYTH

Bacon himself acknowledges at the outset of his *Wisdom of the Ancients* that many readers will think his exposition of classical myths and mythic figures is simply a pleasant amusement, an imaginative exercise of reading various hidden meanings into the myths of the ancients. "I confess," he notes, "this is something I could do if I had a mind to, so that I might intermix these things with more arduous contemplations in order to make more pleasurable either my own meditations or the reading of others."[29] As he suggests, he could use commentary on myths (or what he calls fables) simply as a vehicle to express more serious philosophic observations in an appealing way—in which case, his appeal to fabular or mythic concerns would be little more than a rhetorical or literary device.[30] But Bacon refuses to

28. *Novum Organum*, in *Works*, 4: 31.
29. *Wisdom*, in *Works*, 6: 695.
30. Cf. Farrington, *Philosophy of Francis Bacon*, 121.

admit that his discussion of the myths is an ornamental, rhetorical, or extraphilosophic exercise. Though others have used commentary on the myths to propose their own positions, investing them with the solemnity of antiquity and thereby hoping to lend to their positions a certain credibility, Bacon resolves to avoid such an imposture and chooses to rely on what he calls the evidence of facts and the obvious conformity or connection of fabular names and descriptions with the things he says they signify.[31]

As to the questions of whether ancient authors actually shrouded philosophic mysteries in the cloak of entertaining and even illustrative fables or myths, Bacon professes only a guarded opinion. "Upon the whole I conclude with this: the wisdom of the primitive ages was either great or fortuitous; great, if they knew what they were doing and invented the figure to indicate the meaning; fortuitous, if without meaning or intending it they fell upon matter which gives occasion to such worthy contemplations. My own pains, if there be any help in them, I shall think well bestowed either way: I shall be throwing light either upon antiquity or upon nature itself."[32]

In regard to matters relating to religion and divinity, he notes, the myth or fable form serves as a useful restraint on direct and literal discourse while still providing some means by which to relate matters of divinity and humanity: "Religion," he says, "delights in such veils and shadows, so that whoever removes them almost prevents commerce between things divine and human."[33] But Bacon's main concern in discussing the myths of the ancients is not how the myths provide access to divine wisdom (indeed, even within his own commentaries on the myths of Acteon and Pentheus, and of Prometheus, he warns against their use in this way). Rather, he argues, the use of myths shows something about the development and transmission of human wisdom that would otherwise be overlooked: namely, that the generation of new ways of looking at nature and of communica-

---

31. See Bacon, *Thoughts and Conclusions*, as translated in Farrington, *Philosophy of Francis Bacon*, 86–87 (Latin original in *Works*, 3: 604–5); *The Refutation of Philosophies* (1608), translated in Farrington, *Philosophy of Francis Bacon*, 120–21 (also in *Works*, 3: 574); *Advancement*, in *Works*, 3: 345; *Novum Organum*, in *Works*, 4: 108; and *De Augmentis*, in *Works*, 4: 317.

32. *Wisdom*, in *Works*, 6: 698–99.

33. *Ibid.*, 696; and *Advancement*, in *Works*, 3: 266–68.

ting such discoveries depends on the fruitful use of fables, parables, or (what today we might call) hypothetical models.

At issue for Bacon is not whether the ancients actually attained the insights of natural philosophy and the moral and civil wisdom that he discerns in the myths he treats. Our task, he notes, is not so much to second-guess the intentions or assumptions of the mythmakers as it is to understand how myths can be used to expand human wisdom. "For no learned man, except one of mediocre education, will object to the reception of such a use as something important and serious, free from all vanity, and exceedingly profitable and even necessary to the sciences."[34] What is necessary to the sciences is not whether the ancients actually believed what Bacon sees in the myths. What is necessary is that investigators recognize that, just as in early times when initial discoveries were made and human understandings were incapable of subtleties except in regard to sense, so in Bacon's own time to make new discoveries and explanations requires an appeal to myths, fables, parables, and similes: "Even now," he writes, "if anyone wants to throw new light on any subject into men's minds, and that without offense or harshness, he must still take the same way and resort to the aid of similitudes."[35]

For example, by examining various features of the myths associated with Pan (or Nature), Proteus (or Matter), Coelum (or the Origin of Things), and Cupid (or the Atom), Bacon argues that from a scientific perspective the most promising approach to questions of the nature of reality appears to lie in Democritean atomism. However, because the myths are but the "oracles of sense," such accounts need to be corrected in light of divine revelation.[36] Bacon's treatments of ancient myths (e.g., those discussing Dionysus, Nemesis, the Sirens, the Cyclops, the river Styx, and Metis) point up ways of addressing moral, psychological, or political questions and indicate Bacon's approval of the attempt to keep such topics within the tentative and exploratory contexts of mythic thought.

34. *Wisdom*, in *Works*, 6: 698. In Bacon's revisions of *Wisdom*, left uncompleted at his death, he tones down this claim, noting that such a use of myths is only sometimes (*quandoque*) necessary to the sciences—presumably in generating and communicating new discoveries, as opposed to collecting data and performing experiments to test old discoveries.

35. *Ibid.*; and *Advancement*, in *Works*, 3: 406–7.

36. *Wisdom*, in *Works*, 6: 725.

Other myths—for example, those associated with "Orpheus, or Philosophy," "Atalanta, or Profit," and "Prometheus, or the State of Man"—point to the development of a sensitivity to philosophic method, to restraint in inquiry, and to the need for communal investigation. Such myths provide Bacon with the opportunity to make metalevel observations on the philosophic enterprise itself—all within the linguistically justifiable context of mythic writing (i.e., within the context of a syntactic and semantic framework different from, and presupposed by, strictly logical or philosophic writings).

In this way, mythic thought exhibits the context in which specifically philosophic claims can then be made meaningful within, and be regulated by, the narrower domain of logic. "True philosophy echoes most faithfully the voice of the world itself, and is written as it were from the world's own dictation."[37] Prior to the philosophically meaningful expression of what the world is, there is another, sense-bound language by means of which the world can be said to "speak." Or stated in another way, the world is originally experienced as having a linguistic character or grammar of its own; it is the task of true philosophy to incorporate the mythic characteristics underlying philosophic meaning without completely dispensing with them. Mythic or metaphoric writing and thought, then, cannot be superseded by true philosophy because such writing and thought are recognized within true philosophy as providing the context for rationality or meaning (*ratio*).

In trying to show how his examination of the myths is really an attempt to retrieve man's power of creative insight, Bacon goes beyond discussing the myths (and similitudes in general) only as communication devices intended to illustrate by resemblances and examples what is already known. He wants to argue that the creative source and original power of insight that the thinkers of primeval (preclassical) antiquity communicated to the classical poets is still available to modern thinkers; but it is accessible to the moderns only on the same linguistic (i.e., mythic) basis. The very invention of knowledge, beyond its mere communication, depends on the use of similitudes.[38]

For Bacon, man's understanding of the fundamental nature of the world and of man himself is always to be put within the context of the regulation of an ultimately irresolvable fabular or

---

37. *Ibid.*, 714.
38. *Valerius Terminus*, in *Works*, 3: 218.

mythic mode.   As tentative yet foundational explorations, myths
provide Bacon with the opportunity of a formal strategy to
expand philosophical speculation.   Such an extension of inquiry
occurs, for example, in his discussion of the nature of matter in
"Cupid, or the Atom."   But Bacon makes sure to keep this kind
of inquiry both from threatening the nonfabular aspects of
natural science and from pushing philosophy into the examination
of truths concerning the divine source of, or motive force behind,
matter.

They say that Love [Cupid] was the most ancient of all the gods. . . .
This Love is introduced without any parent at all; only, that some say he
was an egg of Night. . . . The fable relates to the cradle and infancy of
nature, and pierces deep.   This Love I understand to be the appetite or
instinct of primal matter; or to speak more plainly, *the natural motion of
the atom*; which is indeed the original and unique force that constitutes
and fashions all things out of matter.   Now this is entirely without
parent; that is, without cause.   For the cause is as it were parent of the
effect; and of this virtue there can be no cause in nature (God always
excepted):   there being nothing before it, therefore no efficient; nor
anything more original in nature, therefore neither kind nor form.
Whatever it be therefore, it is a thing positive and inexplicable.   And
even if it were possible to know the method and process of it, yet to
know it by way of cause is not possible; it being, next to God, the cause
of causes—itself without cause.   That the method even of its operation
should be ever brought within the range and comprehension of human
inquiry, is hardly perhaps to be hoped; with good reason therefore it is
represented as an egg hatched by night. . . . For the summary law of
nature, that impulse of desire impressed by God upon the primary
particles of matter which makes them come together, and which by
repetition and multiplication produces all the variety of nature, is a
thing which mortal thought may glance at but can hardly take in.[39]

Only within mythic thought and writing are we able to consider
that which permits and grounds causal interactions in nature.
Myth points beyond the formal distinctions addressed in logic
and beyond the physical relationships of the determinate objects
addressed in natural philosophy.   Mortal thought only points to
the divine, aboriginal truths addressed in myth without encompassing them or incorporating them into a rational framework.
In this way, Bacon argues that it is through myth that philosophers
are able to respect the mysteries of nature while recognizing the

39. *Wisdom*, in *Works*, 6: 729–30.

tentative progress of communal human attempts to understand those mysteries.

Just as the examination of nature begins by relying on sense, so the sensible imagery of mythic writing permits explorations of nature in contexts that historically antedate argumentative reasoning. The task with which Bacon presents himself is to describe how a new philosophy is possible, how a renovation of thought about nature and man can be accomplished, and how others might be persuaded to understand those mysteries.

In order to accomplish this task, Bacon turns to the examination of the only period of human history in which such an affirmation of creative human power appears—namely, the state of man before the Fall. Man's complete knowledge of nature (and thus his sovereignty and power over it) before the Fall was based on his immediate contact with nature, that is, on his knowledge of creatures in a way that is unmediated by the abstractions of rational thought or argumentation. As Bacon notes in his *Valerius Terminus* (1603), "Whensoever [man] shall be able to call the creatures by their true names he shall again command them."[40] As authors of each creature's name, men (in the person of Adam) attain a certainty guaranteed by the unity of things of sense and things of intellect.

As Walter Benjamin notes, such a move to a stance prior to the strictly philosophical recaptures the spirit of the mythic poets (whom Plato banished from his Republic) as a spirit eminently and foundationally in accord with philosophic insight at its source: "In philosophical contemplation, the idea is released from the heart of reality as the word, reclaiming its name-giving rights. Ultimately, however, this is not the attitude of Plato but the attitude of Adam, the father of the human race and the father of philosophy. Adam's action of naming things is so far removed from play or caprice that it actually confirms the state of paradise as a state in which there is as yet no need to struggle with the communicative significance of words."[41] To know the true names of things undercuts the very need to struggle with the communicative significance of words because the Adamic activity of naming is not one of discovering some truth signified by language but rather is one of inventing (*invenire*) or constituting the meaning of the referent. The name acts as a

40. In *Works*, 3: 222; *Novum Organum*, in *Works*, 4: 20.
41. Walter Benjamin, *The Origin of German Tragic Drama*, tr. John Osborne (London: New Left Books, 1977), 37.

symbol by which some aspect of reality becomes an object for our experience.[42]

Recapturing this unity of things and words, of sense and intellect, of nature and man, permits Bacon to say in the *Novum Organum* that his method of discovery in the sciences places all *ingenia* (creative and natural wits or minds) and intellects on the same level.[43] That is, because mythic and parabolic writing exposes the original structure and character of intellectual things as fundamentally and regulatively tied to sense, the recognition of the human ability to make myths or fables serves to recall man's "ingenious" (and ingenuous, natural) certainty about his discoveries in nature.[44]

Bacon's attraction to the explication of the myths of the ancients is not based on the assumption that he has been able to penetrate and establish certain knowledge concerning topics with which the mysteries deal. Indeed, despite his ability to provide philosophic interpretations of the myths, Bacon refuses to dissociate his remarks from their generative fabular or mythic settings. Here, the methodological retrieval of mythic assumptions serves to show how mythic or fabular philosophy controls the tendencies either toward revealing or toward obscuring truths generated within careful philosophic investigations. The mythic contexts out of which such reflections develop and to which such reflections continue to remain tied reveal those questions and approaches that offer either the promise of some future communal resolution or the prospect of disappointment associated with inquiries into matters beyond the limits of foreseeable human comprehension. In this sense, Bacon's appeal to myths draws the curtain around certain topics, such as (1) God's causal relationship to the sensible world, (2) the need to resist the temptation to specify moral distinctions and methodological procedures in philosophy beyond rough outlines, and (3) general political questions regarding domestic and foreign policies.

42. See Karl R. Wallace, "Aspects of Modern Rhetoric in Francis Bacon," *Quarterly Journal of Speech* 42 (1956): 401–2. Cf. Ernst Cassirer, *Language and Myth*, tr. Susanne Langer (New York: Dover, 1946), 8, 57; and Susanne K. Langer, *Philosophical Sketches* (Baltimore, Md.: Johns Hopkins University Press, 1962), 157–60.

43. *Novum Organum*, in *Works*, 4: 62–63, 109.

44. *De Augmentis*, in *Works*, 4: 315. On "ingenious/ingenuous," see Robert A. Greene, "Whichcote, Wilkins, 'Ingenuity,' and the Reasonableness of Christianity," *Journal of the History of Ideas* 42 (1981): 227–52.

The need to resist the temptation to specify procedures is epitomized in the myths of Icarus and of Scylla and Charybdis. "The principle of moderation in Morals," Bacon comments, "is represented by the ancients in the path which Icarus was directed to take through the air. . . . In every knowledge and science, and in the rules and axioms appertaining to them, a mean must be kept between too many distinctions and too much generality, between the rocks of the one and the whirlpools of the other. For these two are notorious for the shipwreck of wits and arts."[45] By drawing such a curtain, Bacon intends not to obscure truths already known (and to be protected from vulgar eyes) but rather to provide the cautionary foundations from which to suggest further philosophic explorations.

This characteristic of mythic thinking does not assume that the fabulist appeals to fables in order to present some already discerned truths in ways that make such truths palatable or accessible because of their appearances in fabular or mythic contexts. Bacon's commentary on mythmaking is an attempt not so much to conceal some esoteric doctrine from popular comprehension as it is to point to the possibility of philosophic renovation through the agency of ingenium. The recognition of his wit, ingenuity, or ability to cognize new relationships justifies for Bacon his confidence in his own enterprise of philosophic innovation. That enterprise incorporates as a central and self-transcending feature the methodic insistence on the place of fabular, mythic, or, more generally, poetic insight as a constant spur to philosophic discovery.

Nonmythic or deductive systems of thought and reason itself (with its implicit distinction between words and objects, and between language and truth) become idols so enamored by the mind that the mind abnegates the aboriginal power by which it develops rational structures of thought in the first place.[46] The return to mythic modes of thought is intended to reassert this power of creative insight possessed by the human mind.

Accordingly, Bacon proposes that we imagine remote antiquity before the Fall as the setting appropriately parallel to that required for understanding the assumptions and possibilities of his own reworking of philosophy. In such a setting man is unmediatedly in control of nature in virtue of the natural

45. *Wisdom*, in *Works*, 6: 754–55.
46. See *Novum Organum*, in *Works*, 4: 62–66.

(ingenuous) certainty of that which he himself names. Discovery
and creation come together in the inventive practice of metaphor
and translation, in that phenomena or methods in one art or
science are recognized (ingeniously) as comparable to those of
other arts or sciences in virtue of the unity of sensible nature.
"And these [comparable phenomena or methods] are no allusions
but direct communities, the same delights of the mind being to
be found not only in music, rhetoric, but in moral philosophy,
policy, and other knowledges, and that obscure in the one, which
is more apparent in the other, yea and that discovered in the
one which is not found at all in the other, and so one science
greatly aiding to the invention and augmentation of another."[47]
Discovery, understood as scientific creativity, links man back to
God as a new creator: "Discoveries are as it were new creations,
and imitations of God's works."[48]   As in the creation epics,
man's creativity is not *ex nihilo* but is rather one of ordering and
subduing some primal chaos into a world.   And though the act
of naming begins the process out of which collective or abstract
ideas develop (thus distancing man from his creative control of
nature), just such an act, conscientiously reintegrated by sensitive
thinkers, serves to ensure his epistemological access to nature.

   In short, Bacon wants to show how the belief in the possibility
of radically new conclusions and discoveries about the world is
justified and how a method of discovery might be described.
Because myths unite both sense and intellect, the appeal to mythmaking as a feature in a method of discovery is more promising
than that afforded by relying solely on human reason.

THE PRERATIONAL CHARACTER OF DISCOVERY

   By means of the appeal to the myths of the ancients, Bacon
hopes to point out the type of epistemological presuppositions
necessary for philosophic discovery.   These presuppositions do
not reject reason as much as they attempt to bring to light the

   47. *Valerius Terminus*, in *Works*, 3: 230; also see 228–30, as well as *Advancement*, in
Works, 3: 310, 406.
   48. *Novum Organum*, in *Works*, 4: 113.   See Elizabeth Sewell, "Bacon, Vico,
Coleridge, and the Poetic Method," in *Giambattista Vico: An International Symposium*,
ed. Giorgio Tagliacozzo and Hayden V. White (Baltimore, Md.: Johns Hopkins
University Press, 1969), 130.

aboriginal context out of which reason and philosophical argumentation develop.

Philosophy, particularly as it comes to be identified by Greek thinkers, attempts to remove reason from its ties to sensible things, whereas myth reabsorbs all generalization and abstraction into concrete particulars. In Greek philosophy concrete particulars serve reason only as examples. In myth (i.e., constitutive rhetoric) they are the sources of the imaginative expansion of thought because they are not simply instantiations of abstract universals but are individuals made real by their ties (formal, accidental, and imaginative) to all other things. Literate experience has to penetrate behind reason in order to disclose possibilities for discovery that arise in virtue of the fact that sensible individuals are much more suited to a grammar employing metaphor than are classes, universals, or abstractions. Fables or parables, Bacon notes, "now and at all times do retain much life and vigour, because reason cannot be so sensible, nor examples so fit."[49] In other words, reason is not responsive enough to the inventive possibilities of sense-bound experience nor are examples or instantiations appropriate enough for imaginative thinking that they can substitute for the mythopoetic and prephilosophic methods of discovery.[50]

These methods of discovery are exhibited most obviously for Bacon in a mythic setting. That is, they appear most obviously in an explicitly poetic and imaginative setting in which nature is viewed not only as if it were structured like language (i.e., in terms of a temporarily useful analogy or model easily thrown off once we have penetrated to axioms upon which the interpretation of nature is to be grounded), but also as an authentic creation of imaginative (mythic) language. This latter point indicates how for Bacon the linguistic metaphor is not only to be understood as a helpful clue in formulating new experiments and organizing experimental results about nature on the basis of a "philosophic grammar" that emphasizes the analogy between words and things. Equally important in understanding Bacon's theory of discovery is his insistence that the type of language to which we appeal in developing this philosophical grammar is not philosophically regulated or rationally organized. It is fundamentally poetic and

---

49. *Advancement*, in *Works*, 3: 344.

50. *De Augmentis*, in *Works*, 3: 344–45. Also see Sewell, *Orphic Voice*, 59; and Rossi, *Francis Bacon*, 127–28.

is essentially mythic in its concentration on sensible experience unrestrained by presuppositions of reason.

To say that for Bacon the methods of discovery are based on a language whose grammar is essentially mythic is, as Vico later notes, not to say that these methods are inexplicable, irrational, or lacking in determinate rules. What it indicates is that success in inventive discovery is possible only by means of a reorientation of our assumptions about universal terms, subject-predicate distinctions, and (in general) our ability and willingness to reassert control over nature by calling into question the presuppositions (or "idols") of the philosophic language with which we describe nature. In Bacon's view such a reorientation means reinstating mythic thinking to a position of respect within philosophic reflection. And this in turn ensures the possibility of giving a proper explanation of the occurrence of discovery and of definite methods of exploration that promise to yield those new discoveries.

CHAPTER TWO

Descartes on Myth and Ingenuity

MANY OF DESCARTES' WRITINGS, especially his early ones, reveal his fascination with the philosophic function of dreams, myth, fable, and poetic inspiration. Not only does Descartes repeatedly refer to his physical description of the world as a myth or fable; he also points out that philosophic ingenuity (ingenium), by its very nature, embodies the imaginative character of mythopoesis. For Descartes myth codifies the sensible and provides the activity of figuration or sensible instantiation upon which rational thought is based.

Before Descartes could provide a method for philosophical reflection or the rules for the rational direction of the mind, he had to show the antecedent conditions that made such an enterprise possible. Rational discourse presumes a linguistic network that provides the sense-based background of meanings and the code of rules for their use and application. Because myth and fable do not presume such a prior codification of meaning but rather are self-conscious expressions of the need to establish a system of linguistic signs, they are prephilosophic to the extent that philosophic reflection relies on such a previously established system. To the extent that philosophy seeks to extend or revise such a sign system, it recaptures the spirit of its mythic origins.

Descartes' turn to the mythic and fabular thus not only acknowledges the historical priority of myth as the sign system out of which philosophy developed but also reestablishes the starting point for the philosophical renovation of the procedures by which the cogito can be used as a basis for determining certainty. As in myth, the cogito establishes its own codification of signs, its own system of meaning. The cogito can only tentatively "speak" itself in adopting a role as yet inadequately incorporated into a semiotic system that will in part result from its own creative activity. Through its autobiography, the cogito posits itself as a masked poetic figure on the stage of the world, an element within a system of signs. The speech of the cogito, the "I think," is the word that stands as the sensible sign, the figurative image prior to the positing of meaningful reality and necessary for the emergence of knowable reality.

In order to indicate how this aspect of his thought develops throughout Descartes' writings, I will highlight three features of his use of mythopoesis. First, for Descartes the poetic imagination recapitulates God's creations on its own literally "enthusiastic" feigned creations. Echoing Renaissance thinkers for whom the "heroic frenzy" of the poet accorded well with philosophic innovation, he insists on directing philosophy back to its heritage of wisdom found in mythopoesis. Second, the philosophic reconstruction of the world within the context of *fable* (myth) reveals the poetic foundations of Descartes' physics. As Vico notes, "René Descartes by beginning his physics in the initial movement of bodies, begins it truly as a poet."[1] Third, the poetic feint of the cogito provides the ontogeny of subjectivity, a fable in which the self emerges as determinate out of the aboriginal context of the chaos generated in methodic doubt. As such, not only does Descartes recommend a return to the spirit of classical mythopoesis out of which philosophy can be reborn in renewing human participation in divine creativity; he also indicates how this re-creation of the world and of the self is, like that of the poet, not *ex nihilo* but rather the imposition of semiotic order on a chaos otherwise impervious to rational scrutiny and claims of certainty. My concluding remarks point out how this treatment of mythopoesis in Descartes serves to distinguish Descartes' overall philosophic activity from that of the classical mythologists.

ENTHUSIASTIC INGENUITY

In order to appreciate the full import of Descartes' later use of mythopoesis, we have to turn to his early *Cogitationes Privatae*, his 1619 comments on the poetic origins of the "marvelous science" that becomes the concern of his later philosophic work. The central event described in these private thoughts is the dream-filled night of 10 November 1619, a night, Descartes says, in which he was "completely filled with enthusiasm, having dis-

1. See Yvon Belaval, "Vico and Anti-Cartesianism," in *Giambattista Vico: An International Symposium*, ed. Giorgio Tagliacozzo and Hayden V. White (Baltimore, Md.: Johns Hopkins University Press, 1969), 86.

covered the foundations of the miraculous science."[2]   What this admirable science is that Descartes discovered—whether the rules of the method, universal mathematics, the unity of the sciences, the cogito, or the will to give a practical orientation to his intellectual endeavors—is a matter of debate.[3]   Less debatable is Descartes' belief that this discovery should be explained in terms of the same divine poetic frenzy (*enthusiasmus*) that inspired the ancient fabulators or mythmakers.   A few months earlier he had said as much to Isaac Beeckman when he wrote that he had been devoting himself to his studies/the cultivation of the Muses/the development of ingenuity "more diligently than ever before" (*Musas meas diligentius excolui quam unquam hactenus*).[4] Indeed, as indicated by the title he gave to some of his early thoughts, *Olympica*, Descartes wanted to point out not only their concern with matters sublime but also with the distinctly mythic character of the foundations of his marvelous science.

The dreams of that night in November 1619 embody the spirit of mythopoesis, which underlies and is presumed by rational thought.   They provide a poetic, sense-based sign system typically created in a frenzy of divine inspiration.   Though the dreams themselves originally lack the determinate character that would make their meanings obvious, they do provide the context for the emergence of reason and meaning (*ratio*) both for the self and the world.   Descartes' dreams provide the confused, chaotic, and sense-based horizon necessary for the emergence of a world able to be known with certainty and of a non-sensible cogito capable of becoming determinate.   Fable (or myth) functions in the same way as the dream of the self, with the difference that fable (*fabula*) is the dream of the world.   Myth provides the sensible sign system upon which Descartes' "universal mathematics," physics, or purified geometry of nature can be

2.   See the Charles Adam and Paul Tannery edition of Descartes' *Oeuvres*, 13 vols. (Paris: Cerf, 1897–1913), 10: 179, 217; and Richard Kennington, "Descartes' 'Olympica'," *Social Research* 28 (1961): 172–73.

3.   See Gaston Milhaud, *Descartes Savant* (Paris: Felix Alcan, 1921), 1: 98; Maxime Leroy, *Descartes: le philosophe au masque* (Paris: Editions Rieder, 1929), 105; and Roger LeFèvre, *La vocation de Descartes* (Paris: Presses Universitaires de France, 1956), 129.

4.   Descartes to Beeckman, 26 March 1619, *Correspondance de Descartes*, ed. Charles Adam and Gaston Milhaud, 8 vols. (Paris: Presses Universitaires de France, 1936–63), 1: 5; quoted in Henri Gouhier, *Les premières pensées de Descartes* (Paris: J. Vrin, 1958), 23; also see 26.

grounded.   The dream is related to the cogito as myth is related
to the world-cognitively-accessible-as-certain.

In the most significant of the dreams, Descartes imagines a
dictionary and a collection of poems before him. The dictionary
with all of its specificity of meaning refers, he says, to the
sciences; the book of poetry stands for philosophy and wisdom
joined together, the marriage of revelation and enthusiasm
performed by the ancient poets and lost in the works of those so-
called philosophers who have denied the mythopoetic heritage of
philosophy.

For he [Descartes] did not believe that one should be greatly astonished
to see that the poets, even those who only play the fool, were full of
sentences more grave, more sensible, and better expressed than those
which are found in the writings of the philosophers. He attributed this
marvel to the divinity of enthusiasm and to the force of imagination,
which thrusts out the seeds of wisdom (which are found in the mind of
all men, like sparks of fire in stones) with much more facility, and even
much more brilliance, than reason can do in the philosophers.[5]

Mythopoesis provides the horizon or field of meaning (a world)
within which reasonable action and thought became possible.[6]
The poetic imagination provides the seeds of the sciences in
providing the first figures, signs, words, or notions (for example,
the meanings of straight, movement, here, there, one, several) by
which both sensible objects and intelligible objects can be known.

Just as imagination employs figures to conceive bodies, so the intellect
employs certain sensible bodies to figure spiritual things (for example,
wind, light); from which it follows that, philosophizing in a most
profound manner, we can elevate the mind for knowing the highest
sublimities. . . . The cognition of man regarding natural things occurs
only insofar as they are similar to those things which fall under the
senses; accordingly we think of someone as a truer philosopher who can
with more success assimilate the things which he seeks to the things
known through sense. . . . Sensible things are our most appropriate
means of conceiving the Olympics [things sublime]; wind signifies spirit;

5. *Olympica*, in *Oeuvres*, 10: 179, based on the *Cogitationes Privatae*, in *Oeuvres*,
10: 217.   See Kennington, "Descartes' 'Olympica'," 181–82; and "Descartes's
Olympica," tr. John F. Benton, in W. T. Jones, "*Somnio Ergo Sum*: Descartes' Three
Demands," *Philosophy and Literature* 4 (1980): 164.

6. Cf. Joseph J. Kockelmans, "On Myth and Its Relationship to Hermeneutics,"
Cultural Hermeneutics 1 (1973): 69.

movement in time signifies life; light, knowledge; heat, love; instanta-
neous activity, creation.[7]

Just as intellect uses sensible bodies to come to understand spiritual things, so the imagination must appeal to primitive figures in
order to have some grasp of sensible objects. Though such sensible objects can be sensed without having to appeal to primitive
notions (signs, words, figures), they cannot be known.[8] To know
an object means to be able to compare it with some standard,
some "objective being." But the poet or mythmaker has no
such standard or model upon which to fashion a description.
His or her act of figuration provides the code of the sensible,
the means by which the sensible is known. Such an act is enthusiastic because it de-figures the code of God's creation in its
adoption of a code or sign system by which nature is to be made
accessible to human science.[9]

In terms of the resolution-composition method described in
the *Rules for the Direction of the Mind*, this means that the mythmaker's resolution of objects as given in experience is succeeded
by the exercise of his or her own creative power. Objects are
created in a manner that is purified, designated as real, clearly
and distinctly known, containing no conjecture or mystery. Insofar
as the true philosopher seeks after such clarity, he or she attempts
to remove those notions that are not grounded in sense and that,
for Descartes, mask (*larvatae*) the sciences.

THE FABLE OF THE WORLD

Though Descartes' *Rules* (*Regulae ad directionem Ingenii*, written
before 1628, published 1701) acknowledges ingenium as the activity of the mind insofar as it forms new ideas and associations, his
work shifts the focus away from cognitive invention and discovery
toward the determination of how ingenium can be directed or

7. *Cogitationes Privatae*, in *Oeuvres*, 10: 217–19. See Marcel de Corte, "La
dialectique poétique de Descartes," *Archives de Philosophie*, vol. 13, no. 2 (1937):
119; and Gouhier, *Premières pensées*, 84.
8. See J. Millet, *Histoire de Descartes avant 1637* (Paris: Didier, 1867), 118.
9. See Jean-Luc Marion, *Sur la théologie blanche de Descartes* (Paris: Presses
Universitaires de France, 1981), 266; and de Corte, "La dialectique," 143–47.

trained to attain certainty.[10]   This shift in emphasis colors much
of Descartes' subsequent thinking about the activity of ingenium
and the role of imaginative insight in philosophic discovery.

The *Rules* represents a transition in Descartes' writings from a
concentration on the generation of meaning to an examination
of the procedures regulating certainty.   Specifically, the *Rules*
identifies the procedure by which certain "seeds of the sciences"
provide the foundations upon which are developed discursive
systems.   These "first germs of useful modes of thought" reflect
the activity of divine creativity, for, as Descartes says, "the human
mind has in it something that we may call divine."[11]   This
reappearance of prereflective enthusiasm indicates the way in
which the mythic antecedes, and serves as the point of departure
for, the emergence of the distinctly human mind.   Because the
human mind is oriented toward practical considerations of a
particular nature, such sparks or germs are always tied to some
utility.

What is striking is the fact that the basis for the human
concern for practical particulars is divine—but not divine in the
sense of the spiritually transcendent source of innate ideas or
judgments (which would be concerned with abstract or general
truths), but divine in the sense of the mythic or imaginative
elements by means of which the intellect can develop as human
and rational.   Because figures or signs are the aboriginal images
within which the mind emerges before the organization of
intellect—even before the distinction of intellect and body, which
depends on such images—they display things sublime (the
"Olympics") especially well in virtue of their particularity.   It is
the sensible and particular immediacy of such signs that permits
their application back into practical experience.

Such immediacy also ties the distinctively human mind to the
world of sensible particulars even before any Cartesian attempt to
provide a rational proof of the existence of God or of the
external world.   Indeed, in the imaginative world of sensibly
immediate particulars nothing means anything and nothing exists

10. See the *Rules for the Direction of the Mind*, rule 12, in *The Philosophical Works of
Descartes*, tr. Elizabeth S. Haldane and G. R. T. Ross, 2 vols. (Cambridge: Cambridge University Press, 1967), 1: 39.   Unless otherwise indicated, subsequent
references to *The Philosophical Works* are to volume one.

11. *Rules*, rule 4; *Philosophical Works*, 10.   Cf. *Règles utiles et claires pour la direction
de l'esprit en la recherche de la vérité*, tr. and ann. Jean-Luc Marion (The Hague:
Martinus Nijhoff, 1977), 135.

(including God and external world) apart from the sublime and divine images or figurations.

The distinctively human mind relies on these precognitive elements as points of reference indicating not only the bodily character of the *human* cogito but also the persistence of a divine, mythic, precognitive residue within the human order. These elements of thought are not thoughts themselves but rather serve as the constituents of the modes of thought, which themselves become the fundamental units of judgment. Or to put this in terms of Descartes' later replies to Gassendi's objections to the *Meditations*: The methodic doubt sweeps away only the prejudicial judgments found within all uncritical thinking, not the *notions* "of which it is impossible to divest ourselves."[12] These notions, Descartes observes, are neither judgments nor concepts but are rather particulars such as the lines or figures drawn to introduce a child to the fundamentals of geometry.

The figures of "ordinary mathematics" (lines, circles, triangles, numbers) are "the outer husk rather than the constituents" of the "Universal Mathematics," the characterization of all forms of study in terms of order and measurement.[13] These precognitive signs do not order or measure; they provide the opportunity for ordering and measuring by providing the matrix in which claims of order and measurement come to mean something in the first place. In this way "ordinary mathematics" reveals in a perspicuous but eminently superficial manner the ultimately sensible foundations of thought. Accordingly, in their inception there is no correct order to the arrangement of these "seeds": they are the bases upon which order and measurement emerge as meaning.

Though the *Rules* points to procedures by which discourse achieves philosophic credibility, it does not presume to employ those as yet unfounded principles for determining certainty within expression. Instead, even though Descartes warns against becoming caught up in the numbers and figures to which he often turns, he recognizes the practical pedagogic importance of such a presentation: "As for the outer covering I mentioned ["ordinary mathematics"], I mean not to employ it to cover up

12. "Letter from Descartes to Clerselier" (1646), *Philosophical Works*, 2: 126. Also see 127.

13. *Rules*, rule 4; *Philosophical Works*, 11, 13. Cf. Dalia Judovitz, *Subjectivity and Representation in Descartes* (Cambridge: Cambridge University Press, 1988), 73–85.

and conceal my method for the purpose of warding off the
vulgar; rather I hope so to clothe and embellish it that I may
make it more suitable for presentation to the human mind."[14]
Not only do Descartes' words recall the often repeated justifica-
tions for adopting explicitly mythic and fabular forms of
discourse; they also highlight the poetic and literary aims of
pleasing and instructing one's readers or listeners.

But in Descartes' case, the focus of such pleasant instruction,
the human mind, is embodied and hardly exhibits the features of
the disembodied cogito so familiar in Descartes' later accounts.
The distinctively *human* mind is immersed appropriately in the
signs of sensible figuration, but they appear neither as devices for
deception or displacement nor as indications of the vulgar and
fallen character of the human mind. Rather, these signs en-
hance the possibility that the cogito can return to the integrity of
human sensibility once the endeavor to establish the parameters
of certainty is completed.

In effect, Descartes suggests that the figuration of ordinary
mathematics functions in the same way as any fable or myth, in
that figures and numbers display an order that permits cognition,
reflection, or measurement in terms of a vocabulary within a
discursive formation. Identification of the mythic character of
mathematical figuration does not elevate mathematics to some
preeminent position over other discursive formations; rather, it
reemphasizes how the elements of all discursive formations
aboriginally are differentiations of sense and imagination.

Such an identification accordingly returns pure philosophical
speculation to its imaginative roots. "We make it a rule,"
Descartes claims, "not to recognize those philosophical entities
which really cannot be presented to the imagination. . . .
Henceforth we are to attempt nothing without the aid of the
imagination."[15] Before mind can reason or measure, there must
be something to measure, some imaginative ground that reveals
an order only in the facticity of its arrangement (which arrangement is recognized only after the fact). Without this imaginative
ground, no order emerges as the possibility for measurement
(*ratio*). What at first appears as a problem of measurement,

14. *Rules*, rule 4; *Philosophical Works*, 11.
15. *Ibid.*, rule 14; *Philosophical Works*, 57-58.

then, ultimately resolves itself as a problem of order.[16]   That is, in imaging the order of sensible individuals, the human mind creates the conditions for reasoning.   And it is the creative introduction of order into the chaos of sensible figuration that typifies the invitational or prescriptively moral aspect of mythic expression.

This is not to say that reasoning for Descartes is simply the arrangement or juxtaposition of sensible signs.   Rather, the order or arrangement created within the juxtaposition of the signs becomes the foundation for the systematic association of ideas by means of these signs.   Just as in the case of mythic characters, sensible signs provide the vocabulary of discourses that themselves can be classified as moral, scientific, political, or social only in terms of further discursive formations.   Mythic or fabular expression provides order only to the extent that it lends itself to systematization, repetition, redundancy—in a word, regulation. Descartes' mythic invitation to determine the guidelines of such redundancy in the *Rules* thus serves less as an indictment of the imagination-based figurations at the base of reasoning than an explication of the imaginative ground of cognition.

However, Descartes worries in the *Rules* that an emphasis on the imaginative expansion of knowledge will dilute the process of inquiry into the nature of certainty.   What is needed, he argues, is a regulated method by which the things we already know are "discovered" to be true and can be known with certainty. Ingenuity in itself can be said to guarantee certainty only when we have the means to determine that which is truly the activity of ingenium (as opposed to undisciplined and irresponsible flights of fancy).

Bacon had argued that the type of invention or discovery that simply recovers what we already know is not true discovery at all but rather the manipulation of speech and arguments (rhetorical invention).[17]   True invention, Bacon maintains, brings into our experience new objects, meanings, or ways of viewing the world in order to attain truth by extending our comprehension of the

16. *Ibid.*, 64.   Cf. Michel Foucault, *The Order of Things* (New York: Random House, 1970), 56.

17. See Bacon, *Advancement of Learning*, in *The Works of Francis Bacon*, ed. J. Spedding et al., 7 vols. (London: Longman and Co., 1857–59), 3: 384, 389; Paolo Rossi, *Francis Bacon: From Magic to Science*, 153; and Maurice B. McNamee, S.J., "Literary Decorum in Francis Bacon," *St. Louis University Studies*, series A: Humanities, vol. 1, no. 3 (1950): 11–16.

world. Though symbol, image, and figure do not guarantee certainty in innovation, they do permit the extension of inventive insight beyond the limits of what we already know.

Descartes responds to this type of argument by pointing out the need of a prior criterion for determining true inventive insights. As he notes in his 1648 conversation with Burman, mathematics in particular accustoms ingenium to the habit of recognizing the truth.[18] The study of mathematics, Descartes claims, is prerequisite for making new discoveries both in mathematics and in philosophy in general, because in mathematics are found examples of correct reasoning that are not found elsewhere. Once someone accustoms his or her mind to mathematical reasoning, he or she will be ready to investigate other truths because reasoning is one and the same in every area of investigation. The value of mathematics does not lie in its use of figures to provide an imaginative covering (*integumentum*) of objects or truths inaccessible to sensible description.[19] Its value lies in its procedures, which accustom ingenium to distinguish valid arguments and truths known with certainty from those that are unsound, false, or only probable.

In order to argue that mathematics trains the mind (ingenium) to make new discoveries, Descartes posits mathematical reasoning as that type of reasoning which serves in every domain of discourse to enable the detection of the truth of those discoveries. This universal application of one method of reasoning is precisely what Bacon believes stifles discovery (particularly in physics) in that it removes the proper activity of ingenium from its original and natural context as the source of inventive genius and poetic invention. The formal mathematical model of reasoning thus appears to exclude the imaginative introduction of alternative cognitive models because they are unable to provide justification for their own truth claims.

18. See *Descartes' Conversation with Burman* (1648, first published 1896), tr. John Cottingham (Oxford: Clarendon Press, 1976), 47–49. In *On the Study Methods of Our Time* (1709), Giambattista Vico expresses a similar view, noting that analytic geometry restrains the creative impulse of ingenium and thus provides the training necessary to make ingenium all the more acute after its learning period. See *Study Methods*, tr. Elio Gianturco (Indianapolis, Ind.: Bobbs-Merrill, 1965), 26–27.

19. *Rules*, rule 4; *Philosophical Works*, 11. See Jean-Luc Nancy, "Larvatus Pro Deo," *Glyph* 2 (1977): 23; and Judovitz, *Subjectivity*, 52–53.

However, before going too far in distinguishing Bacon's and Descartes' attitudes toward the activity of ingenium and the nature of discovery, we should note that, for Descartes, the imaginative extension of what is known to be certain should be distinguished from the justifiable claims regarding what is known to be true. "Physics," for example, is nothing but nature understood in a geometrical way. As such, physics (according to Descartes' particular treatment) makes no explicit truth claims about its applicability to the world until it can be demonstrated as deducible from metaphysics (at which time Descartes is then willing to call it "natural philosophy" or simply "philosophy").[20] The task of metaphysics is to show that the deductive unity of explanations in physics (certain knowledge of a possibly existent world) can be tied to the explanation and description of the natural world that actually exists. Within the deductive, mathematical model of reasoning, the activity of ingenium is simply that of attending to ideas that are already formed in order to detect the correctness of their interconnectedness.[21] "In Physics," Descartes explains, "there is no place for imagination," because the imaginative and creative activity of ingenium cannot be restricted within the deductive structure of physics.[22]

But this does not mean that Descartes rules out the imaginative activity of ingenium as a topic inappropriate for philosophic consideration. Indeed, at the very outset of the description of his physics (prior to its incorporation within a metaphysics into a "natural philosophy"), Descartes acknowledges in *The World* (*Le Monde*, 1633; published 1664) that he is sensitive to the imaginative or poetic character of such a description. His correspondence at the time of his work on *Le Monde* often refers to his "reveries," to his fable of the world on which he is working, and to his move away from the "light of Chaos" (the pseudolight provided by the sciences in their ungrounded description of the world, a description in need of a corrective re-creation).[23] What Descartes fails to do in *The World*—and Vico later points this out—is to make explicit or to develop thematically the originative and

20. See S. V. Keeling, *Descartes*, 2d ed. (London: Oxford University Press, 1968), 131–33; and James D. Collins, *Descartes' Philosophy of Nature* (Oxford: Basil Blackwell, 1971), 8–9.
21. *Rules*, rule 12; *Philosophical Works*, 39.
22. *Conversation with Burman*, 48.
23. See Ferdinand Alquié, *La Découverte métaphysique de l'homme chez Descartes*, 2d ed. (Paris: Presses Universitaires de France, 1966), 113, 116.

fabulating nature of ingenium as the secret of poetic invention and the source of inventive genius.

The world that Descartes' physics describes recaptures the spirit of poetic invention and acknowledges its fabular ties to those myths of the ancient poets that serve to make some primal chaos epistemologically accessible. While the primary material out of which this world is fashioned is "the most confused and entangled chaos that Poets ever feigned," all of the things this new world contains are known so perfectly (because of their status as things created within a geometrically regulated and ordered physics) that we could not even feign not knowing the fundamental nature of this chaos.[24] "My purpose," Descartes writes, "is not to explain . . . things which are, in effect, in the true world, but simply to feign one at pleasure, in which there should be nothing which the dullest minds are not capable of conceiving, and which might nevertheless be created just as I have imagined it."[25] Descartes' task as a geometer of nature, like that of the mythic poet, is not to describe the world as it already exists. For the physical geometer and the poet, what exists is only a chaos out of which a world is to be fashioned and upon which (that is, subsequent to which) claims of certainty and truth can be made. In Descartes' description of *Le Monde*, physical bodies are eminently distinguishable and intelligible insofar as they are characterized principally in geometrical terms; but positing their character in geometrical terms is an invention or imaginative (that is, poetic) discovery that retrieves, for Descartes, the spirit of poetic insight operative in the myths of the ancients.

The primary justification for introducing Descartes into the discussion of fabular philosophy rests on his invitation to consider both *The World* and the *Discourse on Method* (1637) as fables. The two works complement each other's fabular features. *The World*, on the one hand, presents some of Descartes' ideas on the philosophy of nature in a way (he says) that is intended to please and entice without completely revealing or justifying the positions with which it is concerned. The *Discourse*, on the other hand, provides a model for possible imitation in the promotion

---

24. See *Discourse on Method, Philosophical Works,* 107; and Jean-Luc Nancy, "Mundus est Fabula," *MLN* 93 (1978): 650.

25. *Le Monde,* in *Oeuvres,* 11: 33. Cf. Sylvie Romanowski, *L'Illusion chez Descartes: La structure du discours cartésien* (Paris: Klincksieck, 1974), 83-99.

of the good conduct of one's reason. Without adopting either the Aesopic apologue or the classical myth as his formal paradigm, Descartes appropriates their fabular assumptions in drawing upon the expectations and qualifications generated by the use of the term *fable* as the designation for his two works.

Instead of turning to the Aesopic animal fables or the classical myths as appropriate contexts in which to renew the fabular enterprise, Descartes substitutes a new form of fabular thinking— one that respects the not-yet fully grounded character of certain discussions about God, nature, and the self, at the same time as it reintroduces some of the didactic presuppositions of Aesopic apologues (but with a diminished emphasis on explicitly moral considerations). Such didactic presuppositions include a sensitivity for making description of the natural world appealing, colorful, intriguing, and yet epistemologically accessible to all.

As an alternative Descartes retrieves the fascination for the fabulous from the ancients by bringing into methodological prominence Bacon's desire to leave some things tentative and as yet unrevealed while incorporating the appeal and educative value of the classical fables. As with Bacon, Descartes' justification for restraining the tendency to expose completely the meanings and implications of fabular thinking does not depend on the inherently inaccessible nature of the objects with which such thinking is concerned. Instead, the sketches drawn in Descartes' fabular philosophy are intended to take into account both (1) Descartes' own movement toward supplying a firm foundation for his thoughts on nature (as expressed, in Descartes' words, in "the fable of my World," *Le Monde*), and (2) the self-constitution and progressive reeducation of the mind (ingenium) as described in the *Discourse*.

Following his nonfabular critique of the reliability of our senses as means by which perceptions are presumed to be related to things, Descartes shifts into a fabular description of nature only after he reaches the fifth chapter of his treatise on the world. Once doubt has undermined the foundations of rational discourse and cleared the way for a renovation of meaning, mythic creativity can then reinstate order in virtue of its control over the adorned figurations of its pronouncements. Pointing out how the move to the fabular perspective permits him to present his discourse in a more appealing way, Descartes infuses his discussion with a character consciously intended to attract and hold the attention of readers concerned more with enlightenment than with exacting demonstrations.

> So that the length of this discourse will be less tiresome for you, I want to envelop a part of it within the invention of a fable, by means of which I hope that the truth be permitted to appear sufficiently, and that it be no less agreeable to sight than if I had exposed it in a completely unadorned way. . . . I do not promise to place before you exact demonstrations of all that I have to say; it will be enough that I open the way by which you shall be able to find them out for yourselves, when you take the pains to seek them. Most minds are displeased when things are made too easy for them. And to paint a picture here which shall please you, it is necessary that I make use of shadow as well as bright colors. Accordingly I shall content myself with following out the description which I have begun, having no other design than to tell you a fable.[26]

As in the case of Bacon's treatment of the fables of the ancients, Descartes' fable (which we subsequently discover to be a treatise on matter, the laws of motion, and the generation of physical bodies) does not aim to provide unadorned truth; rather it provides enough truth to entice others to participate in the attempt to understand nature. And like Bacon, Descartes' fascination with the fabular reaffirms the inventive power of the mind and highlights the need for the communal investigation of nature.

The fabular creation of the world is pleasing to the mind because (for Descartes) it is, in effect, re-creational, a retrieval of the power of ingenium behind the fabular constructions that constitute the ancient myths themselves. Unlike Bacon, who accepts the fables of the ancients as the starting points for developing lines of inquiry, Descartes raises into prominence the feigning mind behind the fabular construction, the mind for whom certainty consists in being the inventor of its own fable.[27] However, in order to prevent such a feint from slipping into a solipsistic exercise, Descartes presents his fable as a didactic invitation to draw out further the colors of the picture, which he is unwilling to fill in at the expense of appearing pedagogic in an enterprise as yet tentative and exploratory.

---

26. *Le Monde*, in *Oeuvres*, 11: 31, 48. Cf. Michael S. Mahoney's translation in his edition of *Le Monde* (New York: Abaris Books, 1979), 49, 77. Also see *Discourse on Method*, in *Philosophical Works*, 107.
27. See Nancy, "Mundus est Fabula," 639–40, 650.

THE FABULATION OF THE SELF

Lacking the philosophical support of demonstrations showing (1) the relationship between the fabular-mechanical explanation of the world and the existential order of reality and (2) God's role in ordering the universe—demonstrations that he finally provides in his *Meditations* (1641)—Descartes cautions against understanding *The World* as a work devoid of fabular assumptions.[28] Far from being solely a prudential disclaimer intended to avoid the fate of Galileo by proposing his theory of the world "as a mere fable or a pure hypothesis," Descartes' appeal to the vocabulary of fable recurs in the *Discourse* and in his later correspondence, and finally appears in a thematic way in a portrait of Descartes done by J. B. Weenix around 1647. The portrait (see frontispiece, p. ii) shows Descartes holding an open book in which is written *mundus est fabula*, an expression that points back to the fabular principles of *Le Monde* through the fabular treatment of the self's relation to the world in the *Discourse*.[29] The *Meditations* and the *Principles of Philosophy* (1644), in providing the metaphysical justification and epistemological mechanism for Descartes' treatments of self and world, move such treatments into a structure of philosophic determinacy that does not disavow its imaginative source in human ingenuity.

Whereas the cautions about the fabular assumptions of *The World* primarily concern the metaphysical positions characteristic of the classical type of myth-fables, the cautions about the fabular assumptions of the *Discourse on Method* address epistemological considerations in distinctly moral-pedagogic (Aesopic) ways. "In this Discourse," Descartes writes, "I shall be very happy to show the paths I have followed, and to set forth my life as in a picture, so that everyone may judge of it for himself."[30] The picture Descartes paints is one with explicitly practical ("moral") and exemplificatory ends in mind. But he warns that, while the fable form is a moral form from which readers can gain certain

28. See Collins, *Descartes' Philosophy*, 7–9.
29. See Nancy, "Mundus est Fabula," 635. Cf. Descartes to Fr. Denis Mesland, May 1645, *Correspondance*, 6: 236.
30. *Discourse on Method*, in *Philosophical Works*, 83. Cf. Andrew E. Benjamin, "Descartes' Fable: The *Discours de la Méthode*," in *The Figural and the Literal: Problems of Language in the History of Science and Philosophy, 1630–1800*, ed. Andrew E. Benjamin, Geoffrey N. Cantor, and John R. R. Christie (Manchester, Eng.: Manchester University Press, 1987), 23–27.

helpful insights, such insights should not be considered universally helpful or universally binding in the same way as precepts of moral philosophy.

My design is not here to teach the Method which everyone should follow in order to promote the good conduct of his Reason, but only to show in what manner I have endeavored to conduct my own. Those who set about giving precepts must esteem themselves more skillful than those to whom they advance them. . . . But regarding this Treatise simply as a tale, or if you prefer, a fable in which, amongst certain things which may be imitated, there are possibly others also which it would not be right to follow, I hope that it be of use to some without being hurtful to any, and that all will thank me for my frankness.[31]

While expressing confidence in the portrait of the self's develop-ment in wisdom in much the same way as *The World* expressed confidence in Descartes' feigned new world, the fable of the *Discourse* makes all the more clear how fabular philosophy adopts a self-restrictive though nonetheless exhortative and didactic stance. The moral of Descartes' *Discourse* fable lies in showing, rather than describing, the value of frankness, the freedom to feign a self, to reestablish the poetic union of description and moral encouragement.[32]

The *Discourse* thus reveals how, for Descartes, the fabular stance does not presuppose that the fabulist assumes preeminence in wisdom in the matters addressed. Instead, it indicates how the fabular philosopher (1) attempts to involve others in the enter-prise by challenging and inviting them to contribute to a project that they must see as worthwhile and yet incomplete, while at the same time (2) attempts to avoid either self-effacement or the appearance of moral (or more generally, philosophical) superiority. Only through participation in a shared and regulated discourse can either the author of the *Discourse* or the reader escape the radical solitude of the self prior to its fabular constitution. As such, the act of the cogito itself cannot be imitated because such an act is the aboriginal, groundless, though mutual means by which the narration/history/discourse of communicating and

---

31. *Discourse on Method,* in *Philosophical Works,* 83. Cf. Étienne Gilson, *René Descartes, Discours de la Méthode: Texte et Commentaire* (Paris: J. Vrin, 1925), 98–99.
32. See Nancy, "Mundus est Fabula," 644–45.

cooperating selves emerges.[33] To see Descartes' move to fabular philosophy simply as a means to protect himself from doctrinal difficulties such as those faced by Galileo accordingly fails to recognize the exhortative, self-corrective, and epistemically necessary assumptions operating within the fabular philosophic context.[34]

By means of the fable of the *Discourse,* Descartes is able to restrain the poetic imagination as it appears to be released from existential reality in virtue of the methodic doubt that threatens to destroy all further access to the world. The fabular structure permits Descartes to doubt the existence of the world without having to lose all sense of how it could be described once it is reincorporated into a metaphysically grounded and epistemologically responsible account.[35] Once clarity, distinctness, and certainty are identified and characterized in isolation from their sporadic appearance in the natural-world-as-unmethodically-examined, then the natural world can be re-viewed as the proper locus of scientific endeavor.[36]

By adopting the stance of the fabulist, Descartes insists (like the ancient poets) that the creative mind must be left to start with something. Everything cannot be wiped away by methodic doubt (nor should it be), for the fabular situation always begins with some chaos upon which ingenium can exercise itself in coming to know itself or a world: Poetic invention is not *creatio ex nihilo.* But no self and no world can legitimately be said to be known except by means of the feint through which they are thought.[37] Prior to the fable there is no self and no world to be known or thought; for the discourse that is the fable serves as the discriminating, determining means by which ingenium (mind-nature) becomes determinate.

The fabular posture returns the cogito to its proper, well-ordered, pure (*mundus*) status, undifferentiated and indeterminately distinguished from, and aboriginally united to, all that

33. See John D. Lyons, "Subjectivity and Imitation in the *Discours de la Méthode,*" *Neophilologus* 66 (1982): 509–10, 520–21.
34. See *Discourse,* in *Philosophical Works,* 106–7. Also see Gilson, *Discours,* 99; Collins, *Descartes' Philosophy,* 8; and Nancy, "Mundus est Fabula," 640.
35. See Donald B. Kuspit, "Epoché and Fable in Descartes," *Philosophy and Phenomenological Research* 25 (1964): 37.
36. *Ibid.,* 49–51.
37. See Nancy, "Mundus est Fabula," 650–52; and Nancy, "Larvatus Pro Deo," 18, 28–31.

which subsequently will provide the determinate objects necessary to allow even the possibility for raising questions about the nature of the self and about the recognition of truth. The fable of the *Discourse* denies the history of the fabulator apart from the fabling: here the transcendental subject makes itself determinate in its narrative. The narrative is a pure creation; it does not model itself on anything else. It is a portrait the subject paints of itself, which at the same time constitutes itself as the original. But the painting or narrative is only a poetic feint, a covering (*integumentum*) or mask the subject paints in the attempt to see itself.[38] The transcendental subject or self that engages in the feint is itself only a shadow, one whom we ought to agree not to see, much like the prop men on stage between acts in a play.[39] Only the masked self, through its pronouncements and activity, provides a *persona* in relation to which determinate claims of truth are applicable or even meaningful.

The problem, of course, is that in trying to illuminate itself the subject can only show itself as positional, an intentional relation to a self as an object identified only as a mask of the self. Because the narrative undermines the effort to establish the self's essence as pure thought, it can reveal only the self as masked, the same self with which Descartes began in the *Cogitationes Privatae*: "Just as actors, when called upon to take up a mask so that people do not see their faces turn red with embarrassment, so I also, mounting the stage of the world where I have hitherto only been a spectator, advance masked [*larvatus prodeo*]."[40] The embarrassment of the self resides precisely in its frankness, the nakedness of Adam after the Fall, after coming to know himself as masked (hidden by fig leaves) and therefore visible to God as another self. We forestall epistemological shame only by agreeing not to identify the fabulator behind the mask, the transcendental self who, like the prop men, makes the play of discourse and the discourse of play possible.

In shadow as well as bright colors, the self emerges in its veiled performances. It must be posited to be known; that is, it

38. See Nancy, "Larvatus Pro Deo," 23–24; Nancy, *Ego Sum* (Paris: Flammarion, 1979), 84–94; and Judovitz, *Subjectivity*, 33–37, 112.

39. See Robert Champigny, "The Theatrical Aspect of the Cogito," *Review of Metaphysics* 12 (1959): 374.

40. *Cogitationes Privatae*, 1 Jan. 1619, in *Oeuvres*, 10: 213. See Dalia Judovitz, "Autobiographical Discourse and Critical Praxis in Descartes," *Philosophy and Literature* 5 (1981): 95, 104; and Gouhier, *Premières pensées*, 67–68.

must be objectivized as a function within a system of signs, even though to make it an object only masks its essence as that which is aboriginal, pure (*mundus*), known only by means of its fabulating activity. The narrative of methodic doubt points to and reveals a purity that cannot be thought or expressed outside of the ruse of the figural, sense-based narration itself.[41] However, in this case the ruse is all there is to begin with, for apart from it nothing survives the critique of doubt that clears away the residues of meaning.

In this sense the self is that which is presupposed by myth, name, and sign, but cannot be captured within mythologizing, naming, or signing. Just as a light source (*lux*) is revealed in its determinate transmitted modes as *lumen* but cannot be described by or in terms of these modes, so the preconditions of determinateness in self and world cannot be described in other than the language of myth.[42] Put in terms of one of Descartes' more common distinctions: the self of the *Discourse* and the fabled world of *Le Monde* have an objective (fabularly based) reality that can be shown, narrated, signed. The formal (pre-fabular) reality of both, however, is (from a cognitive standpoint) hypothetical, though morally and praxicly certain.

To move beyond this moral certitude into claims about the formal reality of world and self (i.e., reality understood as meaningful independent of the sign system describing it) is to exclude temporarily consideration of the mythopoetic foundations of claims about world and self. This is, in fact, what Descartes does in the *Meditations* and in the *Principles*, by providing some metaphysical grounding for claims about the formal reality of the world and self.

The difficulty with such a move, however, is that it has to employ the rather shaky tack of assuming God's existence in order to move from the objective reality of self and world as narrated within a sign system of mythopoetic origin to claims of the formal reality of self and world that are metaphysically grounded through God's creative power. Such a move is required

41. See Ralph Flores, "Cartesian Striptease," *SubStance* 12 (1983): 86. Cf. Romanowski, *L'Illusion*, 194; and Timothy Reiss, "Cartesian Discourse and Classical Ideology," *Diacritics*, vol. 6, no. 4 (Winter 1976), 26–27.

42. On the lux-lumen relationship, see Descartes' letter to Morin, 13 July 1638, in *Oeuvres*, 2: 204–5; and Stephen H. Daniel, "The Nature of Light in Descartes' Physics," *The Philosophical Forum* 7 (1976): 326–27, 336–37.

if Descartes is to establish the self's essence as pure thought and
not as the marks by which the subject tries to illuminate itself as
an object within a sign system of its own making. The illumina-
tion must come from the source of light and being. But the
only way we can recognize the significance of God as the source
of formal reality is by further appreciating our own abilities as
mythmakers, as cocreators of the sign systems that make the self
and world meaningful and determinate within the context of
objective reality.

In the context of the classical understanding of *fabula*, "the
world is a myth" (*mundus est fabula*) indicates that the world,
including the self, is open to signification: Meaning within a sign
system can be established through the use of inventive ingenuity.
Men share this creative ability with the gods when men are
inspired.   But because the activity of mythologizing entails
ordering an already existing chaos into an understandable world,
there is no opportunity to move beyond the objective, signed,
narrated world to the formal reality underlying it.

This is where Descartes goes beyond the classical mythologists.
Not only must he try to explain how the world and self can
emerge out of chaos into determinate meaningfulness under the
direction of philosophical ingenuity. He must also try to explain
the existence of the chaos itself, the formal reality accessible
apparently only through the objective reality revealed in mythopoetic activity.

For Descartes, then, myth constitutes the system of signs that
permits the meaningful understanding of self and world.[43]   But
the recognition of such mythic activity at the base of philosophic
inquiry prompts further investigation into the prior conditions
that permit the possibility of mythopoesis originally. To describe
the metaphysical presuppositions for the emergence of meaning
in mythopoesis would presume the availability of a premythic sign
system, a system of natural signs developed in God's proto-
mythological genesis of a language (or "book") of nature.
While it may underlie Descartes' mythic description of the world
as the metaphysical presupposition of such a description, this
natural sign system (or "order established by God in created
things") cannot itself be described with certainty in terms of the

43. Cf. Romanowski, *L'Illusion*, 70–83; Reiss, "Cartesian Discourse," 23–24; and
Judovitz, *Subjectivity*, 88–89.

sign system by which "my nature" orders into a world the chaotic complex of all the things God has given me.[44] In the aboriginal chaos, nothing is distinguished from anything else; everything that can be known about it is "the pure" (*mundus*), back to which fable prompts us in order to appreciate how self ("my nature," as distinct from the world) and world ("my nature," that world accessible to me) emerge simultaneously as determinate and distinguished in mythopoesis.

Not only does Descartes want to allow a role for religious faith in God as the source of light and being that precedes the Adamic mythopoetic assignment of names within a sign system. He also wants to permit the possibility for philosophic renovations of such a system by pointing out the differences among nature as presupposed source (God), nature as open to the possibility of semiotic integration (the order established by God in creation, the book of Nature), and nature mythopoetically organized within sign systems. In this way the philosophic impulse toward re-creation is encouraged while at the same time being restricted to claims legitimated through the recognition of their mythic origins and character.

44. *Meditations*, in *Philosophical Works*, 192. See Stephen H. Daniel, "Descartes' Treatment of 'Lumen Naturale'," *Studia Leibnitiana* 10 (1978): 95.

CHAPTER THREE

Political and Philosophical Uses of Fable in England

AMID ALL THE LITERARY FORMS used by writers in eighteenth-century England, the rather humble form of the fable (or apologue, as it is sometimes called) held for a brief period a position of some stature and was well regarded by a sizable number of authors. In a 1732 letter to John Gay, for example, Jonathan Swift commented that, while nothing was so difficult to succeed in as fable writing, he esteemed no writing more than he did fables.[1] Gay and Swift—along with other writers such as Sir Roger L'Estrange, John Locke, Bernard Mandeville, Samuel Croxall, Christopher Smart, Samuel Richardson, and William Somerville—all used the form in varying degrees for didactic, literary, or satiric purposes.

With so many innovative writers adopting the form, it should come as little surprise that one of the first problems we face in understanding how fables were used concerns what English authors meant when they claimed to be writing a fable. In some contexts fables were understood simply as lies or, more specifically, as the false religious teachings found in the classical myths. In other contexts a fable was understood in the Aristotelian rhetorical sense of a narrative scheme or sequence of events. And in some works—for example, Dryden's *Fables* (a 1700 collection of translations from Homer, Ovid, Chaucer, and Boccaccio)—elements of both of these understandings appeared.

Though my concern in this chapter is with the common notion of the fable as a story that imparts some moral and that often has speaking and reasoning animals in the dominant roles, I think it is important to note that authors of the period allow the different understandings of fable (as narrative, apologue, and classical myth) to remain united. In the 1695 English translation of his *Treatise of the Epick Poem*, for example, René Le Bossu

---

1. Swift to Gay, 10 July 1732, *Correspondence*, ed. Harold Williams (Oxford: Clarendon Press, 1963–65), 4: 38. The letter is in response to a letter from Gay (16 May 1732) in which Gay noted that fable writing was the most difficult form of writing he had ever undertaken (*ibid.*, 22).

cautions against the narrowness caused by too quick a move to define the different meanings of fable in mutually exclusive ways: "We conclude then, that the Name of *Fable* which is given to the Fable of the *Iliad*, and that of *Aesop*, is neither *Equivocal* nor *Analogous*, but *Synonymous* and equally *Proper*, that all the *Qualities* which make any difference between them, do by no means affect either the *Foundation*, the *Nature*, or the *Essence* of the *Fable*, but only constitute the different sorts of it."[2] As Le Bossu recognizes, and as often becomes apparent in the writings of fabulists and commentators on the fable, the working understanding of fable (such as the one I have adopted in this chapter primarily for heuristic purposes) should permit an interplay of meanings such that authors who speak about the classical myths as fables establish resonances of meaning for understanding Aesopic and rhetorical uses of the term.

In addition, this particular discussion of fables highlights the way in which, in general, generative and moral/pedagogic themes of myth surface in a different way in England than on the Continent. This in part is due to the English impetus toward the popularization of philosophic activity. By extending the proper domain of philosophy to include the immediate literature of social and political debate, the English treatment of myth (specifically mythic philosophy) transforms the context in which myth arises as a topic of philosophic concern. This is a prime example of how historiographic considerations affect who can be counted as philosophically relevant in the study of myth and modern philosophy. For certainly, many of the writers included in this chapter seem more at home in a survey of English literature than in a discussion of the history of English philosophy. Only when the procedures for the study of mythic philosophy are outlined do the contexts for defining the texts appropriate for such a study begin to emerge. In the English case the vocabulary of myth/fable points to the apologue.

The focal use of fables for pedagogic purposes in the late seventeenth century gradually yielded to the use of fables as devices of political satire in the beginning of the eighteenth century. By the middle of the eighteenth century, the use of fables had generally reverted to a more traditional form of

2. René Le Bossu, *Treatise of the Epick Poem* (1695), in *Le Bossu and Voltaire on the Epic*, facsimile reproduction with an introduction by Stuart Curran (Gainesville, Fla.: Scholar's Facsimiles and Reprints, 1970), 22.

children's literature concerned mainly with imparting maxims of socially acceptable behavior—a function that characterizes most fable writing throughout the remainder of the century.

Though this pattern *describes* the historical development of fable use, it does not *explain* how features of the fable form as a form came to be recognized as problematic in themselves.[3] Such an explanation, I suggest, is to be found in the fact that, as fable writers of the period used the form as a teaching and persuasive device that employed animals in speaking and reasoning roles, they came to recognize that the use of the fable form had unsettling implications for epistemology, learning theory, and theories regarding man's place in nature and treatment of animals.[4]

THE POLITICAL USE OF FABLES

When Richardson was asked in 1739 to produce an edition of Aesop's fables that he could commend to children, he turned to the two then most popular collections of Aesopic fables, namely, that of Sir Roger L'Estrange (1692) and that of Samuel Croxall (1722). The thirty years between these two collections were the most active for English fable writers, and L'Estrange and Croxall serve as the two focal figures of the English attempt to combine the literary grace of fable writing (as found, for example, in the works of La Fontaine) with a popular and often political appeal.

To understand how the fable developed into a political tool in the hands of writers such as L'Estrange and Croxall, it is useful to consider how the form developed in the seventeenth century out of a predominantly pedagogic device. Occasional authors such as John Ogilby published Aesopic fables (in 1651 and again in 1667) with what might be recognized as political motives; however, the applications of such fables are questionable and, in any event, do not approximate the developed political positions found in later collections. La Fontaine's translations into French

---

3. On the distinction between the description and explanation of literary change, see Stephen H. Daniel, "A Philosophical Theory of Literary Continuity and Change," *Southern Journal of Philosophy* 18 (1980): 275–80.

4. Cf. Antoine Houdart de la Motte, *One Hundred New Court Fables Written for the Instruction of Princes, and a True Knowledge of the World . . . with a Discourse on Fable,* tr. Robert Samber (London: E. Curll, 1721), 18; and John Toland's undated letter in which one animal writes to another that their philosopher-masters "frequently confabulate" (British Museum Add. MS. 4465, fol. 54).

(from 1668 to 1694) of fables from Aesop and Phaedrus showed how the fable could be developed into a legitimate literary form as opposed to a simply pedagogic one.

Prior to L'Estrange, however, the dominant use of the fable form, at least in the seventeenth century, was for teaching children Latin. L'Estrange himself complained that Aesop's fables were being taught in the schools of his day "almost at such a Rate as we Teach *Pyes* and *Parrots*, that Pronounce the Words without so much as Guessing at the Meaning of them."[5] As L'Estrange perceived the situation, most students failed to incorporate into their everyday lives the morals they translated because they lost the message in the toil of the translation.

Recognizing this problem, Locke recommended that children be exposed to English translations of Aesopic fables not only for reading purposes but also to introduce children to moral principles. Nonetheless, Locke suggested keeping Aesop's fables as practice tools for translation; indeed, he published his own interlinear Latin-English translation of Aesop's fables in 1703, arguing that such a technique could assist in learning grammar. To improve general reading and stylistic ability in students, Locke thus recommended Aesop's fables (but not his own translations) as devices that could hold students' interest as well as impart useful moral maxims.[6] He included pictures in his own translation of Aesop's fables, he said, to entertain children and to make a deeper impression on their minds.[7]

The same impressionist theory of education had been on L'Estrange's mind when he observed that "Children are but *Blank Paper*, ready Indifferently for any Impression, Good or Bad (for they take All upon Credit) and it is much in the Power of the first Comer, to Write Saint, or Devil upon't, which of the Two He pleases."[8] What distinguished L'Estrange from Locke, though, was L'Estrange's use of the fable form as a forum for political commentary. Taken together, his 1692 "Reflections" on

5. *Fables of Aesop and other Eminent Mythologists*, 2d ed. corrected (London: R. Sare et al., 1694), vii. Cf. Thomas Noel, *Theories of the Fable in the Eighteenth Century* (New York: Columbia University Press, 1975), 14.

6. See John Locke, *Some Thoughts Concerning Education* (1693), in *The Educational Writings of John Locke*, ed. James Axtell (Cambridge: Cambridge University Press, 1968), 259, 298.

7. John Locke, *Aesop's Fables* (London: A. & J. Churchil, 1703), third unnumbered page of the preface; also see *Some Thoughts*, in *Educational Writings*, 273–74.

8. *Fables of Aesop*, ii.

the fables in his collection constituted a Tory-verging-on-Jacobite statement of political principles. Embittered by the fall of James II, L'Estrange turned to the fable as a thinly veiled means of expressing his support of absolute monarchy.[9] As Croxall and Richardson were later to remark, it was difficult not to detect L'Estrange's pro-monarchical intent in remarks such as, "The Multitude are never to be satisfied, Kings are from God; and . . . it is a Sin, a Folly, and a Madness to struggle with his Appointments" (Fable No. 19); "There must be no shares in Sovereignty" (No. 206); "As Government is Necessary, Sacred, and Inaccountable, so it is but equal for us to bear the Infelicities of a Male Excess of it, as we enjoy the Blessings of Authority and publick Order" (No. 254). Even for a man of moderate temperament and political persuasion like Richardson, such remarks were intolerable in a work whose avowed intent was the instruction of children.[10]

L'Estrange, however, replied to his early critics in a second series of fables in 1699 and justified his union of moral pedagogy and political satire by proposing that his general concern was for writing about "the Government of Life." Within the compass of the division between the "Training up of Children" and the "Office of a *Political* Discourse," he pointed out, "may be comprehended *all Practical Duties whatsoever: whether the Persons concern'd be Noble, or Ignoble; Men, Women, or Children*, it matters not."[11] In L'Estrange's view, a discourse on the government of life had application to political and governmental matters as much as to the education of children; and because fables were concerned with the practical duties of both children and adults, there was no reason why a fable writer should restrict himself to politically neutral reflections in his fabling.

Fable translations and commentaries like those of L'Estrange introduced fables into the everyday lives of individuals outside of the schools and had the reciprocal effect of opening contemporary social and political life up to the fabulist, either in terms of applications of classical fables or in terms of newly composed

9. See Mary H. Pritchard, "Fables Moral and Political: The Adaptation of the Aesopian Fable Collection to English Social and Political Life, 1651–1722" (Ph.D. diss., University of Western Ontario, 1976), 135–40.

10. See T. C. Duncan Eaves, *Samuel Richardson: A Biography* (Oxford: Clarendon Press, 1971), 35, 77.

11. *Fables and Storyes Moralized* (London: R. Sare, 1699), [viii].

fables intended to highlight features of contemporary events.[12] The translation of fables into colloquial language provided an opening by which the concerns of ordinary life were to become the concerns of fable writers. In addition, Grub Street writers found that the fable form provided some of the distance and ambiguity necessary to protect themselves from official retaliation for their criticism of the government or its members.[13]

Beginning in 1698 a series of anonymous fables set Aesop on a journey through England and the rest of Europe. Through his animal characters Aesop comments on the Jacobite threat, William's government of England, and Louis XIV's ambitions on the Continent. As one writer put it, "It is now the Mode, it seems, for Brutes to turn Politicians," and Aesop was chosen as their main expositor.[14] *Aesop at Tunbridge* (1698) attacked William and Whig principles in general. In the same year *Aesop at Bath* criticized the Jacobites; *Aesop Return'd from Tunbridge* committed the hapless supporter of the Jacobites to Bedlam; *Old Aesop at Whitehall* defended the government; and *Aesop at Amsterdam* objected to the monarchical forms of government supported in one way or another by Whig, Tory, or Jacobite factions. Aesop travelled to Westminster and Islington (1699), where he inveighed against King William's importation of Dutchmen; then he journeyed to Spain, Paris (attacking Louis XIV), and Scotland (1701), and returned to Wales and then to the royal court in 1702. *Aesop the Wanderer* and *Aesop in Portugal* appeared in 1704, and then for a few years fabulists allowed Aesop to rest. In 1709 the itinerant fabulist returned to Oxford, turned up at the Bell-Tavern (1711), became an adversary of Louis XIV again at Utrecht (1712), spoke up at the Bear-Garden in 1715, "masqueraded" as a Tory proponent in 1718, and made a final appearance at St. James's in 1729.[15]

12. See Pritchard, "Fables Moral and Political," 222.

13. See Laurence Hanson, *Government and the Press, 1695–1763* (Oxford: Clarendon Press, 1967), 36, 46; and Frederick S. Siebert, *Freedom of the Press in England, 1476–1776* (Urbana: University of Illinois Press, 1965), 260. Also see Leslie B. Mechanic, "John Dryden's *Fables*: A Study in Political Subversion" (Ph.D. diss., University of Pennsylvania, 1975), 5.

14. *Old Aesop at Whitehall* (preface page), in *Aesop in Select Fables* [ed. Edward Ward] (London: Booksellers of London and Westminster, 1698).

15. See Noel, *Theories of the Fable*, 30–31; Albert E. Graham, "John Gay's *Fables*, Edited with an Introduction on the Fable as an Eighteenth-Century Literary Genre" (Ph.D. diss., Princeton University, 1960), 27–29; and William R. Wray, "The English Fable, 1650–1800" (Ph.D. diss., Yale University, 1950), 192–96.

Complementing several of these six-penny pamphlets concerned with the threat of war or with the Ministry's conduct of the war on the Continent were works such as *Bickerstaff's Aesop* (1709, written probably by the Tory propagandist William Pittis), which attacked the Whigs' conduct of the War of Spanish Succession; and the *History of John Bull* (1712), which satirized Marlborough and the members of the Whig ministry who opposed the peace treaty at Utrecht. As late as 1745, when the Jacobite threat appeared again in the person of the Pretender Prince Charles Edward, Thomas Gibbons composed a fable ("The Vine and the Bramble") portraying George II as the vine that grew and nourished his country but was in danger of being overthrown in favor of a bramble-turned-tyrant.[16]

Some fable writers expanded their treatments of social and political matters to include questions about the power of religious sects (as in the anonymous *Tale of a Nettle*, 1709) and about the well-publicized trial of Henry Sacheverell (as in *The Wolf Stript of His Shepherd's Clothing*, 1710). Most writers, however, chose not to employ fables in theological or religious discussions because, as John Toland maintained, fables tended only to confound religious doctrines and to make them all the more mysterious and inaccessible to ordinary people.[17] Since the political intent of these fabulists was to appeal to the ordinary man in the shops and coffeehouses and was not to address scholars concerned with the intricacies of religious teachings, most agreed with Toland's strictures in practice if not by design.[18]

Samuel Croxall's *Fables of Aesop and Others* (1722) is the standard Whig Aesopic collection of the century. The collection, including the commentary, was compiled (Croxall claimed) as a corrective to L'Estrange's pernicious principles, "Principles, coin'd and suited to promote the Growth, and serve the Ends of Popery, and Arbitrary Power."[19] While repeating the theme from

16. *The Gentleman's Magazine* 15 (November 1745): 607; also printed in *Britannia's Alarm* (London: R. King, 1745), 25–28.

17. See Toland, *Two Essays Sent in a Letter. . . . The Second Concerning the Rise, Progress, and Destruction of Fables and Romances* (London: R. Baldwin, 1695), 29–31; *Clito: A Poem on the Force of Eloquence* (London: n.p., 1700), 16; and "Clidophorus," in *Tetradymus* (London: J. Brotherton and W. Meadows, 1720), 79–87.

18. A notable exception to this is the republican-oriented collection supposedly by a Dutch author, a Johan de Witt, *Fables Moral and Political*, 2 vols. (London: n.p., 1703) 2: 56, 118–20.

19. *Fables of Aesop and Others* (London: J. Tonson, 1722), preface [xxiv].

L'Estrange and Locke that the mind of the child is like wax, soft and capable of any impression that is first given to it, Croxall disputed L'Estrange's claim of having intended his collection for children.[20] According to Croxall, L'Estrange's Jacobite philosophy was instead directed toward an adult readership, as was indicated by the excessive length and cost of L'Estrange's folio volume. But as Richardson later noted, Croxall's collection as well appears to have been inaccessible to children because of its pedantic quotations and Latin passages.[21] Croxall's fables had the distinct tone of dealing with a political philosophy intended for adult readers.[22] Turning the beast fable form around on opponents such as L'Estrange, Croxall argued that the Jacobite understanding of men as stupid or vicious animals failed to recognize the civilizing effect of laws of good government.

In addition to attacks on one another's political parties at large, the fable writers in the early part of the century were expected to concern themselves with public and private satire. The political fables of Jonathan Swift, for example, written during the second and third decades of the century, seldom dealt with any general moral or social themes; instead, particular individuals like Marlborough and groups such as the Dissenters became the targets of his satire.[23] So strong was the pressure to limit fabling

20. *Ibid.*, preface and 205.

21. *Aesop's Fables*, ed. Samuel Richardson (1740; facsimile reprint, New York: Garland, 1975), vi.

22. For example, see his *Fables of Aesop*, 225: "Men originally enter'd into Covenants and civil Compacts with each other for the Promotion of their Happiness and Well-being, for the Establishment of Justice and public Peace. How comes it then that they look stupidly on, and tamely acquiesce, when wicked Men pervert this End, and establish an arbitrary Tyranny of their own upon the Foundation of Fraud and Oppression? Among Beasts, who are incapable of being civiliz'd by social Laws, it is no strange thing to see innocent helpless Sheep fall a Prey to Dogs, Wolves and Kites: but it is amazing how Mankind could ever sink down to such a low degree of base Cowardice, as to suffer some of the worst of their Species to usurp a Power over them, to supersede the righteous Laws of good Government, and to exercise all kinds of Injustice and Hardship, in gratifying their own vicious Lusts."

23. See Colin J. Horne, " 'From a Fable form a Truth': A Consideration of the Fable in Swift's Poetry," in *Studies in the Eighteenth Century*, ed. R. F. Brissenden (Canberra: Australian National University Press, 1968), 198–200; and Albert Ball, "Swift and the Animal Myth," *Transactions of the Wisconsin Academy of Sciences, Arts, and Letters* 48 (1959), 243. Also see the *Poems of Jonathan Swift*, ed. Harold Williams (Oxford: Clarendon Press, 1937), 1: 151–58, 188–91, 207–9; 2: 395–96; Wray, "The English Fable," 71–72; and Swift to Gay, 10 July 1732, *Correspondence* 4: 38–39.

to satire that Anne Finch, Countess of Winchelsea, complained that critics were actually preventing fabulists from addressing classical subjects in literary as opposed to political ways.[24]

However, as the use of fables as a literary form grew in importance—primarily as a result of translations of the works of La Fontaine and La Motte (writers, it should be noted, who were not influenced by the English passion for using fables for specific political and satirical attacks)—writers such as John Gay devoted more attention to the stylistic potential of fables in English. Admittedly, Gay's first volume of *Fables* (1727) combined satiric commentary on social behavior with moral instruction; but when compared with L'Estrange's or Croxall's use of fables, Gay's use is noticeably apolitical in spite of its concern for social morality.

Dedicated to the young prince William, Gay's first set of *Fables* constituted a general guide for the instruction of a gentleman at court, attacking luxury and praising industry. When Gay was unable to gain an appointment from the court after the publication of his first set of *Fables*, he produced a second set, which appeared posthumously in 1738 and which contained numerous satiric attacks on the frauds and cheats among political appointees of the Walpole administration.[25]   In contrast to most of the fables then being published, Gay's second collection appears more fitted to the time thirty years earlier when the fable was recognized as an appropriate political and satiric device.

At the end of the 1730s, Richardson's moves to depoliticize Aesopic fables—as opposed to Gay's attempts to reinstate the fable as political satire—proved to be more in touch with developments in the use of fables by English authors and with the traditional uses of fables.   In his revision of L'Estrange's fable collection, Richardson shows a distrust of party polemics and softens or eliminates L'Estrange's explicit political sniping, noting that "we think it no wise excusable to inflame Childrens Minds with Distinctions, which they will imbibe fast enough from the Attachments of Parents, &c. and the Warmth of their own Imaginations."[26]

---

24. "The Critick and the Writer of Fables" (1713), *The Poems of Anne Countess of Winchelsea*, ed. Myra Reynolds (Chicago: University of Chicago Press, 1903), 153–55.

25. See Sven M. Armens, *John Gay: Social Critic* (New York: King's Crown Press, 1954), 190–96.

26. Richardson, *Aesop's Fables*, xi.

The explicitly political thrust of fable writing in England had given way, by the end of the 1730s, to the use of fables as means of socializing individuals. Or more precisely stated, the shift from political to social themes in English fable writing indicated the rise to prominence of a use of fables that had, in fact, paralleled their political use but that had played, in the early part of the century, a role subordinate to political uses. In particular, writers like Bernard Mandeville refused to limit their use of fables to explicitly political topics and preferred instead to expand their use of the form into discussions of general social and economic themes. As I will argue in my final chapter, this return to the immediacy of individual, passional engagement with fabling allows other English thinkers (e.g., Shaftesbury, Thomas Blackwell, William Warburton) to counter the Lockean inclination to remove myth or fable from the heart of philosophy.

THE SOCIAL APPLICATION OF FABLES

During the same period when many English writers (particularly the Grub Street authors) were turning to fables as satiric tools for criticizing the policies of the parties and individuals within and outside the government, other authors—and at times the same authors—found the fable a useful tool for social commentary. Perhaps the most notable example of this trend is Bernard Mandeville's *Fable of the Bees* (1714), an expanded commentary on his poem, published in 1705, entitled "The Grumbling Hive." In the *Fable* Mandeville was less concerned with the personality conflicts and power struggles of those in government—themes more of interest to Swift and Gay, whose sponsors were members of the government or who sought to ingratiate themselves to particular members of the government—than with the social conditions for civil existence.

As he does in translations of Aesop's fables and in his own original fables (published together in *Aesop Dress'd*, 1704), Mandeville highlights the insatiable character of human desires, the need for integrity and for controlling pride, and the fact of human social interdependence. In his fables, inevitable social inequality allows the rich and powerful to take advantage of their privileged position and oppress the poor and weak. As objectionable as this scenario might be, however, it could easily be worse;

and "The Grumbling Hive" recommends that men not grumble at what they have, for they might always be asking for worse.[27]

Though Mandeville felt uncomfortable about referring to the *Fable of the Bees* as a fable because of its length, he nonetheless continued to identify it in successive editions as a fable, consciously aware of the dominant themes and satirical uses of the form in the period. Just as Hobbes in his *De Homine* had noted that his characterization of men as vicious, self-interested beings governed by fear was not intended to refer to men as men, so Mandeville's adoption of the fable form was intended to describe men's interaction *as if* the prudential morality that characteristically dominates fables were the only or most important standard of moral value upon which men acted or were capable of acting.[28] Mandeville emphasized this point in the second edition of the *Fable* (1714) by noting in the subtitle that his parallels between the bees in the hive and men in society applied specifically only *"during the degeneracy of mankind."*[29] That is, insofar as men were understood in the context of a fable—a form whose most common characters were animals—men were to be understood as concerned primarily with the prudential morality that typically characterizes animals.

The fable form of Mandeville's work not only qualified his positions regarding social relations but also suggested (again in the spirit of Hobbes) that thinkers and educators could see good reason for encouraging the self-regarding and prudential values emphasized in fable writing without implying that such values were the only or most important bases of morality. Rousseau's later objections to the pedagogic use of fables (e.g., in *Émile*, 1762) because of their emphasis on cunning and prudential morality—instead of a morality based on "higher" values—fail to take such a methodological qualification into account.

In matters of economics and trade, the fables of the period praised the man of enterprise who took advantage of opportunities but who was also honest and realistic in his appraisal of his own

27. See John S. Shea's introduction to Mandeville's *Aesop Dress'd*, Augustan Reprint Society Publication No. 120 (Los Angeles: William Andrews Clark Memorial Library, 1966), ix; and Hector Monro, *The Ambivalence of Bernard Mandeville* (Oxford: Clarendon Press, 1975), 26–30.

28. See Stephen H. Daniel, "Civility and Sociability: Hobbes on Man and Citizen," *Journal of the History of Philosophy* 18 (1980): 209–15.

29. See Warren R. Brown, "An Introduction to Mandeville's *The Fable of the Bees*" (Ph.D. diss., Claremont Graduate School, 1977), 20–26.

abilities and dependence on others. Richard Steele, Daniel Defoe, and John Gay repeatedly appealed to the Aesopic fable of the belly and the members of the body (a fable that emphasizes how the arms and legs depend on the stomach for strength and how the belly depends on them for food) as a fable showing the interdependence of the trading and landed interests in England.[30] An occasional fable warned against the mercantilist exploitation of foreign countries and colonies, and numerous fabulists held up the South Sea Scheme as an example of the wages of excessive greed and pride.[31]

As fables of political satire decreased (coinciding with growing confidence in the permanence of the succession of the Hanoverians), fables supporting the political status quo and objecting to actions undermining the established social order began to appear with increasing regularity, thus reinstating a traditional concern of fabling that had been eclipsed during the turmoil of the second half of the seventeenth century. Individuals were encouraged to be satisfied with their place in the natural and social order; they were advised to work hard, to protect their property, and to save for the future.[32] By the middle of the century, fables had become less the means by which writers like Croxall argued that Jacobites should accept their political lot, and more a conservative support for personal material improvement. Yet, as the fables of Christopher Smart maintained (from 1750 to 1763), economic prowess and financial superiority were no match for the simple goodness of homely virtue.[33]

30. See Richard Steele, *The Spectator* (No. 174), ed. Donald F. Bond, 5 vols. (Oxford: Clarendon Press, 1965) 2: 185–86; and Gay's *Fables II* (London J. & P. Knapton, 1738), No. 8.

31. On the misuse of underdeveloped countries by unscrupulous traders, see Caleb D'Anvers's fable about the cow in India, in *The Craftsman* 9 (21 Oct. 1732): 273–77. For South Sea Scheme fables, see Daniel Bellamy the Elder, "The Dog and the Shadow," in his *Young Ladies Miscellany* (London: n.p., 1732), 49; Swift's fable entitled "The Bubble" (1720), printed in Williams's edition of the *Poems*, 1: 248–59, and discussed in Horne, "From a Fable," 201; and Croxall, *Fables of Aesop*, 10.

32. See George E. Bush, "The Fable in the English Periodical, 1660–1800" (Ph.D. diss., St. John's University, 1965), 160–69; and Joan Hildreth Owen, "The Choice of Hercules and Eighteenth Century Fabulists" (Ph.D. diss., New York University, 1969), 9.

33. See Edward G. Ainsworth and Charles E. Noyes, *Christopher Smart: A Biographical and Critical Study* (Columbia: University of Missouri Press, 1943), 53–54; and Arthur Sherbo, *Christopher Smart: Scholar of the University* (East Lansing: Michigan State University Press, 1967), 98.

That simplicity and unaffected virtue so characteristic of many of the animals found in fables of the period continued to attract interest on the part of fabulists. But the insistence that humans learn their place in nature—coming particularly in a genre that turned the relationship of human beings to animals topsy-turvy—demanded some treatment of that relationship itself, a treatment that needed to break free of the imagery and conventions of the fable form. Ultimately the debate concerning this philosophical problem undermined the confidence of some writers in the fable form and no doubt had some influence in the demise of the genre's popularity among writers. In any event, the discussion that emerged focused attention on the pivotal importance of speech for fable characters. This, in turn, thematized the need to examine the question of the origin of language in myth.

THE ANIMAL PROBLEM FROM INSIDE FABLE USE

The animal fable presented authors with both an opportunity and a philosophical problem. The form allowed authors a didactic and satirical device whose persuasiveness and charm lay precisely in its indirect application to human behavior. But the fragile nature of the implied parallel threatened the very project of fable writing and therefore aroused concern that readers would either scoff at the idea of animals acting like human beings or fail to see the methodological limitations imposed on the author's message by the intentional adoption of the fable form. By writing fables fabulists hoped to use animal characters to express various ideas about human beings; but the more authors wrote animal fables—especially fables that encouraged people to avoid pride and to learn their place in nature and in society—the more apparent became the need to address the question of mankind's relationship to animals (a relationship in which human beings were assumed to be dominant but concerning which people were cautioned not to become overly proud).

Animal fables had a reflexive and ambivalent impact on the understanding of the nature of humanity. Either they portrayed animals as superior to human beings (in hopes of embarrassing individuals into good behavior), or they highlighted the natural superiority of human beings over animals (by placing importance on the speaking and reasoning abilities of the fabular characters), or they emphasized the right of members of each species to live according to their places in nature (with the implication that humans needed to curtail the pride that resulted in their disruption of that natural order). Because these different ways of interpreting fable use were not mutually exclusive—indeed, the irony implicit in such ambivalence of intent appealed no doubt to most fabulists—authors were unable to adapt the fable form to reflect changes in attitudes toward the status of animals vis-à-vis mankind.

The beast satire of the sixteenth and seventeenth centuries constantly referred to the similarity between animal and human behavior and pointed out how people often act less rationally than beasts. Edmund Spenser's *Mother Hubberd's Tale* (1591) and John Dryden's *The Hind and the Panther* (1687) suggested that humans could learn a great deal by observing the natural reason of brutes. In describing how beasts refused to be changed back into human beings, James Howell's *Parly of Beasts* (1660) portrayed people primarily in terms of their brains and bodies, as opposed to the animals who had attained a peace of mind that transcended the tumultuous flux of the material order—an almost direct reversal of the Cartesian depiction of animals (vis-à-vis humans) as mindless and soulless machines.

By the time Swift described how the reasonable Houyhnhnms governed debased men (the Yahoos) in *Gulliver's Travels* (1726), the point had been repeatedly made that the justification for using animals in fables to teach individuals wisdom was based on the observation that animals, unlike humans (who, Swift satirically noted in the 1732 fable "The Beasts' Confession to the Priest," can be elevated almost to an equal footing with certain brutes), do not fall victim to their own pride and self-deception.[34]

John Toland reasoned that animals, unlike people, always act in prudential ways; and it is their prudence and cunning that makes them objects of admiration for human beings. Within the domain of the fabulist, Toland noted, prudence is the queen of the virtues; and it is prudential action that creates all the wonderful things in the world: "Prudence may justly be stil'd, The Guide of our Life, the Thread of our Labyrinths, and the Comforter under all Afflictions."[35] The prudential morality of animals

34. See Horne, "From a Fable," 202. Cf. "The Beasts' Confession to the Priest," in *Jonathan Swift: The Complete Poems*, ed. Pat Rogers (New Haven, Conn.: Yale University Press, 1983), 508–14.

35. Toland, *The Fables of Aesop* (London: Thomas Leigh and Daniel Midwinter, 1704), 358; see also 73, 343–52.

exhibited, he concluded, the constancy of mind needed to guide people through the complexities of human existence, and by means of such a morality individuals could avoid "the Capricios of Intemperance and Ambition."

Swift's treatment of animal behavior as exemplary for human beings outlines the fabular context in which Toland made his remarks. Though human nature in fact excels brute nature, animals (in Swift's view) can teach human beings to live up to their calling to moral excellence. But as Swift remarked in discussing the Houyhnhnms, the prudential morality encouraged in animal fables is inferior to the morality of fully reasonable behavior.[36] In moving beyond his fables to *Gulliver's Travels*, Swift highlighted a progression from the fabular endorsement of the prudential morality of animals, through a stage in which humans adopt the morality of prudential behavior, to a culmination ironically outside the fable form in a moral vision characteristic of animals (the Houyhnhnms) but transcending the prudential morality of fabular animals. As such, Swift's writings pointed beyond prudential morality as an ideal by pointing beyond Aesopic fables.

The reflexive reconditioning of fable writing and revision of the understanding of human-animal relationships (such as we find in Swift's writings) are part of the larger movement of fabulists to reevaluate the concept of the order of nature and mankind's place in it. Reintroducing a common practice of fabulists prior to the seventeenth century, authors employed as principal figures not only animals but also gods, humans, abstractions, and inanimate objects. Such fables appeared to make a concerted effort to break down the distinction of species and to throw into question mankind's privileged place in nature. Failing to live in accord with their rightful place in nature, people were challenged to justify their disruption of the natural order. By means of the fable, Gay and others were able to reinstate an order in nature that asserted, in its startling reversal of the relationship of human beings and animals, confidence in the human inclination to goodness but disappointment in the pride and egotism that diverted people from realizing their potential.[37]

36. See Ball, "Swift and the Animal Myth," 243–47; and Wray, "The English Fable," 78.
37. See Bush, "The Fable in the English Periodical," 82–116; and Armens, *John Gay*, 218.

From the fables of Edmund Arwaker (*Truth in Fiction*, 1708) to those of Gay and Smart, the message was clear: The analogy between humans and animals implied in fables is justified by our observation of animal behavior and should occasion respect for, and more humane treatment of, animals.[38]   But Toland had warned, at the relatively early date of 1704, that readers should not press the fabular comparison between humans and animals too far, for to do so would encourage the erroneous belief that, because animals in fables speak and reason, they also speak and reason in real life.[39]   For most fabulists the fabular device of speaking and reasoning animals did not imply their essential similarities to human beings.

However, Arwaker and even Dryden hinted that the metaphorical use of philosophical doctrines such as the Pythagorean theory of the transmigration of souls enabled the fabulist to link the reasoning and speaking abilities of humans with similar abilities in animals.[40]   The recurring portrayal of reasoning and speaking animals in fables was thus to have the effect of pointing out how the issue of the status of animals vis-à-vis humans was not really an issue resolvable within the methodological restrictions of the fable form.

As late as 1760, William Shenstone and Robert Dodsley were debating the merits of granting animals reason and speech.[41] Dodsley argued that the fabulist must give animals the ability to speak and reason in order to establish a striking resemblance between animals and people, a resemblance that makes the instincts of the animal characters intelligible and gives their exemplary actions a determinate focus.   Shenstone, however, was concerned less with the formal requirements of the fable genre than with the philosophic presuppositions implied by the use of the form.   "The grand exception to fables," he wrote, "consists

38. See Graham, "John Gay's *Fables*," 73; Armens, *John Gay*, 229; and Ainsworth and Noyes, *Christopher Smart*, 54.

39. *The Fables of Aesop*, 73.

40. Edmund Arwaker, *Truth in Fiction: or, Morality in Masquerade* (London: J. Churchill, 1708), introduction; and John Dryden, *Fables Ancient and Modern* (1700), in *The Poems of John Dryden*, ed. James Kinsley (Oxford: Clarendon Press, 1958), 4: 1724.

41. See Ralph Strauss, *Robert Dodsley: Poet, Publisher, and Playwright* (New York: John Lane, 1910), 283–84; and Robert Dodsley, *An Essay on Fable* (1761), introduction by Jeanne K. Welcher and Richard Dircks (Los Angeles: William Andrews Clark Memorial Library, 1965), lxvi–lxix.

in giving *speech* to animals, &c. a greater *violation of truth* than
appears in any other kind of writing! This objection is insurmountable.''[42] Vicesimus Knox later voiced a similar complaint
when he noted, "The reasoning and conversation of irrational
animals raise them to a level with the human species; and if
children are to respect reason and speech as most excellent gifts,
they will, in their imaginations, honour the cock, the wolf, and
the fox, as much as man, or else degrade man to the rank of the
cock, the wolf, and the fox.''[43]

As such remarks make clear, both Shenstone and Knox understood fable writing in the context of the extrafabular debates
regarding mankind's relationship to animals and the centrality of
speech as a distinguishing human characteristic. Dodsley, on the
other hand, approached fable writing as a world-defining process
in which the fabulist *creates* relationships and parallels, and thus
controls and regulates the implications of giving speech and
reason to animals. Concerned mainly with the fable *form* and
not so much with the extrafabular relationship of humans and
animals, Dodsley restricted the form to its didactic function in
spite of pressures both within and outside the form to address
the implications of its use.

But as succeeding chapters of my discussion will indicate,
something more was at issue. For it is precisely when the fable
form reveals its educative control of language/speech and reason
that the mythic powers of fabling appear. The fable-myth
embodies in its figural presentation of speech exactly what constitutes reason. The presence of speaking animals challenges the
human monopoly on reason by throwing into question the criteria
by which humanity is defined. In this mythic setting, speech is
not simply some ability that human beings happen to have:
Speech defines the human by defining the rational within the
performance of fable. Fables, like myths, invite a reorganization
of meaning by reverting to moments of creativity, moments when
the speech of the fable recalls the possibility of human invention
and control over meaning.

42. Shenstone to Richard Graves, 3 Oct. 1759, in *The Letters of William Shenstone*,
ed. Marjorie Williams (Oxford: Basil Blackwell, 1939), 523.

43. *Winter Evenings* (London: C. Dilly, 1788), 1: 438–39; also see Wray, "The
English Fable," 173–74, which points out how this position is indebted to
Rousseau's *Émile*.

When the dispute about animals brings the discussions of reason and speech together, the truly mythic character of fabling surfaces. Instead of saying that Dodsley's remarks point to extra-fabular concerns, it would be more correct to say that he (perhaps unknowingly) points to the combination of exhortative (moral, pedagogical) and meaning-constitutive features of fabling. In this sense, what at first seems to be a separate discussion of the literary history of Aesopic fabling in England ultimately leads into the same kinds of questions addressed by Descartes, Vico, Herder, and others I have thematically highlighted in my other chapters.

THE EPISTEMOLOGY OF FABLE USE

In a number of ways Dodsley is a culminating and pivotal figure in the development of fable use in England in the eighteenth century, for his work stands as the last significant attempt to reunite judgment (or reason) and imagination by means of fable writing. Though he insisted that animals be given speech and reason within fables, he also specified that fables should be rational. The fabular treatment of animals, Dodsley argued, should not violate our reasonable expectations of animals. As such, stories of lions who fall in love with maidens, geese who lay golden eggs, or foxes who desire grapes are poorly conceived. According to Dodsley, fable writing and fable reading require both judgment and imagination, whereas simple narrative requires only judgment. Accordingly, the writing form of the fabulist attempts to respect the character of the author both as creative poet and as rational teacher.[44]

However, at least twenty years before Dodsley wrote his fables, David Hume had pointed out that men would not even make a serious effort to imagine something that they knew to be false, and therefore obviously false "creativity" would be at cross-purposes with any attempt at rational pedagogy.[45] When Shen-

---

44. Dodsley, *An Essay on Fable*, xxxvi, lxx.

45. See *A Treatise of Human Nature* (1739–40), ed. L. A. Selby-Bigge (Oxford: Clarendon Press, 1965), 121. Cf. Christopher Smart's fable, "Reason and Imagination" (1763): *Gentleman's Magazine* 33 (July 1763): 355–56, reprinted in the *Collected Poems of Christopher Smart*, ed. Norman Callan (Cambridge: Harvard University Press, 1950), 1: 78–82; and Owen, "The Choice of Hercules," 99.

stone objected to Dodsley's fable-writing project, he was simply applying this same type of reasoning. Dodsley, however, rejected the belief that fables would appeal to the imagination only when they were entirely true; for to limit fables to truth and reality would undermine the assumption upon which fables were based, namely, that imagination entertains and educates reason, and not that reason educates imagination.

The year after Dodsley's *Essay on Fable* (1761), Bishop Richard Hurd highlighted the predicament in which Dodsley found himself when he noted that his age was one in which imagination was forced "to ally herself with strict truth, if she would gain admittance to reasonable company." Referring to the eclipse of imagination by reason, Hurd lamented that "what we have gotten by this revolution . . . is a great deal of good sense. What we have lost is a world of fine fabling."[46] Though the decline in mythic writing was uppermost in Hurd's mind, his comment about the loss of fabling (following in the spirit of Le Bossu's linkage between Aesopic and mythic fabling) applied equally and as forcefully to the Aesopic form, which shared the epic's exhortative character.

Hurd pointed to Hobbes and Locke as sources contributing to the split between the imaginative and the rational; and, indeed, it is in Locke's writings that we begin to detect epistemological doubts (vis-à-vis pedagogical doubts) about fabling. For, in *Some Thoughts Concerning Education* (1693), Locke had recommended that children read fables to improve both their reading abilities and their moral sensibility and not so much to develop their facility with grammar. In contrast, the primary intent of his interlinear translation of *Aesop's Fables* (1703) was to provide readers with an explicitly grammatical, and not a stylistic, introduction to the language. In both works, though, he treated fables as complete parcels of information that, joined with illustrations, could impress upon the minds of readers desirable practical, moral, or linguistic patterns of thinking. In Locke's hands, imagination thus declined from an essential characteristic in the formulation of fables to an auxiliary feature that made the reasonable or truthful part of the fable more entertaining or memorable.

46. *Letters on Chivalry and Romance*, in *The Works of Richard Hurd* (1811) (Hildesheim, FRG: Olms, 1969), 4: 350. See also James Sutherland, *English Literature of the Late Seventeenth Century* (Oxford: Clarendon Press, 1969), 354.

The de Witt collection of *Fables Moral and Political*, published in the same year as Locke's *Aesop's Fables*, assumed (even more than Locke did) the fabular appropriateness of an impressionist theory of knowledge: Fables were understood as instruments used by an author to make deep impressions on the mind. De Witt noted that unless our thoughts are associated with, or represented to us by means of, some corporeal thing or are joined to the words that allude to such thoughts, we have trouble remembering them.[47] In de Witt's view, the sensible imagery provided by fables acts as a mnemonic catalyst for reasoning and thought but does not really serve as a constitutive element in them. The impressionist theory of knowledge in the Locke and de Witt collections thus emphasized the role of the imagination and the fruitfulness of imagery only insofar as the reader of fables needs entertainment in the process of acquiring good sense or needs devices to aid memorization.

In such an approach, however, the fable *form*, by which the reader acquires such truth or good sense, is not an essential contributory factor in the truth or good sense thus learned. The process of fable writing (as distinguished from fable reading) treats the imagination as subordinate to reason, and in fact (in Shenstone's words) actually violates truth in order to impress on the minds of readers the elements of good sense contained within (and almost in spite of) the fable.

When adults were considered as fable readers, the Lockean epistemology (as adopted and modified by other fable writers) focused on the weaknesses, intransigence, or pride of fable readers rather than on the readers' contribution of imaginative insight. In his *Truth in Fiction*, for example, Arwaker employs the light imagery of the Cambridge Platonists in describing how fables filter or disguise truths that men are otherwise unable or unwilling to accept.

The Strength and Vigour of Men's Minds are hinder'd from exerting themselves to Advantage, by a mixture of Weakness and Infirmity: So that few can contemplate Truth in its full Splendour, but must have it convey'd to them by *Medium's*, and its Beams let gently in upon them, as it were through Chinks and Crannies. But they whose Manners are any-way depraved and vitiated, cannot endure the Light that shews them their own Deformity too visibly. . . . So that, to gain admittance to their

47. *Fables Moral and Political* 1, [viii–ix].

Regard, Truth must appear in the insinuating Disguise of Fiction; and, by a pleasing Fable, they must be led insensibly to the Wisdom of an instructing Moral.[48]

Wisdom (for Arwaker) is not to be found in the fable, for the fable form conceals or disguises truth so as to lead the reader toward wisdom: The fable entices the reader through an appeal to imagination to overcome the restrictions of imagination and to transcend the fable-reading process itself in attempting to attain the truth. Through works like Arwaker's, such a description of the role of fable contributed to a tension within the use of the form itself, born out of the recognition of the essentially distorting character of fable writing. It was just such a tension, as Hurd later noted, that opposed fabling to good sense.

In *The Spectator* Joseph Addison in 1712 challenged the assumption that the imaginative character of fables covers or distorts rational truth. Instead of discussing fables as devices by which information is transmitted in an incidentally entertaining way, Addison considers fables first and foremost as works of persuasion. By shifting the focus from information transmission to persuasion and advice-giving, Addison recognizes an essentially communicative character of fabling (including consideration of both fable writing and fable reading).

Instead of suggesting that we study the fable as a finished project, Addison invites his readers to consider the fabling process as a process by which the reader is made to believe that he advises himself. In reading a fable, Addison observes, "The Moral insinuates it self imperceptibly, we are taught by Surprise, and become wiser and better unawares. In short, by this Method a Man is so far over-reached as to think he is directing himself, whilst he is following the Dictates of another, and consequently is not sensible of that which is the most unpleasing Circumstance in Advice."[49] This understanding of the growth in wisdom as an intellectually pleasing process presents the fable as a form whose entertainment lies not so much in its appealing imagery as in the natural gratification of the mind as it becomes aware of its own creative abilities:

---

48. Arwaker, *Truth in Fiction*, ii–iii.
49. Joseph Addison, *The Spectator* (No. 512), 4: 318.

If we look into Human Nature, we shall find that the Mind is never so much pleased, as when she exerts her self in any Action that gives her an Idea of her own Perfections and Abilities. This natural Pride and Ambition of the Soul is very much gratified in the reading of a Fable; for in the Writings of this Kind, the Reader comes in for half of the Performance; Every thing appears to him like a Discovery of his own; he is busied all the while in applying Characters and Circumstances, and is in this respect both a Reader and a Composer. It is no wonder therefore that on such Occasions, when the Mind is thus pleased with it self, and amused with its own Discoveries, that it is highly delighted with the Writing which is the Occasion of it.[50]

Both a reader and a composer, the individual delights in the fabling process as a process of enlightenment in which he or she participates as much as the author. Unlike the accounts of Locke, de Witt, and Arwaker, Addison's treatment describes how the reader's entertainment in participating in the fabling process hinges not on the appeals and enticements of imagery but on the mind's pleasure at its own recognition of the constitutive, creative, and essentially fictive nature that underlies and unites both imagination and reason.

Addison's discussion of fabling presented a perspective different from that found in most of the fabulists following in the footsteps of Locke and L'Estrange. For these latter authors, memory acted as a major regulative factor in fable writing because it united present images with the patterns of thinking acquired in the past.[51] Addison, on the other hand, did not emphasize memory as a regulative factor in the choice of images for fable use because, for him, imagination and the use of imagery did not account for the appeal of fables as much as did the reader's appreciation of the way in which the fable form allows the reader to become conscious of his or her own creative abilities.

Addison thus developed an appreciation of the dialogic character of fables unmatched by any English animal fabulist or fable

50. *Ibid.* As I pointed out in the last chapter, Descartes had recognized this same feature when he remarked in his "fable of the world," "Most minds are displeased when things are made too easy for them. And to paint a picture here which shall please you, it is necessary that I make use of shadow as well as bright colors." See *Le Monde,* in Descartes' *Oeuvres,* ed. Charles Adam and Paul Tannery, 13 vols. (Paris: Cerf, 1897–1913), 11: 48; cf. Michael S. Mahoney's translation in his edition of *Le Monde* (New York: Abaris Books, 1979), 77.

51. See, for example, John Hawkesworth's essay on fables in *The Adventurer* 1 (6 January 1753): 104.

commentator in the eighteenth century except perhaps Mandeville (with whom I will deal in the next chapter). For an extension of this understanding of fabling beyond the author-reader dyad to communities and whole peoples, we would have to look to Dryden and others who speak about the classical myths as fables, or to authors outside England (e.g., Vico and Herder).[52] Both before and after Addison, the fabling stage belongs, as Hurd points out, to those who would distinguish good sense (or reason) and imagination; and insofar as imagination was an expendable accessory to the communal development of good sense, so was the fable form that thrived on it.

THE DECLINE OF THE FABLE FORM

Gay's second set of fables (1738) was the last significant collection of fables directed especially to adults. At the end of the following year, Richardson published his revision of L'Estrange's *Fables of Aesop*, noting that his work was intended primarily for children. As more and more parents decided to educate their children themselves, the demand for texts oriented to children pressured fabulists to avoid political applications and remarks that children would not understand or parents would think inappropriate for a beginning text. Indeed, when John Hall-Stevenson published what must have appeared to some of his contemporaries as an anachronistic collection of fables about economic and political matters, he felt obliged to title his work *Fables for Grown Gentlemen* (1761). Dodsley, who published his study of fables and a collection of fables in that same year, expressed the more commonly held position when he simply assumed that the ordinary audience for fabulists (especially Aesopic fabulists) consisted mainly of children.

The fable collections that appeared after Richardson's—for example, Edward Moore and Henry Brooke's *Fables for the Female Sex* (1744), the anonymously written *Entertaining Fables for Masters and Misses* (1747) and *Fables and Tales for the Ladies* (1750), John Kidgell's *Original Fables* (1763), Thomas Marryat's *Sentimental Fables* (1771), John Langhorne's *Fables of Flora* (1771), William

---

52. See Hayden V. White, "The Irrational and the Problem of Historical Knowledge in the Enlightenment," in *Irrationalism in the Eighteenth Century*, ed. Harold E. Pagliaro (Cleveland, Ohio: Case Western University Press, 1972), 315.

Russell's *Fables Moral and Sentimental* (1772), and John Huddlestone Wynne's *Fables of Flowers* (1773)—dealt with social amenities and sentimental personifications. The force and vitality of the fable collections of the earlier part of the century stand out all the more against these later collections in which delicacy and daintiness become characteristic of a form in obvious decline.

I have suggested that the decline of the fable form in England was due to problems generated by the very way in which the form was used and developed. In the first place, as the short morals of fables were replaced by ever-longer reflections and applications—many of which had little connection with elements in the fables—fable writers recognized that the fable form contained the seeds of its own transcendence. As Shenstone argued against Dodsley, what was important was the moral of the fable; and insofar as the point of the fable was to instill in the reader some truth, then any aspect of the fable that confuted the truth was unacceptable. Particularly in animal fables, the fabular ascription of speech and reason detracted from good sense (which was to be distinguished from imagination); and thus the very nature of "fabulous" writing contained within itself the grounds for raising objections to the fable form as much as to certain uses of it.

In the second place, the fable form was particularly adept at recommending the prudential morality consistent with a concentration on cunning in animal behavior. However, the more fabulists portrayed animals with powers of speech and reason, the more closely animals were to be identified with men. But the more men saw themselves as beasts whose morality was based on cunning and not on benevolence, the more objectionable the comparison appeared. The fable thus presented readers with the dilemma either of thinking of animals on the same level as men or of adopting prudence as more desirable than benevolence. In the face of such a dilemma, many writers simply chose to avoid the fable form.

Finally, my discussion of fables within the broader context of myth arises out of two considerations. First, the moral/pedagogic and creative features of fabling operative in English literature in the eighteenth century resonate with elements of mythic thought. Even in writers such as Addison, the connection between myth and fable at times might appear strained if it were not for the recurring insistence that fables point to originative moments in the formation of personality and moral (and even epistemological) development. Indeed, it is not accidental that fabling is often linked, by Locke for example, to the process of learning language—an association that Herder would capitalize on in high-lighting the fact that a culture's originative vocabulary and literature more often than not stem from its heritage in fabling. As I shall also point out shortly in regard to Mandeville and Vico, the genesis of meaning within fabling or mythmaking is always in some way tied to the question of the origin of human language and speech. The English debate about the propriety of animal speech in fables thus fits quite nicely within the broader discussion of mythic thought.

Second, the more theoretical character of my other chapters on mythic philosophy should not be taken as an underestimation of the significance of the practico-political aspects of myth. In England the fluidity of the various meanings of fable invites such an investigation of mutually suggestive interrelations. Grounded in the so-called "literary" (vis-à-vis "philosophical") works of Bacon, mythic philosophy in England captures the empirical spirit of praxis even if it does not characterize the restrictive literature of philosophical empiricism identified by classical historiography.

To leave the discussion of Aesopic fabling out of the account of mythic philosophy in early-eighteenth-century England is to ignore the distinctive English contribution to the generation of a vocabulary of social and political discourse. Admittedly, as I will point out later, Mandeville and Shaftesbury among others extend the treatment of creativity beyond those bounds. But nowhere other than England do we find such a concerted effort to bring the art of fabling into such close proximity with topics of imme-diate social import.

CHAPTER FOUR

Myth and Rationality in Mandeville

THE FABLE OF THE BEES (1714), by Bernard Mandeville, has settled into an unobtrusive position on English literature graduate reading lists as an example of eighteenth-century wit and satire. Historians of eighteenth-century philosophy make pilgrimages to the *Fable* to find recast versions of Hobbesian self-interest, an amalgam of the problems of trying to integrate social and ethical thought in pre-Kantian form, or a proto–Adam Smith version of economic theory. But despite such attempts to make Mandeville respectable from a literary or philosophic standpoint, he nonetheless commands only polite respect from literary historians who think of his work as more concerned with a turn of phrase than with logical argumentation.

One way of dissolving such artificial distinctions lies in the recent strategy of identifying the philosophic nature of all writing and the literary character of philosophic writing. With such an approach, I would suggest, ambivalence toward Mandeville might finally begin to be corrected. Mandeville's interest in myth (or "fable") serves as an interpretive key. For it is Mandeville's inclusion of his later insights under the title of the *Fable* that alerts us to the fact that "fable" incorporates elements of narrative, apologue, and classical myth.

Mandeville's interest in myth, in particular, unites his concern for writing in a pleasing and useful way with accounts of the conceptual and historical presuppositions of rational analysis and argumentation. By appealing to the vocabulary of myth-fable, Mandeville focuses attention on the expressive and performative character of narrative and the persuasiveness of the literary—all within the context of reflexively highlighting the procedures by which such an account reveals the emergence of meaning.

As I have argued in the Introduction, myths serve a number of functions. First, they provide accounts of origins, especially the origin of giving accounts in the first place; in this way they identify and make explicit the originative character of all discourse. Second, myths introduce order into the chaos of experience through determinate expression. Third, myths identify the community and initiate individuals into it; this is a social function of myth. And fourth, myths provide contexts for defining rationality, meaning, value, truth; as such, myths are not true or false.[1]

Such themes in Mandeville's *Fable* begin to emerge only when its mythic character is recognized. Intensely interested in the conceptual and historical origins of practices, concepts, and language, Mandeville returns again and again to mythic themes and forms of expression. The origins of society, morality, and meaning are revealed in his works as accessible through the language of myth insofar as literature itself is revealed in terms of its all-too-human origins. Mandeville thus pushes the question of the relationship between philosophy and literature back to the mythic, proto-philosophic analysis of the presuppositions of language, meaning, and rationality.

Until we recognize that his effort is concerned less with already meaningfully constituted rational categories of thought than with the lessons to be learned in the accounts of how such categories emerge and function within society, we will not accord Mandeville much philosophic credibility. However, recent phenomenological and hermeneutic research have again raised the issue of the roles of myth and metaphor in the constitution of meaning and rationality. The appeal to the mythic in discourse provides Mandeville with the opportunity to give both a genetic account of the development of language and social practices and a functional account of the socializing impact of myths (including classical ones).

Within such contexts Mandeville can be seen less as a philosopher in the mold of Locke than one addressing concerns later of interest to Vico. Accordingly, he would be understood as a student of proto-philosophy and of the literary character of all philosophy, not a proponent either of the abstract and rational alone or of the literary devoid of its philosophic presuppositions. Insofar as all literature (as language) can be understood as containing philosophic implications, and insofar as all philosophy (as language) is understood as employing literary conventions, Mandeville's work is accordingly made more accessible both to historians of philosophy and to historians of literature and literary theory.

Prior to his publication of "The Grumbling Hive" (1705)—the work upon which the *Fable of the Bees* (1714) is an expanded commentary—Mandeville had experimented with the fable form

1. See the first section of the Introduction.

in at least three publications. In 1703 he published what is probably his first English work, *Some Fables After the Easie and Familiar Method of Monsieur de la Fontaine,* a collection of twenty-seven of La Fontaine's fables along with two fables of his own. This work was succeeded in the following year by *Aesop Dress'd,* an enlarged edition of *Some Fables* including ten additional fables from La Fontaine.[2] The fables in both collections embody the traditional Aesopic fable form and anticipate themes, such as the need for self-honesty and control of pride, that figure prominently in "The Grumbling Hive" and *The Fable of the Bees.*[3]

But in 1704 Mandeville was thinking not only about the Aesopic fable form (or "apologue"). He was also interested in the classical myths, commonly referred to by his contemporaries as fables. In that year he published an English translation of part of Paul Scarron's burlesque poem, *Typhon: or the Wars between the Gods and Giants.* Though he had originally intended to follow this up with a translation of the remaining four parts of Scarron's poem, he produced instead "The Grumbling Hive," which then became the reference point for much of his subsequent writing on the origins of language, rationality, and social practices.

My purpose is to highlight two features of Mandeville's philosophy that appear when we recognize the mythic character of his writings. First, in the expansions of *The Fable of the Bees* Mandeville continues a project begun in *Typhon* in which he recaptures the descriptive and morally exhortative unity of early classical (Homeric and Aesopic) fabling. Second, by means of this new mythology Mandeville is able to describe the origins and development of society, language, and rationality. In the course of these moves he proposes a new Genesis, which circumvents the biblical assumption of man's original rationality in favor of a satire on man's self-deluding attempt to deny his heritage of unreason.

2. Other publications, including *Aesop at Paris* (1701), *The Pamphleteers* (1703) and *The Planter's Charity* (1704), have also been attributed to Mandeville though their authorship is doubtful. In tone they are similar to the authentic works. However, they (along with Mandeville's Latin works on medicine) do not figure in this account.

3. See Philip Harth, "The Satiric Purpose of *The Fable of the Bees,*" *Eighteenth-Century Studies* 2 (1969): 321–22; John S. Shea's introduction to Mandeville's *Aesop Dress'd,* Augustan Reprint Society Publication No. 120 (Los Angeles: William Andrews Clark Memorial Library, 1966), ix; and Hector Monro, *The Ambivalence of Bernard Mandeville* (Oxford: Clarendon Press, 1975), 26–30.

The artificial distinction between literature and philosophy is thus overcome through Mandeville's identification of the mythic origin of both meaning and rationality. Such an understanding of his intention begins to explain why literary and philosophic scholarship has appraised Mandeville's work and importance ambivalently.

THE MYTH PROJECT: *TYPHON* THROUGH *THE FABLE OF THE BEES*

Mandeville points to the mythic origins of human communicability and rationality by highlighting the exemplary and didactic character of proto-philosophic literature. The fables of *Aesop Dress'd*, for example, portray animals with human characteristics—the powerful oppress the weak, prudential morality appears to govern all action—only to emphasize, in the words of the *Fable*, that such a picture applies specifically only "*during the degeneracy of mankind.*"[4] Such a moment of degeneracy can, of course, be understood historically in terms of postlapsarian man, but for Mandeville such a proto-rational condition always lies beneath the veneer of civilized politeness. The self-regarding and prudential values praised in the fables characterize proto-man, mankind in its moral and linguistic childhood. *Typhon*, he says, is addressed to a "Society of Fools"—individuals "above a Monkey, and yet below a Rational Creature."[5] For Mandeville, fable-man is not a man of rationality. Tied to sense and limited to self-interest just as Typhon and the giants are mired in earthbound nonreflection, mythic/fabular man is a hybrid of divine aspiration and mundane sensibility.

Even though this picture of man dictates the complementary literary form of fable or myth, it also indicates through its didactic and sometimes satiric tone how the form itself points to its own transcendence in philosophic literacy. In passages paralleling no text in Scarron's original, Mandeville ("your Favorite *Homer*") describes this development in human understanding as part of a pattern in which moral degeneracy plays a central role:

4. Cf. the title page of the 2d ed. of *The Fable of the Bees* (1714), ed. F. B. Kaye (Oxford: Clarendon Press, 1924) 2: facing 392.
5. "Epistle Dedicatory," in *Typhon: or the Wars between the Gods and Giants* (London: J. Nutt, 1704), ii.

Man grows worse and worse; you flatter
Your self, and cry they will grow better;
And so they will, in Understanding;
But as for any other mending,
You'll find, they'll do that ev'ry hour
As small Beer that begins to sowr.[6]

Within the context of the myth-fable, such a description of man serves less as a criticism of earth-bound prudential morality than as an indictment of the absence of commerce between divine reflection and earthy sensuality. "What Business has *Jove* here below?" asks Typhon. The gods would prefer to have little to do with earthly inhabitants. Indeed, the whole story about the war between the gods and giants in *Typhon* provides Mandeville with a mechanism for reestablishing contact between rationality and sense-bound communication within a moral context. Just as Aesopic fables serve to accomplish this in introducing children to the linguistic and moral community, so mythic accounts of mankind's infancy identify the prudential and figural bases of language and morality that can reinvigorate contemporary discussions of ethical and social progress.

In *Typhon* characters of the classical myths (e.g., Jove, Mercury) play roles normally assigned to animals in Aesopic fables. As Mandeville says, "There you shall see Gods no wiser than some of us turn'd into Bears, Bees, Storks, and such like Creatures resembling one another."[7] Gods, men, animals, even inanimate objects—all are reduced within Mandeville's myth to the equal status characteristic of inhabitants of the aboriginal chaos traditionally assumed as the context out of which the mythologist brings forth order, meaning, and rationality. "I have provided you," Mandeville remarks, "a little *Ragow of Gods, Pins, Speeches, Stars, Meal-tubs,* and other Nick-nacks all jumbled together."[8] By jumbling all things together in fable (understood as combining elements of Aesopic apologue and classical myth), Mandeville reinstates the preclassical status of myth as not only an account of the origins of nature and man but also as a moral-pedagogical device. He thus throws into doubt the hierarchical order of beings in terms of which gods, giants, and men make claim to

6. *Typhon*, 24. Cf. *Oeuvres de Scarron*, 7 vols. (Paris: J.-F. Bastien, 1786) 5: 430.
7. *Typhon*, vi.
8. *Ibid.*, v.

intellectual and moral superiority and delude themselves about their worth and importance.

Myth imposes an order on original chaos in its attempt to explain the origin of the set of conditions by which meaning is made possible in subsequent nonmythic accounts. By making explicit such a turn in *Typhon*'s account of the gods and in the continuing saga of the fable of the bees, Mandeville appeals for a reexamination of (1) the origins of human rationality, (2) the presumption that the world is meaningful by virtue of human activity, and (3) the arrogance of the sense of human superiority, which supports the questionable pride men take in bestowing order and meaning on the world.

Mandeville's fascination with the myth-fable thus has three implications. First, because fabulation or mythmaking jumbles the conventional expectations of the behavior of animals, men, and gods, it serves as a form of philosophical renovation. Accordingly, Aesopic fables (such as those in *Aesop Dress'd*) explicitly challenge human pride based on claims of natural superiority. Second, the turn to myth recaptures the spirit of chaos underlying classical myths about the origins of nature and man. In order to recount the story of the genesis of society, virtue, and language, Mandeville returns to the classical form used for such a task. Third, myth not only assumes a chaos out of which rationality emerges; it also identifies itself as the form appropriate for describing the emergence of such order. In myth man reasserts control over himself and nature by establishing the context in which explanations of his condition can have meaning.

Like the Homeric poets, Mandeville sees such an undertaking as extending far beyond a satirical attack on human hypocrisy, pride, and self-ignorance. It calls for an exposition that explains Mandeville's own interest in Scarron's *Typhon* and in the folly of gods, giants, and men. It calls for a new creation myth in which "mere" men of flesh and passions, "ignorant of the true deity," enjoy the comforts of their Eden-like existence, believing that they are "bless'd with all the Virtue and Innocence that can be wish'd for in a Golden Age."[9] But such a golden age is not one of superficial civility or rationality; instead it is an age unselfconscious of any distinctive importance it might have.

9.   *Fable of the Bees*, 1: 6–7.

As Mandeville points out, the main design of *The Fable of the Bees* is to reveal how mythic immediacy in sensation degenerates into dispassionate and unchanging rationality. Mandeville does this by recalling for socialized man the self-interested principles of human behavior described in the Homeric myths and all too easily glossed over in the polite shallowness of a golden age become civilized. Mandeville's *Fable* strips away such coverings, exposing the so-called Eden of the hive as morally corrupted by self-congratulatory but socially beneficial pride. As the Muse-inspired spokesman for the gods, Mandeville recounts the epic of prerational, premoral man before his fall into sociable self-delusion.[10] Whereas *Typhon* only hints at the possibilities for this mythic revelation, Mandeville's commentary on "The Grumbling Hive" expands his application of the classical tragic flaw (lack of self-knowledge, specifically, failing to know one's origins) to the status of myth itself.

This attempt to unite mythic characters and concerns with those of the Aesopic fable points to assumptions underlying "The Grumbling Hive" and *The Fable of the Bees* that do not become apparent until we consider the possibility that, for Mandeville, *The Fable of the Bees* is as much a mythic form of writing as it is an Aesopic fable form. Fresh from their participation in *Typhon* the year before, Jove and Mercury do not just happen to reappear with the manlike bees of the hive; rather, they signify the link between myth and apologue in Mandeville's early English writings. Instead of treating "The Grumbling Hive" solely as a story that imparts some moral and that has speaking and reasoning animals (and even gods) in the dominant roles, Mandeville proposes the work also as a new myth itself, to which he adds the growing mythology found in the 1714, 1723, and 1729 expansions of the *Fable*. This new mythology recounts the genesis of human pride by challenging appeals to morality and rationality as bases upon which to justify claims of human superiority in the order of nature.

It is crucial for Mandeville that he present his indictment of human pride in the form of a fable because only within fable (as myth and apologue) can he recapture the root of human self-

10. Cf. Elias J. Chiasson, "Bernard Mandeville: A Reappraisal," *Philological Quarterly* 49 (1970): 508; John Colman, "Bernard Mandeville and the Reality of Virtue," *Philosophy* 47 (1972): 129; and Thomas A. Horne, *The Social Thought of Bernard Mandeville* (London: Macmillan, 1978), 23.

deception. The beelike gods of *Typhon* and the godlike and Jove-transformed bees of "The Grumbling Hive" embody Mandeville's marriage of Homer and Aesop, of classical myth and apologue. But it is in *The Fable of the Bees* that Mandeville's fabular description of man becomes most explicit. For it is in the *Fable* that he (1) emphasizes the aboriginal, self-corrective, and self-constituting nature of emerging rationality and (2) cautions against the self-deception and pride in human rationality that permit the very success of the fable form as a moral-pedagogical device.

In short, it is not enough to describe Mandeville's philosophy of human nature without explaining why he chooses to present it in the form of a fable including features of both myth and apologue. Admittedly, the designation of fable has to be extended beyond "The Grumbling Hive" to include the extensive commentary on the poem, the essays on the origin of moral virtue and the nature of society, and the dialogues on the origins of language and rationality—all of which Mandeville himself includes under the title of the *Fable*. Considering the fact that Mandeville published other works between 1705 and 1729 on a number of topics, it is all the more revealing that he chose to include treatments of the origins of virtue, society, and language within the ongoing *Fable* project.

In fact, Mandeville says that his *Enquiry into the Origin of Honour* (1732), published three years after part II of *The Fable of the Bees*, employs the very same interlocutors and presumably continues the dialogue begun in the *Fable*. It thus appears that when Mandeville wanted to address questions distinctively appropriate for treatment in mythic forms, he returned to the *Fable*.

"YOUR FAVORITE HOMER" AS AESOP

In the course of the writings associated with the *Fable*, Mandeville presents a mythic (self-consciously originative and exhortative) account of man, society, and the genesis of rationality and language. From the first sentence of the *Fable* Mandeville makes clear his intent to treat man as artificially abstracted from education, socialization, or religious training.[11] Understood simply as a being of flesh and passions, "meer Man" lacks not

11. *Fable of the Bees*, 1: 3–4, 40.

only a natural fondness for other members of his species but also capacities of thought, reflection, and speech necessary for the very possibility of large-scale coexistence. Like Hobbes, Mandeville consciously restricts his description of man to characteristics that can be counted on by those who cunningly manage the body politic on a large scale.[12]

It is not that Mandeville believes all men lack the rationality or concern for others that Shaftesbury, Addison, and Steele describe. Rather, Mandeville's point is that no large-scale political management based on such an image of man can succeed. Unlike these contemporaries, Mandeville equates manageable and dependable (i.e., knowable) society solely with the body politic, that large-scale domain of human interaction dominated by the constants of irrationality and self-interest.

The *Fable* is myth, however, not because it describes natural man solely as a proto-participant in large-scale societies, but because it describes the origins and development of rationality itself in the genesis of the language, meaning, society, and virtue that permits the possibility of Aesopic fabling in the first place. That is, the Aesopic understanding of fable relies on the mythic understanding of fable insofar as mythic man appears to be developing into a reasoning, speaking, and socializing being capable of the virtuous behavior encouraged in Aesopic fables.

The link between men and normally irrational animals that is presumed in Aesopic fabling can succeed only to the extent that, for example, the man-bee connection can be grounded in social-anthropological exegesis. It is not enough for Mandeville to highlight the similarities between human and animal social behavior because, even if there are certain parallels, the analogy breaks down under the strain of presupposing that rational behavior can characterize any behavior other than human. Unlike other Aesopic fabulists, however, Mandeville cannot simply portray the bees (or gods and giants) as naturally reasoning (i.e., human) agents, for his point is that nature does not bestow on men any innate rationality (even if it does bestow on them the passion of pity). The parallel therefore cannot be drawn between individual animals and individual men. Instead, just as order and design characterize the overall social activity of the hive, so also human

12. *Ibid.*, 41, 347; and Stephen H. Daniel, "Civility and Sociability: Hobbes on Man and Citizen," *Journal of the History of Philosophy* 18 (1980): 209–15.

social activity reflects such traits. In both cases, however, no organizing power or conscious decision by individuals contributes to such an end.

The myth of the *Fable* shifts the focus of mythic descriptions of the origins of man away from the solitary Adamic progenitor of humankind to the social nexus in which meaningful and rational behavior emerge and develop naturally though unconsciously. In this way Mandeville supports the appeal to Aesopic fabling and the form's practice of drawing parallels between animals and men without jeopardizing his claim that men individually cannot boast any natural superiority: "The fitness of Man for Society, beyond other Animals, is something real; but . . . it is hardly perceptible in Individuals, before great Numbers of them are joyn'd together, and artfully manag'd. . . . This real Something, this Sociableness, is a Compound, that consists in a Concurrence of several Things, and not in any one palpable Quality, that Man is endued with, and Brutes are destitute of."[13] Nature brings forth order and rationality within social contexts. Because such social contexts need not be human, Mandeville's appeal to the Aesopic use of social animals such as bees not only is justified but also reinforces his point that rationality, virtue, and honor, though characteristically human traits, are insufficient grounds for a justified sense of superiority.[14]

In telling the story of socialized and rational man's development from his natural state, Mandeville cautions against relying on human reason and sociability as bases for large-scale political administration. In fact, part of Mandeville's satirical intent in consciously choosing the fable as his form of writing is to expose the irrational and selfish foundations grounding the rational and virtuous ideal of man normally put forward in Aesopic fables.

Like the Greco-Roman myths, Mandeville's *Fable* describes the early ages of man. But unlike the classical myths, which Mandeville's contemporaries treated as corrupt versions of the Bible or as savage and foolish attempts to explain the human condition, the *Fable* does not assume man's original rationality or ability to speak: "Man is a rational Creature, but he is not endued with

13. *Fable of the Bees*, 2: 188. See F. A. Hayek, "Dr. Bernard Mandeville," *Proceedings of the British Academy* 52 (1966): 129–30; and Martin Price, *To the Palace of Wisdom* (Carbondale: Southern Illinois University Press, 1964), 117.

14. Cf. W. H. Greenleaf, *Order, Empiricism and Politics* (Westport, Conn.: Greenwood Press, 1980), 24.

Reason when he comes into the World; nor can he afterwards put it on when he pleases, at once, as he may a Garment. Speech likewise is a Characteristic of our Species, but no Man is born with it."[15] Rationality and the ability to speak are not distinguishing characteristics that men have naturally. Like Vico and Herder, Mandeville insists that the sociability, rationality, and moral sensibility of men emerge only gradually, coinciding with the development of language. The fact that men develop such traits is less a testimony of their innate abilities than an indication of the lengths they must go to in order to survive communally despite their individual inclinations to the contrary.

Mandeville's development of the temporal character of the evolution of human rationality increases in the course of his expansion of the *Fable*. It is as if the Aesopic dimension of fabular thinking emphasized in "The Grumbling Hive" is supplanted by the mythic dimension of fabling in the dialogues that end the *Fable* project. The *Fable* begins as a characteristically Aesopic apologue whose moral is to show the incompatibility of prosperity and virtue. In large societies, Mandeville argues, prosperity is possible only when truly virtuous actions (i.e., those based on unselfish motives) are replaced by the pride men take in their self-restraint and use of reason. But he has to explain why self-restraint and the use of reason prove successful, and he shows in "The Grumbling Hive" how an attack on pride in human rationality undermines the very confidence in rationality that permits the success of, and requires Mandeville's turn to, fabling in the first place.

Typically the fable form assumes the educability of the mind. But whereas other authors (e.g., Addison, Steele, and Berkeley) emphasize the excellence of such growth and ability, Mandeville focuses on the inadequacy of the mind which requires the appeal to the fable form originally.[16] As far as Mandeville is concerned, his disputants allow this inability and intellectual reticence to disappear too quickly from the process of the education of the mind. Mandeville sees a real fabular value in keeping before us

15. *Fable of the Bees*, 2: 190. See Burton Feldman and Robert D. Richardson, *The Rise of Modern Mythology: 1680–1860* (Bloomington: Indiana University Press, 1972), 3, 51.

16. See *Fable of the Bees*, 1: 52–53; Mandeville, *A Letter to Dion*, ed. Bonamy Dobree (Liverpool, Eng.: University Press of Liverpool, 1954), 48; and A. K. Rogers, "The Ethics of Mandeville," *International Journal of Ethics* 36 (1925–26): 7–9.

not only the prospect of dexterously managed private vices turned into public benefits but also the residually fragile wisdom that men have based on a pride that has lost touch with its fabular (and rhetorical) origins.

Mandeville's *Fable* corrects the assumption that the imaginative and exploratory presuppositions of fabular philosophizing should be replaced with a self-satisfaction that, in effect, attempts to move beyond the fabular context itself. *The Fable of the Bees* thus has the reflexive effect of making the reader analyze critically the fictive constructs of his or her own understanding of the world.[17] However, with Mandeville, the very ingenuity that introduces rational argumentation and the discriminations of understanding into the world is shown to degenerate into pride, hypocrisy, and self-deception. Mandeville's *Fable* thus serves to recall the inventive ingenuity that fashions a world but that nonetheless remains self-conscious of the ease with which the inventive impulse can become complacent and filled with pride concerning its creative activity.

Mandeville does not limit the intended audience of his description of the educability of the mind to his readers; instead he shows by means of his repeated additions to the *Fable* that the fabulist himself never completely transcends his fabular origins. Indeed, Mandeville's final turn to dialogue is intended to make explicit the cooperative exchange that occurs in fabular philosophy between author and reader and between the author and prior or subsequent authorial selves.

In all of these ways Mandeville reveals how the assumptions implicit in fabular writing push the reflective and cautious author beyond the static effect of moralizing pedagogy and authorial pride. In particular, the strictures concerning human pride, present from the beginning in "The Grumbling Hive," extend throughout the development of the *Fable*. Together they provide such a critique of other fables that *The Fable of the Bees* serves to produce an antifable effect within fabular philosophy. That is, the moral of the *Fable* points to the need to reestablish a self-critical restraint on the temptation to take pride in the wisdom

17. See Robert W. Uphaus, "Satire, Verification, and *The Fable of the Bees*," *Papers on Language and Literature* 12 (1976): 142; and Harth, "Satiric Purpose," 340. For more on the ironic and satiric character of this, see Louis Schneider, *Paradox and Society: The Work of Bernard Mandeville*, ed. Jay Weinstein (New Brunswick, N.J.: Transaction Books, 1987), 219–22.

that men imply they have in teaching moral maxims in Aesopic fables and dismissing the inventive insight of the ancient myths. It is thus noteworthy that Mandeville's *Fable* does not teach traditional moral maxims. Instead, it acts as a self-correcting teaching device that (1) criticizes the very intellectual ability that permits its own continued success as a fable (namely, the pride generated by the mind's coming to experience its own power) and (2) undermines the moral principle (pride) with which it is concerned:

The more we are taught to admire ourselves, the more our Pride encreases, and the greater Stress we lay on the Sufficiency of our Reason: For as Experience teaches us, that the greater and the more transcendent the Esteem is, which Men have for their own Worth, the less capable they generally are to bear Injuries without Resentment; so we see in like manner, that the more exhalted the Notions are, which Men entertain of their better part, their reasoning Faculty, the more remote and averse they'll be from giving their Assent to anything that seems to insult over or contradict it.[18]

The very wisdom that fables are intended to provide sets up the condition for the growth of pride in our reason and the reluctance to learn more. The requirement of self-critical fabular philosophy is thus the same as that of self-protective fabular philosophy (i.e., philosophy written in the form of a fable in order to escape political sanctions): The justification for adopting the assumptions of fabular language within a philosophic context stems from the recognition that philosophic writing is often debatably tentative, if not always for the author then at least always for readers. To move beyond that tentative stance, for an author, is to become dogmatic and condescending or, for readers, to be carried away by the embellishments or jargon of rhetoric. The temptation to make determinate, once and for all, the objects of reason (including the virtues taught in Aesopic apologues) can best be restrained, for Mandeville, by the appeal to just such a fabular form that points out its own deficient assumptions and points back to a use of fabling that places less, not greater, stress on the adequacy of our reason.

18. *Fable of the Bees*, 2: 15. Also see Harth's introduction to his edition of *The Fable of the Bees* (Harmondsworth, Eng.: Penguin, 1970), 17; M. J. Scott-Taggart, "Mandeville: Cynic or Fool?" *Philosophical Quarterly* 16 (1966): 221; and A. Keith Skarsten, "Nature in Mandeville," *JEGP* 53 (1954): 567.

THE MYTHIC DEVELOPMENT OF RATIONALITY AND LANGUAGE

Mandeville's appeal to the mythic aspect of fabling, especially in the dialogues of the second part of the *Fable*, reveals the tentative progress and ultimate insufficiency of human rationality. Insofar as men are encouraged to take pride in their rationality, he notes, they can be socialized.[19] But it is not men's rationality that allows them to engage in large-scale peaceful coexistence. They become rational—that is, they engage in reflective and justifiable actions—because of education and socialization: "Men become sociable, by living together in Society."[20] Social organization (i.e., institutionally based management of individual vices) is possible because men are taught to take pride in adhering to rules of conduct that are the products of the halting advances of generations trying to live in groups: "Human Wisdom is the Child of Time. It was not the Contrivance of one Man, nor could it have been the Business of a few Years, to establish a Notion, by which a rational Creature is kept in Awe for Fear of it Self, and an Idol is set up, that shall be its own Worshiper."[21] Institutions and rules concerning social practices of honor and shame were not deliberately (artificially) formulated by wise men in ancient times; nor were they natural in the sense of being uncaused by men. Rather, they resulted from the management of human behavior in ways that proved successful.[22]

For Mandeville rationality is essentially social: It is the ability to persuade oneself and others to act in socially beneficial ways, especially when this means acting contrary to one's own self-interest. Solitary man has no need for rationality, just as he has no need of speech. Though he adopts his social and linguistic behavior to promote communal ends, he does so for his own welfare. But such a turn cannot be considered rational because that would mean that his motive for doing so would be understood and accepted by others as justification for his actions.

19. *Fable of the Bees*, 1: 42–43. Cf. Schneider, *Paradox*, 86–90.
20. *Fable of the Bees*, 2: 189.
21. Mandeville, *An Enquiry into the Origin of Honour* (London: J. Brotherton, 1732), 41. Cf. *Fable of the Bees*, 2: 322, and Kaye's note at 1: 47. Also see Sterling Lamprecht, "The Fable of the Bees," *Journal of Philosophy* 23 (1926): 567; and James Noxon, "Dr. Mandeville: A Thinking Man," in *The Varied Pattern*, ed. Peter Hughes and David Williams (Toronto: A. M. Hakkert, 1971), 252.
22. *Fable of the Bees*, 2: 177, 183–88. See Hayek, "Mandeville," 133–35; Price, *Palace*, 115; and Schneider, *Paradox*, 91–92.

Others, however, would not approve of the solitary individual's self-interested motive for behaving in non-self-interested ways; they would not, therefore, view his action as rational unless (as in fact occurs, in Mandeville's view) the nonrational motive of individual selfishness is "artfully managed" to promote peaceful co-existence. Such artful management transforms selfishness into the productive pride in oneself (or *amour propre*), which members of society are encouraged to adopt in order that honor and shame can regulate their behavior. The seemingly idiosyncratic motive of selfishness is accordingly replaced in society with communally instilled reasons of honor and shame as the springs of human action. Such a development shows the emergence of rationality insofar as it identifies the procedure men use to justify their actions to one another by providing reasons rather than simply describing the motive causes of their actions.

The story of the natural (though at times unintended) process of the management of human actions and motivations is the story of the genesis of society, virtue, and language. As governing structures emerged among men, so did laws (rules of conduct) and the spoken and written forms of language needed to make such laws determinate.[23] Originally recognizing no need for language beyond simple gestures, primitive men slowly identified forms of behavior that improved their condition as social beings. When they encouraged such behavior in one another through the use of flattery, social practices emerged that supported the development and internalization of feelings of pride, honor, and shame.

In order to stir up in one another the idea of recommended though absent ways of behaving, they developed the rudiments of verbal communication. For primitive man as for modern man, speech specified the referent object to be acted upon, the behavior to be adopted by others, or the fact to be believed. Men did not adopt language merely to communicate thoughts, for that would have presupposed that their ideas were already determinate, specific, and meaningful—characteristics that were made possible only by the development of language in the first place. For Mandeville, a speech act is a performance that designates a public and definite reality: "If by Man's *speaking to be*

---

23. *Fable of the Bees*, 2: 269. See F. B. Kaye, "Mandeville on the Origin of Language," *Modern Language Notes* 39 (1924): 138; and Hayek, "Mandeville," 138.

understood you mean, that when Men speak, they desire that the Purport of the Sounds they utter should be known and apprehended by others, I answer in the Affirmative [viz., that men do speak to be understood]: But if you mean by it, that Men speak, in order that their Thoughts may be known, and their Sentiments laid open and seen through by others . . . I answer in the Negative."[24] Even for modern man—but especially for primitive man—speech identifies the nature of the reality with which man is in contact; in fact, it defines such a relationship by linking society to a world that can be acted upon because it has some identifiable nature by virtue of having been named.

On this point Mandeville reveals a close understanding of the importance of naming and language in creation myths: Mythical accounts of the origin of language repeatedly return to the observation that in knowledge of the word (i.e., language) lies control and power over society and nature. As he points out, "The first Sign or Sound that ever Man made, born of a Woman, was made in Behalf, and intended for the use of him who made it; and I am of Opinion, that the first Design of Speech was to persuade others, either to give Credit to what the speaking Person would have them to act or suffer, if they were entirely in his Power."[25] Language carves out of chaos an order, a world accessible to human social action and mythic expressions of power and control. To tell the myth is to recapture the power of language and speech, the power of exercising control over oneself and others.

When Mandeville describes mythically the emergence of language as a means of persuasion, he is at the same time providing the basis for explaining how the Aesopic fabulist justifies moral teaching. Anticipating a point that Vico will also emphasize, Mandeville argues that the mythic language of ancient man makes no distinction between a suggested course of action and an accomplished fact.[26] The Aesopic fable of "The Grumbling

24. *Fable of the Bees*, 2: 289. See E. J. Hundert, "Bernard Mandeville and the Rhetoric of Social Science," *Journal of the History of the Behavioral Sciences* 22 (1986): 312–14.

25. *Fable of the Bees*, 2: 289. For a comparable view of the mythic character of fable, cf. Alexander Pope's translation of the *Iliad* (1715), in *The Poems of Alexander Pope*, ed. Maynard Mack (London: Methuen, 1967), 7: 5.

26. Cf. *The New Science of Giambattista Vico*, tr. Thomas Bergin and Max Fisch (Ithaca, N.Y.: Cornell University Press, 1968), pars. 401, 808, 814. Cf. Schneider, *Paradox*, 170–73.

Hive" can recommend a course of action in its moral only to the extent that it assumes that man is already socialized and able to distinguish human behavior as it is from what it could be. By turning the latter parts of his *Fable* into myth, Mandeville provides a genetic account of social morality itself. This, in turn, explains how the Aesopic fable's emphasis on the possibility of virtue and honor relies on the unity of fact and value within mythic language.

To trace man's origins back to his prelinguistic, prerational, and premoral state means, for Mandeville, to construct a new myth that parallels those of the classical poets. Like classical myths Mandeville's *Fable* not only seeks to explain human origins by explaining the origin of rationality, language, and moral sensibility; it also seeks (in true Aesopic form) to provide an instructive moral, namely, "the Necessity, not only of Revelation and Believing, but likewise of the Practice of Christianity, manifestly to be seen in Men's Lives . . . [and] the Insufficiency of Human Reason and Heathen Virtue to procure real Felicity."[27] This last minute appeal to Christianity highlights Mandeville's belief that the turn to religion is better served by understanding human nature unencrusted with those superstitions that are intended to support the process of socialization by encouraging the development of pride and the sense of honor. In order to achieve this most Christian of ends, Mandeville suggests replacing the biblical account of Genesis with a new mythology that does not assume man's original (or even postlapsarian) rationality or moral sensibility.

Even as early as *Typhon*, Mandeville had drawn a connection between his mythic-fabular activity and his renovation of religious institutions. Speaking of his Aesopic projects, he remarks, "I have made no more *Fables* since, than I have built Churches."[28] Such a remark indeed sounds odd until it is understood in the context of Mandeville's insistence that authentic religious and moral sensibility are grounded in the constructive and figural activity of mythopoesis. Accordingly, revitalized Christianity would correspondingly call for a new mythology such as the one proposed by Mandeville.

27. *Fable of the Bees*, 2: 356.
28. *Typhon*, v.

The moral of the *Fable* as Aesopic apologue thus finds its support and justification in the genetic account of the *Fable* as myth: The origins and supporting institutions of human rationality and social morality are much too base to inspire any attitude other than a profound humility in being human. The satire of the *Fable* lies in the implication that its audience can be morally better by being made to comprehend a genealogy of morals in which the selfish bases of rationality and socially acceptable behavior are established institutionally and not primarily as a result of conscious human decisions. For Mandeville this picture of the human condition only emphasizes all the more the need to turn to extrahuman sources of insight in order to escape the self-deception so characteristic of human ingenuity.

CHAPTER FIVE

Narrative and Mythic Figuration in Vico

IN GIAMBATTISTA VICO WE FIND perhaps the first modern thinker who attempts to incorporate myth into a historical account of the philosophic enterprise. In place of attempts to provide rational explanations of the ancient myths, either as perversions of religious truths or euhemeristic exaggerations of actual persons or events, Vico challenges the fundamental assumption underlying such accounts of myth: namely, that they are products of a rational mind. At issue for Vico is more than simply the status of myth. For if myth is the language of a prerational, sense-based form of thought, no rational explanation of mythic activity can provide an appropriate account of it. Insofar as myth eludes such an Enlightenment account, it throws into question not only the historical legitimacy of philosophy's claim to the pursuit of truth (including the truths revealed in myth) but also the purity of rational, enlightened inquiry itself.

Vico refuses to allow philosophy the self-delusion that linguistic figuration can be transcended or ignored. He insists that the grammar of all meaningfulness (including both myth and philosophy) is generated in the history of a community's expressions or commonplaces *(topoi)*. Because that history is a history of narrative figuration, any attempt to ignore the etymological surface of language will likewise result in an inability to account for the ingenious generation of novel meanings or insights.

Indeed, Vico's examination of myth, which is so prominent throughout the *New Science* (1725, rev. ed. 1744), is an exploration into the procedures whereby meaning in language emerges so as to permit knowledge. Myth and its abbreviated form, metaphor, express the interrelations of objects at the level of the genesis of meaning: They are true narrations in the sense that such language carves out of indeterminate experience a reality, a referent. Mythic language is symbolic of divine creativity and permits nature to present to itself objects to be perceived.

Vico's discovery of mythic forms of thought historically at the base of rational inquiry opens the possibility that such sense-based metaphorical forms still infect the character of thought. This suggests that philological and etymological analyses reveal the close ties between the language of myth and the language of supposedly purified philosophical discourse. The language of philosophy itself emerges as meaningful in this Vichian account only in terms of its genetic association with the image-based metaphors of prerational thought. In a move that has been compared to that of Derrida, Vico makes the ancient myths accessible not by portraying them as rationally intelligible but by highlighting the inherently metaphoric character of philosophic language. A philological examination of words (including philosophic terms) reveals their metaphoric bases in ways that undermine the attempt to rescue philosophic discourse from rhetorical tropes of literature. Insofar as both myth and philosophy are publicly accessible, they share the tropes implicit in all language. And though this provides Vico with a route to mythic understanding, it also undermines further attempts to identify the linguistic bases for distinguishing mythic and philosophic discourse.

THE CENTRALITY OF LINGUISTIC FIGURATION

As I have noted in previous chapters, writers for whom mythic thinking serves as an important methodological concern are aware of the distinguishing and excluding meanings that other authors of the period give to the use of "fable"—for example, classical myth, narrative, falsehood, or moral exemplar. Against the move (by Hobbes and Locke, for example) to divorce wit from judgment and imagination from reason, fabular thinkers appeal to the generative source underlying human cognitive activity in general.[1] Their attempt to reinstate the foundational creativity of *ingenium* (the ability of the mind to cognize new relationships) resists the tendency to isolate such meanings of "fable" from one another.

Vico, for one, relishes the opportunity to retrieve the polysemous character of fable as myth, narrative, and moral exemplar. He first has to show, however, why fable and myth have a reputation among philosophers like Hobbes and Locke as a dissembling

1. See Thomas Hobbes, "Answer to the Preface to Gondibert" (1650), in *The English Works of Thomas Hobbes*, ed. William Molesworth, 11 vols. (London: John Bohn, 1839–45), 4: 499–500; John Locke, *An Essay Concerning Human Understanding*, ed. John W. Yolton, 2 vols. (New York: Dutton, 1964), 2: 105–6 (III.10.34). Also see Hayden V. White, "The Irrational and the Problem of Historical Knowledge," in *Irrationalism in the Eighteenth Century*, ed. Harold E. Pagliaro (Cleveland, Ohio: Case Western University Press, 1972), 312–16.

device, the false rhetorical flourish that occasionally pleases and instructs but more often conceals the truth.

For Vico the task begins with understanding the object of philosophy: "Philosophy," he notes, "contemplates reason, whence comes knowledge of the true."[2] This knowledge of the true assumes a structure of determinate concepts removed from the life-blood of human ingenuity. Philosophic reasoning reveals "the true" only by ignoring how the meanings of concepts originate and how the procedures whereby novel combinations of terms create new semantic possibilities and interpretive techniques. That is, philosophic reasoning undermines attempts to elevate human creativity to a level of intellectual respectability by ruling out such concerns as inappropriate for philosophic inquiry.

As such, the turn to the fabular entails penetrating through philosophy to its philological foundations, where "human choice is author, whence comes consciousness of the certain."[3] Poetic (fabular) invention ensures access to its own creations as objects of immediate consciousness. They are apprehended with certainty because the content of consciousness is not yet incorporated into a formalized structure whose author (or authority)—human choice—is effaced by itself in adopting the mask of reason. Insofar as fabular ingenuity does not presuppose the static existence of "the true" (by means of which ingenuity is supposed to guide its own activity), it is mistakenly identified by some philosophers as the source of falsehood and mere storytelling or fictionalizing.

In defense of the move to philosophy, though, it should be noted that the very turn to "the true" is an attempt to negate the presence of the author in order to affirm the meaningfulness of a text independent of all humanity. Doubt (even about the "truth" of Descartes' cogito) cannot be eliminated as long as the gap between sign (language as figuration) and thing exists. So Vico turns to the mythic character of language as the condition by which speech is made anonymous though still responsive to human interests.[4]

2. Vico, *The New Science of Giambattista Vico* (1744), tr. Thomas Bergin and Max Fisch (Ithaca, N.Y.: Cornell University Press, 1968), par. 138. Some of the translations I refer to are silently changed in my quotations based on Vico's original text.

3. *Ibid.* See Donald Philip Verene, *Vico's Science of Imagination* (Ithaca, N.Y.: Cornell University Press, 1981), 172.

4. Cf. Eric Gould, *Mythical Intentions in Modern Literature* (Princeton, N.J.: Princeton University Press, 1981), 42–43, 87.

By means of the cogito, for example, I am conscious of my existence as something certain but I cannot be said to have achieved "the true," for the true is the anonymous domain of philosophic reason, of which I am not the author.[5] In fact, from the perspective of philosophy (vis-à-vis myth), no one is the author of meanings: Meanings exist in virtue of their structural relationships to one another. The origin of or "authority for" the structure itself or genesis of meaning in general cannot be explained philosophically. Though it provides the mechanism for determining truth, philosophy cannot provide certainty because it is unable to justify the claim that meanings generated within the structure of language in fact refer to a world. Philosophic language is thus open to skeptical challenge in virtue of its very insistence on structural closure of meaning. It is as if philosophical discourse attempts to conceal the very gap it creates between itself as linguistic sign system and the things it signifies.

In order to close the gap between sign and thing, language has to regain its authority (authorship) as mythic, poetic inventiveness unrestricted by "the true." This is precisely the importance of Vico's celebrated discovery of the true Homer, the author of the classical myths: The myths are not authored by any individual but are rather the anonymous products of the Greek peoples.[6] Grounded self-consciously in human choice, mythic language expresses the anonymity of communal experience while retaining control over the reflective philosophic tendency to divorce conceptual structures from their sense-based origins. Unlike philosophic reason, mythic activity ensures the anonymous *but human* authorship of meaning by refusing to blind itself to language's creative and metaphorical origins and continued openness to interpretation and development.

This Vichian concentration on mythic expression reasserts the priority of language over thought, signification over reflection, figuration over intellection. According to Vico, that which is said (*dictum*) is that which is certain (*certum*) and determinate (*deter-*

---

5. Vico, *On the Most Ancient Wisdom of the Italians* (1710), tr. Leon Pompa in *Vico: Selected Writings* (Cambridge: Cambridge University Press, 1982), 58–59. Cf. Vico's original text in *Opere,* ed. Giovanni Gentile and Fausto Nicolini, 8 vols. in 11 (Bari, Italy: Laterza, 1911–41), 1: 139. Also see Max H. Fisch, "Vico and Pragmatism," in *Giambattista Vico: An International Symposium,* ed. Giorgio Tagliacozzo and Hayden V. White (Baltimore, Md.: Johns Hopkins University Press, 1969), 130.

6. *New Science,* pars. 873–75.

minatum), whereas that which is meant-by-word (*verbum*) is that which is made (*factum*) as the true (*verum*).[7] Vico thus challenges both Cartesian and Lockean epistemologies by questioning the belief that private thought is meaningful prior to its expression within mythic language.

Private choice of meaning would be much too uncertain and indeterminate to ensure the practical achievement of communal goals. "Human choice," Vico notes, "by its nature most uncertain, is made certain and determinate by the common sense of men with respect to human needs and utilities."[8] That is, communal needs specify the immediate, sense-based experience highlighted as "topoi" or commonplaces within language. Such linguistic commonplaces relate seemingly unrelated things in imaginative, problem-solving ways. These topical devices do not provide access to "the true" because they do not assume that the emergence of language as a function of common sense presupposes reflective rationality: "Common sense is judgment without reflection, shared by an entire class, an entire people, an entire nation, or the entire human race."[9] Discourse is made meaningful within the determinate though anonymous context of the communal dictum of mythic expression. Conceptual (rational) meaning presumes this "mental dictionary," which is prior to reflection and which identifies the commonplaces of group experience that serve as origins of the articulated languages.[10] The sense or meanings of expressions summarized within such a dictionary are not mental in the sense of internal or private. Rather, as the prereflective judgments of the common experience of a people, they establish the context within which reflection and private mentality can emerge.

Vico's sensitivity to the poetic (fabular) foundations out of which rationality has grown, and of which it has lost touch, reemphasizes the need for a critique of what he calls the "barbarism of reflection" that fills men with pride and makes them more inhuman rather than less.[11] Humanity is characterized primarily not in terms of its rationality but in terms of its

7. *Ancient Wisdom*, 77 (*Opere*, 1: 189).
8. *New Science*, par. 141.
9. *Ibid.*, par. 142.
10. *New Science*, pars. 35, 145, 161–62.
11. *Ibid.*, par. 1106. See Ernesto Grassi, "The Priority of Common Sense and Imagination: Vico's Philosophical Relevance Today," *Social Research* 43 (1976): 571.

communal procedures for creative problem solving. Creative ingenuity highlights the similarities of things rather than their differences. Learning the topoi of a community not only initiates an individual into the mental vocabulary of the community but also reiterates the essentially communal character of humanity and the integral unity of all things that men sense.

The barbarism of the intellect isolates the individual from the sense of human community by turning his or her attention to the true as if it could be discussed devoid of its commonsense grounding in the figural (poetic) language of practical certainty. This attempt to "subdue the sharpness of minds still bound to the body" undermines the unity of *humanitas* provided by the figuration of language.[12] Minds trained in the humane character of letters and language (the commonplaces or poetic wisdom of a people) penetrate categories established in the critical attempt to insulate statements about the true from their sensible origins.[13] Such ingenuity identifies otherwise unnoticed similarities by appeal to their metaphorical union in the commonsense topoi of a language.

To appeal to the linguistic basis of philosophical criticism is to regain for philosophy the opportunity to tap the natural creative power implicit in its metaphorical and mythical origins. Far from questioning the value of reason or understanding, then, Vico's account reasserts the grounds for the possible inventive expansion of reason by pointing to the originative unity of ingenuity.

CERTAINTY WITHIN MYTH

Shortly after Vico became acquainted with Bacon's *On the Wisdom of the Ancients*, he composed his own *On the Most Ancient Wisdom of the Italians* (1710), in which he describes ingenium as the natural human faculty responsible for the generation of artificial things in the same way that nature is responsible for the generation of physical things. Just as God is the artisan of nature, so

12. *New Science*, par. 159. Cf. Verene, "Vico and Marx on Poetic Wisdom and Barbarism," in *Vico and Marx: Affinities and Contrasts*, ed. Giorgio Tagliacozzo (Atlantic Highlands, N.J.: Humanities Press, 1983), 258.

13. Vico, *On the Study Methods of Our Time* (1709), tr. Elio Gianturco (Indianapolis, Ind.: Bobbs-Merrill, 1965), 13–14, 24, 42; and *Ancient Wisdom*, 74 (*Opere*, 1: 212).

man in virtue of his ingenious ability to cognize order and harmony is the God of artifacts.[14]

Insofar as he is the cause of those things he makes, man makes them to be true. When someone says he knows something as the true, he is justified in making such a claim only if he knows the causes of that which he knows.[15] To be able to know something as true is to cognize the form by which a thing is made, to be its author, its creator. Men do not simply discover or find (*invenire*) the true, they make it (*facere*).

Those things that men make, they know through the agency of their natural ingenuity: "This ingenium," Vico writes, "has been given to men for knowing, that is, for making."[16] Those things that men do not actually make or create (i.e., natural objects), they "invent" (*invenire*) by means of this same faculty. Invention or discovery in natural philosophy (i.e., concerning the things that we do not make) is the product of that same ingenium by which we are able to know those things that we do make. To discover something, Vico argues, means to see an object *ex genere*, that is, in contexts and relationships different from those that specify the genus according to which truth judgments about the thing are normally made.[17]

In establishing the principles of mathematics, for example, man sets up the conditions for determining the true in that the validity of his claims holds only within the parameters of the system. Likewise, the historian creates history insofar as he or she uses principles to determine what constitutes an event and then selects those events that can be understood in terms of certain (determinate) causes.[18]

This example of history as an artifact of human ingenuity serves as a key for understanding Vico's insistence on the central role of poetic language (especially myth) within his critique of the modern divorce of inventive discovery from critical judgment.

14. *Ancient Wisdom*, 70 (*Opere*, 1: 179); and Vico's 1711 replies to criticism of the *Ancient Wisdom*, "Polemiche relative al *De antiquissima Italorum sapientia*," *Opere*, 1: 212.

15. *Ancient Wisdom*, 58 (*Opere*, 1: 140); also see 75 (*Opere*, 1: 185).

16. *Ibid.*, 51, 57–59, 75 (*Opere*, 1: 132, 139–40, 185, and particularly 192).

17. *Ibid.*, 74 (*Opere*, 1: 183); and *Vici Vindiciae* (1729), in *Opere*, 3: 303–4. See Grassi, "Common Sense," 561.

18. See Pompa's introduction in *Vico: Selected Writings*, 26; and Sandra Rudnick Luft, "A Genetic Interpretation of Divine Providence in Vico's *New Science*," *Journal of the History of Philosophy* 20 (1982): 159, 168.

Against such an insistence some might argue that the historian arranges data in ways that make history intelligible, but he or she certainly does not "make" history: The events occur whether the historian or anyone else knows about them or understands why they occur.

Vico, though, challenges such a view by undermining the distinction between history as a sequence of events, and subsequent accounts or understandings of these events. To construct a rational arrangement of events assumes that the events have already been identified as events. To be so identified as certain and determinate events means that they would have been identified as of practical interest to a community. According to Vico, the community does not *make* the event be of interest; if it is of interest it becomes an event, and if it is not of interest, no event would be recognized as having occurred.

As such, events cannot be either true or false; truth and falsity are reserved for the rational constructions of history. To make history, therefore, is to apply principles of interpretation to events that are assumed to have occurred because they are already found in the commonplaces (topoi) of a community. Common sense has no access to the true because, for the commonsense mentality, no topoi could be false: There is only the certain, determinate dictum, the memory of a culture contained within the "true and severe narrations" of its myths or fables.[19]

This cultural memory is not a rational reconstruction of events. It is the communal cognizance of the sensible or figural forms of meaning expressed by and on the surface of poetic language. More precisely, there is only surface meaning expressed in poetic language because the imaginative language of myth cannot imply a meaning more certain or true without throwing into doubt its own act of figuration. Memory, Vico notes, is imagination or *phantasia*, the springing up or discovery (*inventio*) of the sense-based meaningfulness of inventive expression as a response to the necessities of life.[20] As such, the memory of a culture exists in its figural expressions.

The very act of poetic or mythic expression not only recounts the meanings or topoi of the community; it also shows how the

19. *New Science*, par. 814. Cf. Verene, "The New Art of Narration: Vico and the Muses," *New Vico Studies* 1 (1983): 28.
20. *New Science*, pars. 699, 819. Cf. Ernst Cassirer, *Language and Myth*, tr. Susanne Langer (New York: Dover, 1946), 28–29, 38, 57, 83.

topoi are related to one another. The "grammar" of myth does not reside as a "deep structure" below the surface of its figural (spoken, written) expression. As Vico points out, "Grammar is defined as the art of speaking, yet *grammata* are letters, so that grammar should have been defined as the art of writing."[21] The juxtaposition of letters or expressions creates a grammar of the figural. Within such a grammar all expression is metaphorical in that the very juxtaposition of the letters or expressions creates the relationships by which a "crossing over" (*meta-phor, translatio*) is possible as historical. The figural juxtaposition presents the emergence of a grammar on the superficies of history: that is, the expressions constitute history within figural juxtaposition. Because no grammar aboriginally exists beneath the grammar of figural juxtaposition, nothing challenges the metaphorical character of all expression: There are no parallel similes to which the metaphors can be reduced. Just as the first men viewed every change in facial expression as a new face (subsequently incorporated into the myth of constantly changing Proteus), so every metaphor whether written or spoken displays a myth (fable) in brief, a dictionary-cum-grammar legacy of the community.[22]

To learn to speak the topoi is far different from learning how to make noises. To speak the topoi means becoming literate in the grammata, the figural expressions that identify the community in virtue of its topoi. In order to understand the very meanings of expressions, then, Vico suggests first learning what it means to speak the topoi and then training adolescents in the common-sense experience or wisdom contained in the myths: "The first science to be learned should be mythology or the interpretation of fables," because such knowledge or science (*scienza*) puts us in immediate contact with the origins of communal meaning.[23] The community becomes a "nation" (a birthing) out of its mute origins in speaking the topoi according to the regulation of writing: "All nations began to speak by writing since all were originally mute."[24] Without the stabilizing influence of writing—

21. *New Science*, par. 429. Cf. White, "Foucault Decoded: Notes from Underground," *History and Theory* 12 (1973): 23.

22. *New Science*, par. 404.

23. *Ibid.*, par. 51; *Study Methods*, 13.

24. *New Science*, par. 429. Cf. Jacques Derrida, *Of Grammatology*, tr. Gayatri C. Spivak (Baltimore, Md.: Johns Hopkins University Press, 1976), 355; Margherita Frankel, "Vico and Rousseau Through Derrida," *New Vico Studies* 1 (1983): 54; and Christopher Norris, *The Deconstructive Turn* (New York: Methuen, 1983), 123.

or its oral equivalent, restricting permission to recite the myths to
selected individuals—meanings could not be protected from uncertain or indeterminate expression.

The Greek philosophers, however, according to Vico, stabilized
meanings by replacing imaginative ingenuity with critical reflection.
Instead of relying for knowledge on relationships of figural
(linguistic) particulars expressed in the myths or topoi of the
community, the philosophers created structures of universals as
criteria for judging the truth of particular expressions. Such a
move identified as proper objects of knowledge hypostatized
universals that were only accidentally related to linguistic expressions.

This displacement of particularized expressions by universal
concepts implied that, insofar as sensible expression itself cannot
be used as the criterion for judging its own truthfulness, figuration then serves as an obstacle to knowledge. Poetry's attention
to its own sound and appearance, accordingly, stands less as an
indication of the importance of figuration than as a rhetorical
hindrance to precision in conceptualization. As the cost for such
precision, reflective criticism dissociates judgment from inventive
ingenuity.

As long as speaking the topoi—reciting the myths—is seen as
establishing meaning in the very act of showing how particular
characters are figurally related, judgments about meanings are
understood as highlighting the similarities that permeate all (and
only) named things. Similarities permeate the world in virtue of
the similarity of figural expressions that give meaning to the
things in the world. Things are themselves sensible figurations,
the icons, tokens, or "dicta" of nature. The particular topoi of
a people express how the similarities of all figural expressions
become certain and determinate as judgments of communal
importance. The myths or topoi do not separate inventive
phantasia from judgment. In fact, they make judgment possible
by specifying how the ingenious (poetic) mind relies on figural
characters to cognize things that are made similar by their
associated appearance within the topoi.

In rational Greek philosophy, however, topics (the art of
discovering similarities based on commonplace association) is
replaced by criticism's emphasis on distinction or dissimilarity as
the principle of knowing. "The divorce of discovery from judgment which began with the Greeks," Vico argues, "occurred only
because they failed to attend to the faculty proper to knowing,

the faculty of ingenium, whereby man is capable of apprehending things and making them similar."[25] To know (*scire, sapere*) means to apprehend things as related in the figuration of poetic expression. The sensible expression unites them as things made meaningful within and because of mythic discourse. As such, judgment cannot be divorced from discovery without divorcing knowledge from figuration.

Within philosophic rationality this divorce creates a gap between reflective, universal meanings and the things to which such meanings are intended to refer. In "topical" judgments, on the other hand, certainty is guaranteed because of the sense-based immediacy implicit within the poetic identification of figural expression and thing. Mythic expression *shows* the grammar of things by means of a "language with natural significations."[26] Things are related to one another not in terms of some natural order independent of mythic expression; indeed, it is mythic expression that figures their relatability by identifying them as meaningful things in the first place. Nature itself is the "language of the gods," and its signs are "real words."[27] Nature is thoroughly linguistic, semiotic, *figural*, just as mythic language is thoroughly natural, original, creative, divine. To speak the topoi is to make both language and nature determinate and certain insofar as figural expression reveals the semiotic character of meaningful nature.

For Vico each new arrangement of signs, letters, gestures, or sounds contributes to the grammar of nature, the grammar of myth. To search for a logic abstracted from the etymology of figuration ignores the historical character of expression and reveals what Derrida has called the logocentric bias of Western philosophy. For any culture sensitive to the origins of meaning, it is the act of narration or figuration that first creates such meaning and that accounts for changes in meaning. For Vico, just such a sensitivity has been lost in Western philosophy's "barbarism of reason," for the appeal to a meaning (*logos*)

---

25. *Ancient Wisdom*, 73–74 (*Opere*, 1: 183); and "Polemiche," in *Opere*, 1: 212. See Ernesto Grassi, *Rhetoric as Philosophy: The Humanist Tradition* (University Park: Pennsylvania State University Press, 1980), 41–45; and Michael Mooney, *Vico in the Tradition of Rhetoric* (Princeton, N.J.: Princeton University Press, 1985), 131–38.

26. *New Science*, pars. 381, 431.

27. *Ibid.*, par. 379.

behind the superficies of figuration distances any inquirer from the immediacy and historicity of experience and the world.

The union of sense-based language and sense-based nature within figuration constitutes a metaphysics of imagination and poetry, a non-self-conscious metaphysics, a metaphysics in which knowledge is identical to poetry because knowledge is identical to mythic or topical figuration. The rational metaphysics of the Greeks, however, displaces the particularity and certainty of poetic metaphysics with intelligible class concepts intended to provide access to the true. In so doing, rational metaphysics separates the meaning of concepts from their figural expressions as commonsense topoi. In order to restrain the proliferation of mythic expression unregulated by the consensus (*con-sensus*) embodied in the topoi, rational metaphysics divorces the sense-based ingenuity of figural expression from universal concepts whose meanings are fixed within a structure. Unable to account for its own genesis, such a structure cannot permit the syntactical crossovers common in poetic and mythic expression; and because of this, philosophic novelty or ingenuity is reduced to a rehash of what is already known.

It might be argued that even within mythic thought discovery amounts to little more than recalling the commonplaces of a people's experiences. The difference between philosophic and mythic ingenuity, for Vico, lies in the fact that by its figural nature, mythic expression continuously reveals its inventiveness by displaying the origination of meanings in each new arrangement of signs, letters, gestures, or sounds. Deviations in that which is said acquaint the mythic mentality with new meanings, relationships, and realities. Mistakes and feints have no meaning when each pronouncement is a "true narration" or origin of meaning. Poetic "violations" of grammatical structures can occur only when such structures become conventions. The essentially figural nature of myth, even as expressed in the topoi, retains the tension of an ever-present possibility of emerging human ingenuity. As such, ingenium is not some inner, spiritual capacity of man's mind as much as it is the possibility of novel figuration inherent in, and on the surface of, human language.

The rational attempt to internalize and universalize meanings cuts man off from his immediate contact with the world to which such meanings refer. The identity of sign and signified is broken, and in its place skeptical doubts about the referential meaning of language threaten to undermine the meaningfulness of any signifier.[28]   Confronted with the vacuous possibility of linguistic signification of nonbeing, rational metaphysics models conceptual relationships on structures of its own creation (e.g., algebraic analysis). This substitution of the true for the certain, of intellection (*intelligere*) for knowledge (*scire*), attempts to ignore the gap between signifier and signified by replacing the *dictum-certum* unity with the *verbum-verum* relationship.[29] Within mythic expression no such gap exists because what is said (*dictum*) is the icon or sign signifying its own character as thing signified. There is no distinction between signifier and signified because there is no distinction between sign and signifier.

The mechanism for the creation of the true, however, avoids doubt only by denying commonsense interests. In its search for truth, rationality cuts man off from the immediacy of sensible contact with the world and isolates individuals from the topoi of *humanitas*, the "humane letters" that unite a community linguisti- √ cally. As Vico notes, to create the true requires that I create or cognize something in terms of a structure in such a way that "there will be no possibility of my doubting it since I am the very one who has produced it."[30] A rational reconstruction of experience along Cartesian lines cannot, therefore, produce certainty about the world without assuming erroneously that I cause the world. Such certainty about the world would require that all claims of subsequent truth be prefaced by an appeal to the mythic presuppositions of such claims. From this perspective it is only fitting that Descartes himself characterizes his description of the physical world as *une fable*, a feint of figuration intended to appeal to the senses and to provide utmost certainty.[31]

NARRATIVE INGENUITY

Bacon's retrieval of the spirit of discovery underlying classical myths provides Vico with a focus for his own doctrine of fabular ingenuity. When Vico refers in his *Autobiography* to Bacon's

28. Cf. Grassi, "Vico, Marx, and Heidegger," in *Vico and Marx: Affinities and Contrasts*, ed. Giorgio Tagliacozzo (Atlantic Highlands, N.J.: Humanities Press, 1983), 240–41; and Gould, *Mythical Intentions*, 43, 67.

29. *New Science*, par. 363.

30. See Vico's 1712 replies to criticism of his *Ancient Wisdom*, in *Opere*, 1: 258.

31. See René Descartes, *Le Monde* (1633), in *Oeuvres*, ed. Charles Adam and Paul Tannery, 13 vols. (Paris: Cerf, 1897-1913), 11: 31, 48.

Wisdom of the Ancients as "more ingenious and learned than true," he demonstrates that he considers Bacon's concern for the fables of the ancients as much more than a misdirected exercise of wit.[32]   From Vico's point of view, Bacon's turn to the myths to explore nature is an "ingenious" move, a move intended to open natural philosophy up to new and imaginatively based avenues of investigation.   Such a move only indirectly has a chance of revealing the true.   Thus Bacon's appeal to a mode of thinking that does not assume the rational categories of true and false is appropriate, as far as Vico is concerned, and is properly identified within a fabular context.   It is ingenious in that it points to the fabular methods by which new discoveries in nature are to be made.

Since men are not themselves the causes of nature, they cannot know natural things in terms of the true.   But they can describe the certain insofar as they examine nature as accessible to man, that is, nature as creatively and mythically organized. Thus for Vico to say that Bacon's descriptions in the *Wisdom of the Ancients* are ingenious is to say that Bacon correctly restricts himself to the certain (i.e., nature made cognitively accessible through fabular, figural organization) without making claims about that which he does not create.   Furthermore, it is to maintain that Bacon correctly recognizes the creative and natural intelligence associated with the fabular process of construction and commentary.

For Vico, however, Bacon does not go far enough in explaining how the emergence of language and the process of naming actually permits Bacon to speak about the power of the ancients to call creatures by their "true names."   Vico himself alludes to the facile way of explaining the situation: God simply granted Adam the power to name things "according to the nature of each."[33]   But Vico all along eschews such an approach in describing the origin of gentile languages because it adopts the rationalistic presumption of the peripheral importance of figuration: It portrays naming as accidental to the emergence of meaningful realities.   The mythic mentality does not use names to try to guess or approximate the essential natures of things in order to identify their "true" names.   Rather, the human act of

32. See *The Autobiography of Giambattista Vico* (1725), tr. Max Fisch and Thomas Bergin (Great Seal Books; Ithaca, N.Y.: Cornell University Press, 1963), 148.
33. *New Science*, par. 401.

naming (making figural, legible) creates things as meaningfully accessible to sensibility in virtue of their "extrinsic" figuration. Even divine understanding presumes the figuration of a "litera-ture" of nature insofar as God is able to understand (*intelligere*) by "reading completely" (*perfecte legere*) the intrinsic as well as extrinsic elements of things.[34]

In other words, Vico notes, "Created things [*facta*] are God's *dicta*," which become divine *verba* only when God's utterances are formalized as a grammar in which words are divorced from things in terms of their case endings.[35] Case endings identify the fate (*fatum*) of *dicta* as inexorably removed from and as pointing beyond the immediacy of the figural. *Dicta* originally do not have case endings because *dicta* establish the topoi upon which the for-malization of meanings (*verba* with case endings) is based. Only when man both arranges and makes the formalization (e.g., in mathematics) does the distinction arise between *verba* and *res* in which words (*verba*) are seen as symbols of ideas, and ideas are seen as symbols and tokens of things. Only God can properly lay claim to "true names," words (*verba*) of the mind as opposed to the *dicta* of figuration, insofar as, in the divine mind, the *dictum* is the figuration (*nota*, icon, token) or thing itself: "The word of the mind is made properly in God but improperly in man."[36] For man to read the *dicta*, on the other hand, is to (re)collect the figurations or "outermost elements of things" by which they become determinate (*certum*) and able to be thought.

Insofar as the constructs of the mind and of nature are identified within the same creative and imaginative act, ingenium refers to both mind and nature.[37] To speak a name is to show mind-nature in the process of carving out of indeterminate chaos (meaninglessness) determinate linguistic order. From the stand-point of nature, this cutting away, sharpness, or penetration (*acutezza*) appears as the shaving away of matter. From the standpoint of mind, it appears as the discerning of relationships. But just as the natural object does not exist before it is carved out of indeterminate matter, so the relationships cognized (note: not "recognized") by the mind do not exist before their figural expression. Nature (divine ingenium) emerges as meaningful not

---

34. *Ancient Wisdom*, 51 (*Opere*, 1: 131).
35. *Ibid.*, 77 (*Opere*, 1: 189).
36. *Ibid.*, 51–52, 76 (*Opere*, 1: 131–32, 187).
37. *Autobiography*, 148 (*Opere*, 5: 34); *Ancient Wisdom*, 70 (*Opere*, 1: 179).

only in a way similar to but also identical to the emergence of human ingenium: Divine providence shows itself in human history. Ingenium is the creation of significance, the identification of the communally important within the context of imaginative signification.

This signification is imaginative in the sense that mythic language *shows* nature being figurally made meaningful. Physical objects are signs as much as are gestures because the life and creative (divine) power of something stems from its efficacy within speech.[38] Signs are not meaningful in virtue of their having referents. Rather, signs are meaningful in virtue of being referents. In mythic or poetic language, words give one another meaning within textual figuration and as such reveal the creativity of the speech of phantasia. Insofar as nature itself is seen to "speak" in a language of natural signification, it reveals its own meaningful structure as linguistic.

Mind and nature, thought and world are thus united in the self-referential figuration of mythic expression. Without the certainty and determination of such a figuration, language lacks signification. Myth is "natural speech," the speech of nature as itself a signifying language without which signification fails and the world and man remain mute (*mutus*). In fact, Vico points out, *mutus* comes from *mythos*, an indication that speech was born in mute times when attention was focused on the indistinguishable unity of idea and figural expression.[39] When critical rationality separates idea and figural expression, this etymological connection of *mythos* and *mutus* persists, now to reveal another function of myth: namely, to be a testimony to the "metaphysics of absence" or self-effacing failure of referentiality implicit in every sign.[40] To compensate for this vacuum in philosophical rationality, the appeal to myth attempts to reclaim figuration from the prospect of muted signification by concealing the lack (or negativity) of natural signification brought on by the divorce of meaning from figuration.

Vico's characterization of Bacon's work on fables receives renewed attention when Vico responds (in his *Vici Vindiciae*, 1729) to the charge of a reviewer of the first edition of his *New Science*

38. See *New Science*, pars. 401, 431; cf. par. 376.
39. *Ibid.*, par. 401. Cf. White, "Foucault Decoded," 45, 48.
40. Cf. Gould, *Mythical Intentions*, 195; Frankel, "Vico Through Derrida," 54–55; and Verene, *Vico's Science of Imagination*, 69.

(1725) that he "indulges more in that which is clever than in the truth" ("ingenio magis indulget quam veritati").[41] Vico uses the occasion to rescue ingenium from the poor reputation given it by other thinkers as wit lacking discernment, wittiness, or cleverness, and turns the criticism into a compliment of both Bacon and himself by restoring ingenium to its classical status as "divine parent of all invention," the source of all intellectual freshness and discovery.[42]

Accordingly, it would be misleading to translate Vico's use of the word *ingenium* simply as "mind," even though that is a standard practice in regard to other seventeenth- and eighteenth-century uses. For example, Descartes' *Regulae ad directionem ingenii* is generally rendered as *Rules for the Direction of the Mind*. The availability of other terms (e.g., *mens*) and the appearance of similar discussions with alternative titles (e.g., Spinoza's *Tractatus de emendatione intellectus*), however, caution against the assumption that Descartes and other thinkers use ingenium to refer indiscriminately to all human mental activity. Indeed, when Descartes speaks about the need to direct ingenium by rules or to restrain ingenium through training in mathematics, he gives the impression that ingenium is anything but that purely spiritual or intellectual character of human beings designated as mind. When purified of its tendencies to make imaginative leaps between ideas, ingenium takes on the character of mind insofar as its operations are guided by the ideal of attaining certainty.

In the course of Descartes' transformation of ingenium, though, ingenium loses the distinctively creative or inventive character it has for earlier thinkers who are concerned with describing the human capacity to generate novel and inventive solutions to pressing practical matters.[43] In order to avoid the charge that his description has undermined the proper function of ingenium, Descartes appropriates the view (traceable through Raymond Lull back to the Stoics) that *inventio* (discovery) occurs only to the extent that an observation finds a place in a system of ideas. This notion of inventiveness as finding a place for

41. *Vindiciae*, in *Opere*, 3: 295; and *Autobiography*, 188 (*Opere*, 5: 68). Also see Mooney, "The Primacy of Language in Vico," *Social Research* 43 (1976): 587, 590.

42. *Vindiciae*, in *Opere*, 3: 303; and *Autobiography*, 140 (*Opere*, 5: 27); *Ancient Wisdom*, 70 (*Opere*, 1: 179); *New Science*, par. 816. Also see Grassi, *Rhetoric as Philosophy*, 10, 44–45.

43. See, for example, Grassi, *Rhetoric as Philosophy*, 10–14.

something already known underlies Descartes' claim that the study of mathematics is prerequisite for making new discoveries, in that mathematical reasoning accustoms the mind to reveal the step-by-step connections that link ideas to one another.[44]

Such a view of inventive ingenuity is not, of course, limited to Descartes. Bacon had also suggested that an orderly, deductive "interpretation of nature" finds places for otherwise isolated bits of information that, when left outside such a structure, could not contribute to further insights and thus hardly could be termed discoveries. Bacon recognized that imaginative leaps of ingenium at times provide a "thread" through the labyrinth of nature, which, when systematically followed up, could provide knowledge that could justly be termed scientific. Such "anticipations of nature," however, are not dependable enough to ground any program of research even though ingenious insights can serve as hints of possible avenues of investigation.

But where Bacon is willing to admit that ingenium manifests itself in ways that do involve leaps of imagination, properly called inventive genius or discovery, Descartes is not because, for Descartes, discovery is defined in terms of the recognition of truth. Insofar as ingenium is not regulated according to standards that support claims of truth, it does not promote true discoveries. Descartes' recharacterization of ingenuity thus excludes non-rational judgments from the domains of philosophy proper only by subsuming the art of inventing (referred to by Cicero as Topics) under the regulation of procedures of judgment.

The significance of such a shift in meaning appears most graphically when we compare dictionary entries for *invention* from before and after the onset of the Cartesian influence. For example, Robert Cawdry's *A Table Alphabeticall* (1604) defines *invention* simply as imagination; whereas Elisha Coles's *An English Dictionary* (1701) defines the act of invention as a procedure of "finding out a device."[45] Imagination and unregulated ingenuity are replaced by regulated structures of reasoning, which define discoveries in terms of judgments of their truth. How the insights themselves first occur before they are brought before the tribunal of reason to determine whether a device can be found for their

44. See *Descartes' Conversation with Burman*, tr. John Cottingham (Oxford: Clarendon Press, 1976), 47.

45. Robert Cawdry, *A Table Alphabeticall* (London: Edmund Weaver, 1604); and Elisha Coles, *An English Dictionary* (London: Peter Parker, 1701).

incorporation into the system of thought is a matter outside philosophy's proper concern.

This relegation of imagination, rhetoric, and the art of topics to the status of proto- or para-philosophy overlooks those interesting and productive aspects of ingenium that highlight the naturally creative aspects of human thought. Insofar as Descartes and Hobbes develop philosophies modeled on the critical or mathematical restraint of ingenium, they portray ingenium as wit, the ability to find quickly and deductively what is already known.[46]

Such an understanding of ingenium overlooks the distinctively creative function of genius—a function that is recognized only in appreciating the confluence of the meanings of *ingenuus* and *ingeniosus*. *Ingenuus* (ingenuous) refers to the innate ability to solve problems and to abide by reason willingly; as such, it implies nobility of mind and a frankness unencumbered by artificial constraints. It is precisely this frankness, this freedom of mind to express nature creatively, that links *ingenuus* to the *ingeniosus* (ingenious) character of mind.[47] The ingenious mind is inventive, just as Descartes had suggested. But his treatment severs the classical Latin union of the inventive/creative aspect of mind and the free and noble activity of nature operative in human thought.

In order to reunite these ideas, Vico recalls that the Latins identified ingenium with *natura*.[48] Nature itself is inventive; that is, it "finds" its objects by carving out of indeterminate experience objects of its own making. Human ingenuity is thus "acute," "sharp," or "penetrating" insofar as it is able to discern relationships *ex genere*, that is, by piercing through the ordinary structures by which things are rationally associated with one another.[49] Such rational association is due to an emphasis on the art of criticism, that art modeled from Descartes' analytic

---

46. See Kineret S. Jaffe, "The Concept of Genius: Its Changing Role in Eighteenth-Century French Aesthetics," *Journal of the History of Ideas* 41 (1980): 585.

47. See Robert A. Greene, "Whichcote, Wilkins, 'Ingenuity', and the Reasonableness of Christianity," *Journal of the History of Ideas* 42 (1981): 227, 240, 251–52.

48. *Ancient Wisdom*, 70 (*Opere*, 1: 179).

49. *Ibid.*, 74 (*Opere*, 1: 183); *Autobiography*, 148 (*Opere*, 5: 34). See Alfonsina Albini Grimaldi, *The Universal Humanity of Giambattista Vico* (New York: S. F. Vanni, 1958), 122.

geometry and Arnauld's Port Royal Logic; according to Cicero, it can be traced as far back as the Stoic concern for judgment to the exclusion of the study of topics.[50]

The art of discovery (which Vico equates with the art of topics, the art of finding in anything all that is in it) is the special domain of the ingenious (*ingegnosi*): "To discover new things," he says, "is the power [*virtus*] of ingenium alone."[51]   But in spite of its acuity, ingenium does not cut things apart; rather it cuts through the artificial rational divisions that separate topics. In short, ingenuity concerns itself less with the restrictions of truth (which assumes rational, critical discrimination) than with the presumption of the unity and harmony throughout nature, which permits the ingenious person to bring together things that, "to those lacking this faculty, seemed to have no relation to one another at all."[52]

In order to express the unity that is prior both to the discrimination of things in nature and the differentiation of objects of knowledge, ingenium employs metaphor as its proper language. The use of metaphor does not assume the propriety of the rational distinctions of things because it recognizes that rational distinctions themselves are the creative product of the discerning (acute) activity of ingenium in the first place.   If any faculty of mind is specifically philosophic, then, it is certainly not regulated by the critical art of geometrical method; rather it is the capacity to perceive similarities between matters that appear very dissimilar.[53]

Prior to any rational judgment of truth, the mind posits a pure, natural metaphorical unity of things upon which claims of knowledge can be based.   As such, before knowledge of things as determinate and distinguishable from one another is possible, ingenium posits a common, sense-based and imaginative context by means of which knowledge claims (claims of similarity and difference or, in general, claims of relatability) can be made. When Vico says, then, that "ingenium has been given to men for knowing, that is for making," he means that ingenium participates

50. See Mooney, *Vico in the Tradition of Rhetoric*, 51–54.

51. *Autobiography*, 124 (*Opere*, 5: 14).   Also see *Study Methods*, 26 (*Opere*, 1: 87); and *New Science*, par. 497.

52. Vico, "Polemiche," in *Opere*, 1: 212; Ernesto Grassi, "Critical Philosophy or Topical Philosophy?   Meditations on the *De nostri temporis studiorum ratione*," in *Giambattista Vico: International Symposium*, 49.

53. *Study Methods*, 24 (*Opere*, 1: 86).

in the divine activity of creating nature so as to make it accessible to human knowing.[54]

The unity of nature creatively posited by ingenium is thus expressed in the language of metaphor, learned in the study of topics, and experienced universally as "common sense." Such a unity serves as the presupposition of knowledge insofar as knowledge is communicable and imagination- or sense-based. Through the study of the commonsense and imaginative bases of language, then, we learn about the genesis of meanings: We relive genesis in tapping into ingenuity as expressed during the adolescence of mankind.

In the adolescence both of mankind and of every individual, common sense and imagination naturally (i.e., frankly, free of rational or critical constraints to speak the "truth") generate meanings based on verisimilitudes.[55] Training in topics conditions the mind to extend its grasp of connections widely so as to apprehend the matters on which critical judgment and reasoning can be employed. As far as Vico is concerned, the education of adolescents in the art of criticism before they have had the chance to develop their imaginative grasp of the interconnectedness of things frustrates the natural course of the mind's development (which is to know things before judging them).[56] The study of topics, on the other hand, renders the mind ingenious and, as the primary operation of the mind, uncovers those things necessary to human life prior to the appearance of critical judgment (the second operation of the mind).[57]

Because Vico considers the study of topics and the imaginative and metaphorical invention of the preconditions of truth as prior to and more fundamental than judgments of truth, he relishes the comments of critics who charge him with wit (ingenuity) rather than a concern for truth. Such criticism appeared not only after the first edition of the *New Science;* it had also appeared in almost the same form after Vico's publication of *On the Ancient Wisdom of the Italians* (1710). In response to this earlier jibe, he tersely responds: "Topical minds are more

---

54. Vico, *De antiquissima Italorum sapientia*, in *Opere*, 1: 192. Also see Verene, *Vico's Science of Imagination*, 105.

55. *Study Methods*, 13 (*Opere*, 1: 81).

56. *Ibid.*, 14 (*Opere*, 1: 81); and *Autobiography*, 24 (*Opere*, 5: 14).

57. *New Science*, pars. 496, 498, 699.

copious and less true."[58]   Minds employed in the generation of topics attempt to extend the domain of meaningful discourse underlying the possibility for discussion of truth claims.   But this generation of discourse literally *bespeaks* its own extension with disregard for questions of truth.[59]

To *know something*, Vico argues, means to be acquainted with the causes from which it arises; and to *know something as true* means to cognize the thing in terms of the form by which it is made.[60]   The imagination-bound speech embodied in myth and metaphor thus defines or causes objects to emerge as epistemologically accessible insofar as speech carves out of the flux of reality determinate (i.e., formally definable) objects or events.[61] But, as was mentioned earlier, even though that which is said (*dictum*) is the same as the certain (*certum*), it is not equivalent to the true (*verum*).   The true is that which is known in terms of its causes; and since original speech (myth/metaphor) is not self-conscious speech—that is, speech conscious of its form as ingenious or creative cause of the determinateness of its referents—it provides only consciousness of the certain or determinate, not knowledge of the true.   When speech becomes self-conscious by means of the regulation of formal structures (rules recognized as such in grammars and syntax), it distances itself from its imaginative, native, and free origins as its own authority; it blinds itself to the fact that human choice or ingenuity creates language in response to human needs.   Language thus becomes the domain of reason in virtue of its formalized structure; but in such a state it cannot account for how meanings are generated other than in synchronic, formalist, or structuralist terms.

Philosophy, especially the critical version of Cartesianism that Vico fears has captured the modern mentality, is unable to account for the origins or genesis of the meanings contained within the structure of language because uncertain and

---

58. Vico, "Polemiche," in *Opere*, 1: 271; quoted in Grassi, "Critical Philosophy," 49. Also see *Autobiography*, 188 (*Opere*, 5: 68).

59. *Autobiography*, 148 (*Opere*, 5: 34).

60. *Ancient Wisdom*, 51, 58 (*Opere*, 1: 132, 140).

61. See Gianfranco Cantelli, "Myth and Language in Vico," in *Giambattista Vico's Science of Humanity*, ed. Giorgio Tagliacozzo and Donald P. Verene (Baltimore, Md.: Johns Hopkins University Press, 1976), 62; Donald P. Verene, "Vico's Philosophy of Imagination," *Social Research* 43 (1976): 415–21; and Patrick H. Hutton, "The *New Science* of Giambattista Vico: Historicism in Its Relation to Poetics," *Journal of Aesthetics and Art Criticism* 30 (1971–72), 363.

unsystematic (free, frank, ingenuous) human choice is the author of such a system of meaning. It is the task of philosophy, then, to study that of which human choice is the author "whence comes consciousness of the certain." Ingenium relates the mind to an object of its own making in the sense that the mind becomes conscious of an object in terms of its connectedness (its communality) with all else that the mind is conscious of through its awareness of the "commonplaces" or topics that summarize the human experiences of a nation or a period in imaginative or poetic language.

Vico distinguishes consciousness of the certain from knowledge of the true in much the same way that Foucault distinguishes *connaissance* and *savoir* (for Vico, *coscienza* and *scienza*): Consciousness relates the mind to its object without explicitly enunciating the conditions whereby such an object can be given to consciousness.[62] Such an enunciation occurs only at the critical or philosophic level, the level at which rational judgment replaces the common sense of the nation or period in the philosophic search for the discriminations that make truth claims meaningful.

It is thus left to philology to discern the proto-philosophic genesis of meaning that characterizes consciousness rather than knowledge. Philology, Vico notes, studies the history of words, the narration of which is its own creation and, as such, contains its own certainty.[63] To narrate the history of ingenious (mythic/ metaphoric) language is to remember the imaginative ties (or topics) by which men who have common needs associate things with one another. "Hence memory is the same as imagination. . . . And imagination is likewise taken for ingenuity or invention," because the study of topics recaptures the spirit of imaginative and free ingenuity organized around a history of the common experiences (or "common sense") of a nation.[64]

Because the study of topics provides the mind with the "commonplaces that must all be run over in order to know all there is in a thing that one desires to know well," such a study recapit-

62. See Michel Foucault, *The Archaeology of Knowledge*, tr. A. M. Sheridan Smith (New York: Harper and Row, 1972), 15n. On Vichian aspects of Foucault's thought, see White, "Foucault Decoded," 48–52.

63. Cf. *New Science*, par. 349; and the first edition of the *New Science* (referred to as the *First New Science*, 1725), tr. in *Selected Writings*, 139 (*Opere*, 3: 145).

64. *New Science*, par. 819.

ulates the common sense of the nation.[65]   But such a common
sense is not the proper object of philosophic study because, as
noted above, "common sense is judgment without reflection."
To treat common sense philosophically would be to treat it as
having a rational structure, which (in turn) would mean treating
it according to rules intended to restrain the inventive character
of ingenium.

The whole point of Vico's appeal to topics as the expression of
a common sense is to show how the mind can retain its ingenious
(free, creative) character while still having definite guidelines by
which it can be taught and can be exercised inventively.   The
guidelines are learned only in learning the topics, the commonplaces of a people, the common sense of a nation as expressed
in the etymology of its language.   The comparison of different
languages occasionally reveals radical discontinuities of meaning
that simply cannot be ignored in philosophical attempts to
impose a rational order or structure onto common sense.   The
New Science that Vico proposes incorporates both philology and
philosophy in its description of the pattern of cultural development and decline.   Within such a pattern critical or reflective
thought loses touch with the creative and inventive character of
ingenium that originally invigorates a culture.   Science (or
knowledge, *scienza*) itself needs to dip back into its ingenious and
ingenuous origins through the imaginative use of topics if it has
any hope of avoiding what Vico calls the barbarism of reflection
and the sterility of intellect.   This is precisely the effect of Vico's
retrieval of the original Latin meaning of *ingenium*.

FIGURATION AND THE TRUE

For the mythic mentality, objects of knowledge are both
certain and true because nothing is conceivable that is also
inaccessible to a creative construction of the mind.   "In regard
to the true," Vico writes, "we may hence conjecture that the
sages of ancient Italy identified the true with the made."[66]   The
very construction of objects and meanings is an activity of meta-

---

65. *Ibid.*, par. 497.
66. *Ancient Wisdom*, 51 (*Opere*, 1: 131).   Also see *New Science*, par. 403; and
Verene, "Vico's Science of Imaginative Universals and the Philosophy of Symbolic
Forms," in *Giambattista Vico's Science of Humanity*, 304.

phorical ingenuity—where metaphor does not presuppose a meaningful relation of things that exist behind or beneath the supposedly poetic imagination implicit in the use of metaphor.[67] Where there is no conception of an organized world apart from one's creative apprehension of it, truth and thought merge into each other. Just such a situation is precisely what we find, Vico explains, when we examine the epistemological presuppositions underlying the appeal of the ancient fables or myths. The fables are "ideal truths" that identify a character or condition (a meaning): "Poetic truth, and physical truth which is not in conformity with it, should be considered false."[68] Even the statements of rational metaphysics must respect the meanings established originatively in the poetic or "imagistic metaphysics" of mythic expression.

The proper meaning of *fabula*, according to Vico, must be traced to *logos*, understood as active and effective word, implemented idea, true narrative. "The definition of *mythos* is 'true narration' but it has continued to mean 'fable,' which everybody has hitherto taken to mean 'false narration,' even though the definition of *logos* is 'true speech' and is commonly taken to mean the 'origin' of 'history of words.' . . . Fables and true speech mean the same thing and constituted the vocabulary of the first nations."[69] Fables as such do not *describe* the world, as if the fabular construction were distinct from a meaningfully organized world. Rather, they constitute or give origins to the world as meaningful and epistemologically accessible. As the sense-bound narrative expression of the world, fable certifies reality as meaningfully accessible.

In fact, the *fabula* does not include the possibility for a distinction between imagined and real world, or between what ought to be and what is. Myth, narration, and moral exhortation are contained complicitly within the understanding of the active, effective, emotive, constructive expression.

'Logic' comes from *logos*, whose first and proper meaning was *fabula*, fable, carried over into Italian as *favella*, speech. In Greek the fable was

67. See Verene, "Vico's Philosophy of Imagination," 432–33. Cf. Cassirer, *The Philosophy of Symbolic Forms*, vol. 1: *Language*, tr. Ralph Mannheim (New Haven, Conn.: Yale University Press, 1953), 107.

68. *New Science*, par. 205; also par. 375.

69. Vico, *First New Science*, in *Selected Writings*, 139 (*Opere*, 3: 145).

also called *mythos*, myth. . . . *Logos* means both word and idea. . . . *Logos* or word meant also deed to the Hebrews and thing to the Greeks. . . . Similarly, *mythos* came to be defined for us as *vera narratio*, or true speech. . . . The first age invented the fables to serve as true narratives, the primary and proper meaning of the word *mythos*, as defined by the Greeks themselves, being 'true narration.'[70]

Figural expression is deed, thing, actuality: there is no way in which it can be false (within the fabular setting) because there is nothing other than itself against which it can be measured as real or feigned.   Within such an understanding—for instance, that of Descartes when he feigns a world like that found in *Le Monde*—it makes no sense to ask the question "But is your fabular world the real one?"   Truth and falsity are not at issue here; there is only the certain, that which is, immediate figuration. "The true" is a derivative concept, made possible by and generated through the emergence of reason and of abstracting, discursive ways of thinking.

Within a rational metaphysics—that is, a metaphysics in which human reason considers determinate things and ideas in a discursive way—human beings treat things in the world as distinct from themselves and as apart from their creative control.   To understand (*intelligere*) things in the world thus involves the assumptions (1) that those things exist in some meaningful way apart from the activity by which they are understood, and (2) that in order to understand them, man must extend his mind to take them into himself.   Such an extension means going beyond the sensible, the figural, the communally experienced, to that which does not fall under the senses.[71]   Such a move to the intellectual has to blind itself to the sensible basis of meaning within figural expression in an attempt to extract a common or universal quality found in, but not restricted to, any sensible instance of expression.

This move to the intelligible, however, completely misses the point that within figuration there are no analogical expressions. Each figuration (metaphor, myth/fable) identifies a univocal meaning in virtue of the figuration itself.[72]   All chiefs of war, for example, are not simply like Godfrey—they are Godfrey; otherwise

70. *New Science*, par. 401; also see pars. 408, 808, 814.
71. *Ibid.*, par. 363.
72. *Ibid.*, pars. 205, 210, 403, 460.

they are not chiefs of war. Poetic style creates its own meaning
and thus cannot rely on another standard apart from itself to
relate its particular expression to other "similar" expressions.
The meaning of poetic characters (figural icons that serve as
imaginative genera) lies on the etymological surface of mythic
expression. Such meanings are "not philosophical but historical,"
in that they emphasize (in their storytelling, narrating, or fabling
character) how the origin and development of meaning is one
ongoing historical process.[73] The sheer temporality of figural
expression shows how *logos*, true speech, could commonly be
understood to mean "the origin or history" of words: To speak
the topoi is to pass time with figurations that identify words as
meaningful. As such, to recount the myths is to live through the
very time (not just a similar time) in which the poetic characters
achieve meaning.

Within the imaginative metaphysics of fabling, man does not
understand things, as if they were originally distinct and determinate apart from him. Myth undercuts the need to understand
by undercutting the presupposition that ingenium (mind) and
nature (ingenium) are not originatively united.[74]

Rational metaphysics teaches that man becomes all things by understanding them (*homo intelligendo fit omnia*), but imaginative metaphysics
shows that man becomes all things by *not* understanding them (*homo non
intelligendo fit omnia*); and perhaps the latter proposition is truer than
the former, for when man understands he extends his mind and takes
in things, but when he does not understand he makes the things out of
himself and becomes them by transforming himself into them.[75]

To speak about understanding is to adopt a certain type of
language (viz., that of truth and reason) that loses touch with the
perceptual immediacy of mythic invention.[76] To adopt the stance
of *not* understanding, of transforming oneself into all things by

73. *Ibid.*, par. 34. Cf. Derek Attridge, "Language as History/History as
Language: Saussure and the Romance of Etymology," in *Post-structuralism and the
Question of History*, ed. Derek Attridge, Geoff Bennington, and Robert Young
(Cambridge: Cambridge University Press, 1987), 183–211.
74. See *Autobiography*, 148 (*Opere*, 5: 34); *Ancient Wisdom*, 70 (*Opere*, 1: 179).
75. *New Science*, par. 405. See Gillo Dorfles, "Myth and Metaphor in Vico and
Contemporary Aesthetics," in *Giambattista Vico: International Symposium*, 587; and
Verene, "Vico's Science," 296.
76. See Cantelli, "Myth and Language in Vico," 62; and Verene, "Vico's
Philosophy," 415.

identifying human ingenuity with figuration, is to reinstitute the mythic, poetic, or fabular spirit of invention.

The fragmentation of the meanings of fable (as classical myth, narrative scheme, Aesopic apologue, and falsehood) is thus overcome in Vico's suggestion that mythic narrations constitute particular individuals (heroes, gods, men, Aesopic animals) as meanings or linguistic exemplars ("imaginative genera"). These accounts of individuals, in turn, prescribe modes of behavior by providing the bases for the practical (including moral) ordering of the world. As such, in their original condition, the fables of Aesop and Homer display a fundamental unity.[77]

As poetic or mythic language, Homeric and Aesopic fabulation have three aims: (1) to sensitize members of the community to the meanings or topoi by which the community is imaginatively and figurally united; (2) to recount the origins or "ultimate circumstances" of why things are as they are—that is, to show how understanding origins is crucial in understanding meanings; and (3) to call individuals to noble behavior by presenting such ideals in imaginative ways.[78] As long as the imaginative metaphysics of figural expression restricts meaning to figuration itself, questions of epistemological or moral truth simply cannot arise. However, as distinctions begin to develop between spoken word and idea, between imaginative genera and intelligible genera, myths/fables (in virtue of their figural character) remain tied to their imaginative sources. Distinguished from the intelligible or rational development of the human mind, they become contrasted to the means of defining the true, and under the critical gaze of Greek rationality are subsequently considered as false.

Vico's philological examination of fables proposes that the most important stage in the development of the concept of the fable (as the moderns know it in its different forms) occurs after articulate languages are invented but before human reason is fully developed.[79] Communally shared speech permits men at this stage to attain consciousness of the certain and does not as yet raise questions about knowledge of the true; for, the meaning of figural expression at this intermediate state depends on its use and communicative power, not on its validity as expressive of some reality outside itself. There is no *humanitas* other than that

77. *New Science*, pars. 424, 816. See Grimaldi, *Universal Humanity*, 215, 222–26.
78. *First New Science*, 139–40 (*Opere*, 3: 146), and *New Science*, par. 376.
79. *New Science*, pars. 138, 1045.

which exists in and through the topoi of a community's expressive figurations.

Because Bacon, Vico, and even Descartes recognize that the communicative power of language limits us to consciousness of the certain rather than providing access to knowledge of the true, they address the question of philosophic discovery or invention as an issue related to the role of fabling within philosophy. What changes from Bacon to Vico is how assumptions regarding the role of fabling are understood and employed. For Bacon, the fables of the ancients serve as boundary markers for the type of questions for which investigators should seek certain but not true answers. Descartes proposes his inquiries within fabular settings in order to highlight the human context of such inquiries. But such a procedure must be justified if it is to avoid the charge of being arbitrary.

In providing such a justification by undercutting the dichotomies of reason and imagination (and, to a lesser extent, even the dichotomies of man and nature, knower and known), Vico reveals the epistemological foundations upon which fabular philosophy is built. He accomplishes this without proliferating fabular forms or jeopardizing the functional integrity (and at least the heuristic value) of existing meanings of "fable." As such, Vico makes thematic the philosophic reluctance to posit a final closure on meaning by insisting on the foundational indeterminacy of fabular referents. In a complementary move, he also cautions against restricting fabular thinking to any meaning that itself would encumber future philosophic innovation and discovery. The cost of such freedom, however, is high, because it requires a return of philosophy to its original rhetorical-philosophical commitments. Only by reaffirming the figural nature of thought can such an attempt be made to regain access to the certainty lost by the adoption of critical rationality.

CHAPTER SIX

Herder and Hamann on Linguistic Mythology

WITH THE POSSIBLE EXCEPTION OF VICO, no eighteenth-century thinker extends the notion of myth to as many topics as J. G. Herder (1744–1803). In Herder's view myth encompasses poetics, history, philosophy, and psychology insofar as language expresses a physiology of individual and social experience. Language exhibits reason within history and experience insofar as sensible, passionate images and sounds provide a vocabulary by which thought is not only made possible but also made available to creative revision in each new juxtaposition of images. Such a recharacterization of reason retrieves, for Herder, the sense in which myth orders a chaos of images into a creative narrative with a distinctively moral purpose. In this way, myth incorporates the rhetorical and pedagogical characteristics of fable while highlighting the order of figuration within a narration. The mythic concentration on the physiology of linguistic experience thus allows Herder to reinterpret empiricist psychology within its originative context of poetics.

Because J. G. Hamann's (1730–1788) emphasis on the immediacy of linguistic experience influences and clarifies some of Herder's positions, I have included Hamann in this discussion of the centrality of myth. For Hamann (like Herder), mythology elevates language to its primordial preeminence: It reaffirms the unity of thought and feeling, fact and value, description and recommendation; it reappropriates the creative capacity of language in the actual determination of both nature and history. To adopt the mythic attitude means, for Hamann, to recognize how nature and history are ordered within a divine grammar with which human linguistic expression is not only analogous but also identical.

Whereas Hamann often focuses on the distinctively religious character of *logos* within language, Herder attends more to the anthropological implications of such language-centered historiography. Both thinkers, though, expand the concept of mythology to include lived experience as linguistically ordered in social, historical settings. As such, their comments about epistemology, poetics, or philosophy of history point to, rather than begin from, a redefinition of myth. Through just such an approach they counter the classicist ideal of starting with a definition of myth or fable and deducing its characteristics and proper applications.

Insofar as creativity and ingenuity characterize the process by which human rationality is ordered in experience, poetics and philosophy become identifiable (particularly for Herder) as rational only in terms of modes of expression explicitly concerned with the invention of such order. Mythology, Herder argues, provides the "poetic heuristic" by which our creations order experience: "In short," he claims, "we should study the mythology of the ancients as a poetic heuristic [*Poetische Heuristik*] in order to become inventors ourselves."[1] Herder's own invention of mythology as heuristic guides his discussions of the poet, the philosopher, and the historian as themselves mythologists, creators of order within the communal framework of language as a moral/educational organon.

For Herder, accordingly, myth embodies the originative, creative aspect of language and experience as opposed to the rationalistic petrification of language and experience into deductive categories of fixed syntax. His "new use of mythology" reinstates poetic expression to the center of epistemology and history by recalling the sensuous (physiological) origins of individual and communal life. As such, his treatments of Aesopic fables, individual sensation and cognition, and human historical development exhibit different ways in which he reveals the mythological character pervading his entire philosophy.

My presentation parallels roughly the development of Herder's own writings in terms of three interconnected themes. In his early writings he takes up the idea espoused by Hamann (with whom he became friends in 1762) that all of reality is ordered linguistically; and for Herder this means that the linguistic traditions of imagery ordered in poetics or mythology reveal the sources of grammars by which all experience is meaningful. He then extends the discussion of the sequential ordering of images into a "psychological physiology" in which reason and thought emerge together as products of fabular figuration. Just how such patterns emerge to provide the bases both of historical under-

---

1. Herder, "On the New Use of Mythology," in *Fragments Concerning Recent German Literature* (*Über die neuere deutsche Literatur; Fragmente*, 1766–67), in *Sämtliche Werke*, ed. Bernhard Suphan et al., 33 vols. (Berlin: Weidmannsche Buchhandlung, 1877–1913), 1: 444. Unless otherwise noted, references are to the German texts.

standing and of a philosophy of history serves as the focus for
Herder's later work and for the return to Hamann's synthesis of
nature and history as the language of God.

MYTHOGRAPHY: THE POETICS OF EXPERIENCE

By focusing attention on mythology and the sensuous immediacy
of language, Herder challenges the Enlightenment views that
thought exists prior to speech or history, that reason is independent of language, and that the eternal and immutable provide
the a priori conditions for meaning within the historical and
expressive.   In order to reassert the centrality of the figural
within experience, Herder reverses the places of mythology and
philosophy: Philosophy begins in, and is never able fully to transcend, the sourcing powers with which it is confronted within
experience. But such an observation does not simply reassert the
empiricist program of beginning with passive sensations.   Instead,
it regains for philosophy the possibility for creative regeneration
and development by identifying the source of meaning and rationality within the actual order of sensible imagery immediately
presented in experience. Visual and auditory images serve not
only as the sources of thought but also as the determinants of
what can come into being. As such, they function in the same
way as sense-based creators (i.e., mythic divinities).
   At the same time, this extension of mythology as poetic heuristic
does not denigrate reason but instead recognizes the importance
of speech and writing as sources of the signs by which nature
and thought are made intelligible. In *Fragments Concerning Recent
German Literature* (1766–67), Herder boldly claims, "Through
language we learn to think."[2]   Language provides both the
individual and the culture with the distinctive characters for
identifying the components and relationships of cognition.[3]
Without the sign system that language provides, thought is

2.   *Fragments*, in *Sämtliche Werke*, 1: 147. Cf. Joe K. Fugate, *The Psychological Basis
of Herder's Aesthetics* (The Hague: Mouton, 1966), 82.
   3.   See James W. Marchand, "Herder: Precursor of Humboldt, Whorf, and
Modern Language Philosophy," in *Johann Gottfried Herder: Innovator Through the
Ages*, ed. Wulf Koepke and Samson Knoll (Bonn: Bouvier, 1982), 25; and Wulf
Koepke, *Johann Gottfried Herder* (Boston: Twayne Publishers, 1987), 48.

impossible because thought is nothing more than the arrangement of such signs in a narration, a plot, a fable.

Prior to examining the implications of such a position, it is useful to note that Hamann had been developing this theme for some time before he met Herder. In 1758 he notes: "God reveals himself; the creator of the world is a writer"; "All of nature is full of signs and reveals itself as writing [*Schrift*]."[4] As a written and spoken sign system, the world becomes intelligible, for Hamann, only to those who approach it in terms of its linguistic character. He accordingly writes to Kant (who himself becomes Herder's teacher and friend in 1762): "Nature is a book, a letter, a fable [*Fabel*] (in the philosophical sense)."[5] That is, the philosophical sense of fable captures the creative, scriptive (and thus scriptural) character of nature. The fabular/ mythic exhibits nature as writing, a communication in sensible signs. Hamann's appeal to the fabular in its distinctively philosophic sense accordingly prohibits the reduction of such a remark to an entertaining and easily dismissed metaphor about nature. Indeed, the depiction of nature as fable illuminates the central feature of metaphor, namely, the *identity* of sign and signified. For therein lies the key for understanding the poetic sensitivity to visual and auditory figuration in forms of writing and speech. The true writer creates characters (meanings, relationships) in the use of characters (letters, signs), and in doing so properly identifies the genesis of reason itself.

For Hamann, the origin of reason can be explained only in terms of the creative and poetic capacity of linguistic expression to order signs by which a chaos of sights and sounds becomes a cosmos, a world. "Without the word," he comments to Jacobi, "there is no reason, no world. Here is the source of creation and government!"[6] To Herder he later writes: "Language is the organon and criterion of reason."[7] And in criticizing Kant's

---

4. Hamann, "Biblical Reflections," in *Sämtliche Werke*, ed. Josef Nadler, 6 vols. (Vienna: Herder, 1949–57), 1: 9, 68. Also cf. 1: 5. In order to distinguish this edition of Hamann's works from the Suphan edition of Herder's writings, I will refer below to the Nadler edition of Hamann's *Sämtliche Werke* simply as *Werke*.
    5. Hamann to Kant, end of Dec. 1759, in *Briefwechsel*, ed. Walther Ziesemer and Arthur Henkel, 7 vols. (Wiesbaden: Insel, 1955–75), 1: 450.
    6. Hamann to Jacobi, 2 Nov. 1783, in *Briefwechsel*, 5: 95. Cf. James C. O'Flaherty, *Unity and Language: A Study in the Philosophy of Johann Georg Hamann* (1952; reprint, New York: AMS Press, 1966), 31.
    7. Hamann to Herder, 8 Dec. 1783, in *Briefwechsel*, 5: 108.

failure to take note of the importance of figurative expression in the analysis of reason, he concludes, "Not only the entire ability to think rests on language . . . but language is also the center of the misunderstanding of reason with itself."[8] In Hamann's view, to ignore the poetic character of reason divorces thought from the immediacy of feeling implicit within the awareness of the figurative and narrative character of language. All language presents a narration in showing in visual and auditory figuration a sequence, an order, a plot. Ignorance of this constitutive factor within reason withdraws philosophy literally from the sensation of thinking.

To appreciate the possibilities of reason thus means to understand the poetic origins of rational structures. Insofar as such structures presume the visibility of linguistic figuration, reason cannot be properly understood apart from the fabular imagery that provides the mythic context from which philosophy mistakenly tries to distance itself. As Hamann concludes, "No reason is invisible or without language."[9] Those forms of language (such as myth and poetry) that highlight their own visible presence counteract the impulse to displace figuration in favor of some thought or reason supposedly behind language. In myth and poetry, the identity claimed in metaphor emerges in the act of self-disclosure, a text that unites the sensible and the rational in the immediacy of the linguistic.

As such, reason is nothing more and nothing less than language: "If I were as eloquent as Demosthenes," Hamann writes to Herder, "I would do no more than repeat one sentence thrice: Reason is language, Logos. On this marrow-bone I gnaw, and I will gnaw myself to death on it."[10] Reason emerges not because a statement is somehow intuitively obvious or true in spite of its utterance; rather, the redundant incorporation of the narrative sequence into a linguistic tradition establishes it within the parameters of syntax that constitute meaningful discourse. Reason occurs in the retelling of a narrative. This originative

---

8. *Metacritique of the Purism of Reason* (1784, published 1800), in *Werke*, 3: 286; cited in Ronald G. Smith, *J. G. Hamann 1730–1788* (New York: Harper and Bros., 1960), 216. Cf. the comments by O'Flaherty, *Hamann's "Socratic Memorabilia": A Translation and Commentary* (Baltimore, Md.: Johns Hopkins University Press, 1967), 40.

9. Hamann to Jacobi, 27 Apr. 1787, in *Briefwechsel*, 7: 168.

10. Hamann to Herder, 8 Aug. 1784, in *Briefwechsel*, 5: 177. Cf. O'Flaherty, *Unity*, 99.

moment in the genesis of meaning fascinates Hamann and opens up for him the possibility that reason can reappropriate its lost sense of beauty, proportionality, and eloquence.

Hamann's reappropriation of eloquence in reason is made possible only within his ongoing critique of reason understood as eternal, unresponsive to linguistic change, and unconcerned with its own sensual origins. Within such an understanding of reason, so-called rational expressions attempt to efface their very presence as figural expressions. In this regard he writes to Kant: "Lies are the native language of our reason."[11] That is, insofar as reason points to something supposedly behind language, rational expressions displace themselves in falsely affirming their own transparency. As Hamann notes to Jacobi, "We still lack a *grammar* of reason," insofar as reason's continual historical development in figural expression frustrates attempts to absolutize the structure of meaning.[12] Philosophic systems that assume that reason is ahistorical imply the possibility of such a grammar at the expense of affirming a role for creativity in reason.

The linguistically based grammar of figuration, on the other hand, provides an alternative to this misplaced ideal of a grammar of reason. Or more precisely, it identifies the means by which a grammar of reason is possible only within a revision that acknowledges the poetic tropes grounding reason. Parables, analogies, and allegories make explicit the role of language in the development and communication of meaning. But insofar as reason has lost touch with its fabular origins, parables and allegories are seen only as indictments of man's fallen state. Rather than reasserting human participation in the creation of meaning, such rational discourse accepts the displacement of reason from language as a result of original sin.[13] Authentic, living reason, like effective eloquence, can be regained, Hamann argues, only by renewing the philosophical commitment to the use of what he calls "metaschemata."[14] Such devices recall philosophy to its Aesopic and Socratic origins, in which language adorns itself in the eloquence it embodies as the source of meaning and reason:

11. Hamann to Kant, 27 July 1759, cited in Smith, *Hamann*, 240.
12. Hamann to Jacobi, 1 Dec. 1784, in *Briefwechsel*, 5: 272; cf. O'Flaherty, *Unity*, 68.
13. Cf. W. M. Alexander, *Johann Georg Hamann: Philosophy and Faith* (The Hague: Martinus Nijhoff, 1966), 44.
14. Cf. Hamann to Herder, 28 Jan. 1776, in *Briefwechsel*, 3: 215; also see O'Flaherty, *"Socratic Memorabilia,"* 89.

"Aesopic and Socratic language beautifies itself [*verschönert sich*] as an organon of genuine, living, and proportional reason."[15] In this affirmation of the original unity of fabular and philosophic language, Hamann invites a return to a mythic sensitivity to the presence of language as a moral and aesthetic force. As his *Socratic Memorabilia* reveals, such a reaffirmation also demands a reassessment of Socrates (and subsequent philosophers) from a perspective that presumes a unity between narrative account and fabular moralizing. Hamann's juxtaposition of Aesop and Socrates accordingly reintegrates philosophy into the historical, sensual, and creative environment of mythopoesis.

Herder, in his turn, makes the connection among mythology, language, and philosophy even more explicit. "Homer," he says, "creates in narration."[16] The mythic poet provides the grammar by which all communication or thought—including that of philosophy—retains its immediate contact with the world. Rather than withdrawing us from the world of our experience, the mythologist places us immediately before the linguistic expressions loaded with and indiscernible from the passions and interests that have called them forth.

Especially in his *Essay on the Origin of Language* (1770; published 1772), Herder takes up Hamann's theme when he says, "Without language man has no reason"; but then he quickly adds, "and without reason man has no language."[17] In fact, without language/reason, there is no such thing as man, for the concept and word, the thing and the name, are the same. Before man the actor appears, there are actions, sounds, verbs without nouns; and this sounding, acting, stirring nature brings man into being at the same moment as the whole mythic pantheon of poetic characters and linguistic figures.[18]

The oldest dictionary was thus a sounding pantheon. . . . For what was this language of ours other than a collection of elements of poetry?

15. Hamann to Jacobi, 27 Apr. 1787, in *Briefwechsel*, 7: 168.
16. *Critical Forests*, "First Grove" (1769), in *Sämtliche Werke*, 3: 152; cf. Martin Schütze, "The Fundamental Ideas in Herder's Thought: II," *Modern Philology* 18 (1920): 299.
17. *Essay on the Origin of Language*, tr. Alexander Gode in *On the Origin of Language* (New York: Frederick Ungar, 1966), 121. Cf. Wulf Koepke, "Herder's Craft of Communication," in *The Philosopher as Writer: The Eighteenth Century*, ed. Robert Ginsberg (Selinsgrove, Pa.: Susquehanna University Press, 1987), 98–99, 115.
18. *Origin of Language*, 127, 132.

Imitation it was of sounding, acting, stirring nature! Taken from the interjections of all beings and animated by the interjections of human emotion! The natural language of all beings fashioned by reason into sounds, into images of action, passion, and living impact! A dictionary of the soul that was simultaneously mythology and a marvelous epic of the actions and the speech of all beings! Thus a continuous fabulation [*Fabeldichtung*] with passion and interest!—what else is poetry?[19]

The narration of mythology creates not only the syntax by which expression becomes meaningful but also the very elements constituting the dictionary of terms in which myth is expressed. The chaos of sounding, stirring nature appears as the speech of beings and the being of speeches, the passion-filled order that emerges simultaneously as reason. Furthermore, and contrary to Condillac and Rousseau, Herder claims that the structural order of language (reason) is not the product of emotion or imitation. Nor is it due to convention or social agreement, for no determinate prior thing exists to be imitated, no society exists to employ sounds and images as conventions.[20] The creative, poetic, and expressive character of language affirms itself as the source of order and reason in the world. In fact, the world as cosmos (ordered unity) traces its origin back to an epic populated by actions or active events/powers (the gods) governed by chance, fate, absurdity; it is certainly not governed by reason, for reason emerges only in virtue of these actions. In the "epic of actions" that constitutes myth, the gods are verbs and not nouns, forces in continuous flight within the passing of the narrative. The plot or "fable" is the simultaneously immediate presence of sounds and images of the narration, filled with passion and interest, which points to no rationale beyond itself for its own legitimation.

The grammar of any philosophy based on such mythological presuppositions recognizes language as something distinct from and additional to being, only to the extent that language is allowed to encourage its own displacement through the use of the past tense. However, the true nature and vitality of language, as Herder points out, lies in the use of the present tense: "The present is something one shows; the past is something one must

19. *Ibid.*, 133, 135–36. Cf. *Sämtliche Werke*, 5: 55–57.
20. See *Origin of Language*, 118. Cf. Luanne Frank, "Herder's *Essay on the Origin of Language:* Forerunner of Contemporary Views in History, Aesthetics, Literary Theory, Philosophy," *Forum Linguisticum* 7 (1982): 22.

relate."[21]   To treat language as a medium for communicating thought or emotion or for imitating nature withdraws man from the creative immediacy of the present tense and condemns creativity to an irretrievable past.   The various forms of the past tense stand as indictments against attempts to reinstate the present expressive word as man's aboriginal link to divinity.   In short, the past tense reminds us of man's fallen state, of the state of language fallen from the presence of divine creativity.

Through his renewal of mythology and poetics within the figuration or graphic character of discourse, Herder thus reclaims the creative prerogative of philosophy.   In doing so, he redefines mythology: He replaces the study of the origins of meaning and rationality seen in terms of past events with the study of the immediate creative capacity of present linguistic figuration.   Insofar as myth or mythology focuses attention on anything other than the ritual of its own performance as the origin of intelligibility, it distances man (specifically, the community) from the sensual immediacy that passionally unites graphemic expression and action.

This new "mythography" places philosophy back into the domain of divinity without demanding that such a move transcend the immediacy of experience.   The word (*logos*) continues to be the activity of the gods in creation.   But by means of its reorientation as mythography, philosophy can not only relate the history of rationality but also show the very process of the constitution of reason.

Herder's renovation of philosophy applies not only to subsequent endeavors but also to the interpretation of creative moments in the writings of previous thinkers.   Interpretation demands re-creation in historiography in order to reveal the emergence of reason in history.   About Berkeley's philosophy, for example, Herder writes: "I regard his system as being, like the systems of *Spinoza, Fénelon, Leibniz,* and *Descartes, fictions,* as being poetry [*Dictung*]—for what system is anything else or should be regarded as anything else?—and in Berkeley the poetry is great, keen, and thoroughly sustained."[22]   Herder's designation of

21.   *Origin of Language,* 161.
22.   Herder, review of James Beattie's *Essay on Truth* (1772), in *Sämtliche Werke,* 5: 461; quoted in Robert T. Clarke, *Herder: His Life and Thought* (Berkeley: University of California Press, 1955), 178.   On the contrast between mythology and mythography, see Burton Feldman and Robert D. Richardson, *The Rise of Modern Mythology: 1680–1860* (Bloomington: Indiana University Press, 1972), xxiv.

philosophical systems as fictions and poetry obviously does not belittle them in his eyes; instead it elevates them to their appropriate stature as sources of rational insight. They are such sources not in virtue of what they reveal of a world that they try to mirror or describe but in virtue of the sign system constituted in their very presentation: Their mythographemic character overrides the self-effacing tendency of mythology understood as simply the collection of or commentary on ancient myths.

In portraying the world as a system of signs employing a divine vocabulary, Berkeley (for example) recognizes this. What he fails to notice, in Herder's view, is the poetic and originative (i.e., mythic) character of such philosophy. Insofar as philosophy limits itself to the empiricist presuppositions of imagery and sign, though, it retains the means for recovering the eloquence of and fascination with its mythic origins.

PRESENCE IN SENSATION

In writings from the 1770s, especially *On the Cognition and Sensation of the Human Mind* (1778), Herder identifies how the sense-based character of language justifies a philosophical reclamation of inventive creativity only within an epistemology that refuses to extend cognition beyond sensation into faculty psychology. As the creative source of reason, the human mind is nothing other than the integration of sensations, images, or signs. For Herder, to argue that faculties of the mind have sensations of a determinate world distinct from mind not only presumes unjustifiable claims of both metaphysics and epistemology but also raises insurmountable difficulties concerning why human sensations should exhibit any passional connection with a world apparently ordered independently of human creativity. At issue are not only questions of epistemic skepticism but also questions of moral indifference—questions he will raise repeatedly in his later criticisms of Kant. For why should human beings care about a world disconnected from and unrelated to their immediate passionate experience?

In place of faculty psychology Herder offers a "psychological physiology" in which the order of imagery produced by "the harmonious contact and communication between our senses" yields the grammar of experience designated as reason.[23]   In the course of the apparently random sequence of physiological events—a sequence in which sense data establish a "communication between the senses" only in that some order is momentarily achieved— patterns emerge as language/reason.   Such patterns are purely physiological and sensual and in no way imply the emergence of a psychology as anything other than physiology: "No *psychology* is possible which is not definitely *physiology* at every step."[24]   The mind, as such, exists only as the narrative sequence of images.

The poetic foundation of such a narration consists in the fabular character of self-constitution.   Since language is originally a narrative sequence of visual and auditory images, the process of image formation must have exactly the same structure or topology as reason.   Images, like nouns, do not simply appear in passive cognition; rather, they emerge out of the chaotic cacophony of proto-nature as moments of sensual redundancy.   The redundancy of sequences of indeterminate experience establishes the harmonic network by which images are constituted and mind is defined. These images are not images *of* anything, for nothing determinate exists apart from that which is immediately accessible to and accessible as mind.   Redundancy in indeterminate experience occurs, Herder argues, because of unifying forces (*Kräfte*) that order and harmonize sense impressions as historical narratives ("epics of actions").[25]

Within fable the narration brings into being the entities about which the narration speaks.   Just as philosophical systems create the worlds they describe in virtue of their fictional and poetic ingenuity, so even physics (Herder claims) is "a kind of poetics" in virtue of how it calls forth a world in its very language.[26]   But to the extent that physics attempts to narrate a natural history

23. Herder, "Concerning Cognition and Sensation in the Human Mind" (1774 version), in *Sämtliche Werke*, 8: 250; and "On Image, Poetry, and Fable" (1787), in *Sämtliche Werke*, 15: 526.   Cf. Martin Schütze, "Herder's Conception of 'Bild'," *Germanic Review* 1 (1926): 24–25; and Fugate, *Psychological Basis*, 37.

24. Herder, *On the Cognition and Sensation of the Human Mind*, in *Sämtliche Werke*, 8: 180.

25. See Clarke, *Herder*, 225–26, 314–16; Clarke, "Herder's Conception of 'Kraft'," *PMLA* 57 (1942): 737-52; and H. B. Nisbet, *Herder and the Philosophy and History of Science* (Cambridge: Modern Humanities Research Association, 1970), especially 8–17.   I will discuss the relationship of *Kräfte* and "epics of actions" in the next section.

26. Herder, "Image, Poetry, Fable," in *Sämtliche Werke*, 15: 533.   See Nisbet, *Herder and the History of Science*, 41–57, 101–11.

blind to the historicity of its own narrative performance, it undermines the very principles by which initial interest in its projects begins.

As indicated in Herder's 1787 essay, "On Image, Poetry, and Fable," mythology and poetics function epistemologically in the same way as they do linguistically. The continual flow of images that constitutes the mind appears in the form of an unceasing allegory, which, he claims, is the essence of poetry. Thoughts, language, and life itself are thus constructed on a poetic foundation: "Our entire life is, so to speak, a poetics: we do not see, rather we create images for ourselves. . . . Hence it follows that our soul, as well as our speech, continually allegorizes."[27] We do not see but rather create images for ourselves because prior to the narrative activity of fabulation there is no thing to be seen. Here Herder adopts a Leibnizian idea insofar as he identifies the process of imagination as an activity of self-explication. Genuine novelty emerges in the world as the imagistic complexus of reason. But unlike Leibniz, Herder is unwilling to allow reason a divorce from its sensual bases, for even consciousness and self-reflection necessarily continue to employ sensual imagery in their attempts to distance themselves from sensibility.

The attempt to distance the self from its figural foundations is crucial for the emergence of a vocabulary of self-reflection and human self-consciousness. The formation [*Bildung*] of the self requires just such an act of displacement whereby language is objectified as distinct from the act of its objectification. This is the moment that language as such first appears and with it self-reflection and humanity.[28] The self as such is an image-formation, the creation/education of sensibilities. Only in recognizing the self-consciously creative character of poetry or myth can we properly capture the self-constitutive character of this displacement of language. For myth itself implies no distinction between its content and the linguistic vehicle by which such a content is transmitted. Furthermore, myth presumes no author behind its text, no intention "obscured" by its medium. In the figural

27. Herder, "Image, Poetry, Fable," in *Sämtliche Werke*, 15: 526; quoted in Thomas Noel, *Theories of the Fable in the Eighteenth Century* (New York: Columbia University Press, 1975), 129. Cf. Frank, "Herder's *Essay*," 22.

28. See Michael M. Morton, "Herder and the Possibility of Literature: Rationalism and Poetry in Eighteenth-Century Germany," in Koepke (ed.), *Herder: Innovator*, 48–49, 52; and Koepke, *J. G. Herder*, 64–65.

masking of myth lies the possibility of the displacement of the self. In this way, the author is self-consciously revealed behind the language by means of which reason and humanity are possible.[29]

To say that the mind as well as speech continually allegorizes means that the sequential juxtaposition of figures, in either mind or language, allows for further expansion, application, interpretation, and restatement of the sequence. Each renewal of the sequence itself, like each retelling of a myth, constitutes a new sequence—in Hamann's terms, a "metaschema"—that appropriates and exceeds all prior schemata. This unavoidable impulse toward creative novelty permits the expansion of connections among all elements of any sequence.

Connections that the poet makes and that offend the rational sensibilities of the philosopher or violate the approved syntax of the absolutist grammarian not only express the creative impulse of myth and allegory but also recall the moral prescriptions implicit within such uses. For the allegory and the fable self-consciously expose the moral character and rhetorical power of sensual, linguistic, figurative, and performative immediacy.

The point of the allegory and the moral of the fable reside, for Herder, on the perceptually immediate level of felt expression. Any fable or allegory that points beyond itself for its justification contravenes the mythic principle that assumes a unity between action and injunction. In fact, the power of mythopoesis lies in the facticity of its very presence as a form out of which moral and linguistic order (reason) is fashioned. This commitment to ontological and moral regeneration within each linguistic performance captures precisely the intent of the mythological turn in philosophy. In myth, expressiveness or passionate commitment is embodied in, and exists in no other way than through, the linguistic expression. This unity of feeling and thought in expression provides the means by which reason and emotion again speak in one voice.

---

29. See Morton, "Herder and the Possibility of Literature," 53–54, 58. Cf. Denis Diderot's description of genius' access to reason only in terms of such masking in *The Paradox of Acting* (1778, first publ. 1830), tr. Walter H. Pollock (New York: Hill and Wang, 1957), 18; and Lionel Gossman and (especially) Elizabeth MacArthur, "Diderot's Displaced *Paradoxe*," in *Diderot: Digression and Dispersion*, ed. Jack Undank and Herbert Josephs (Lexington, Ky.: French Forum, 1984), 115–17.

In fact, this is why Herder prefers to speak about the songlike character of thought; for song draws attention to itself as a truer form of expressive language than the "dead literary verse" of artful cultivated thinking. For example, in 1773 he writes:

The more distant a people is from artful cultivated thinking, language, and letters, the less will its songs be written for paper—dead literary verse. The lyrical, the living and therefore rhythmical elements of song, the living presentness of the imagery, the continuity and force of the contents and invention, the symmetry of words, syllables, even letters, the melody and the hundreds of other things that belong to and disappear with the living word, the songs of a language and a nation—on this and this alone depends the natures, the purpose, the whole miraculous power of these songs.[30]

In song the living word is present in a way that emphasizes the indispensability of words, sounds, and letters for uniting the imagery of a culture to its ideals. The real, in such a context, is the imagistic. As such, Herder does not contrast the written and the oral, for the written word is as much a figural expression as is song. Instead, he suggests, when figural expressions (e.g., songs, hieroglyphics, linguistic performances) are ignored as presential powers, they become the dead literary verse easily disposed of by thinkers intent on undermining the essentially rhetorical foundations of philosophy.

TRADITIONS OF FIGURATION AS HISTORICAL UNDERSTANDING

With the introduction into psychological physiology of the question of narrative's moral dimension, Herder transforms his epistemological study of individual cognition into a social psychology in which the language of a culture serves as the key to its understanding. However, such a language reveals the genius of a people only in the expressive forms found in its own literature. Furthermore, a nation's poetic heritage is embodied in its literature precisely to the extent that its linguistic figuration (in speech and writing) constitutes a literary tradition. Herder's fascination with the folklore and myths of various peoples testifies to his attention to the creative sources of a tradition, which

30. Herder, "Excerpt from a Correspondence on Ossian and the Songs of Ancient Peoples," cited in Feldman and Richardson, *Rise of Modern Mythology*, 228.

themselves occasion the possibility that reason within a literary history can emerge.

As in the case of individual cognition, the key for the possibility of the development of reason lies in the sequential narrative of figuration. But this time the issue is clouded by the fact that a history of figuration—a nation's sequential speech or "epic of actions"—exposes the historian's prejudice for a distinctly human teleology. What is needed, instead, is a philosophy of history that extends beyond human ends to include providential purposes.[31]

This same issue arose in my previous discussion about the procedure by which sensations are organized in experience. The order that appears as the fabular sequence of images in time becomes identifiable as language, reason. The success of certain sequences in achieving redundancy cannot be due to their approximation of the way things really are, for things themselves come into existence in mythic figuration, that is, in virtue of the redundancy of the sequences.

However, Herder says that the "harmonious" contact of the senses produces images without which experience remains inarticulate and chaotic. This implies that something accounts for the harmony—something that Herder refers to as force *(Kraft)*. This force or energy powers the organic evolution of history through which reason appears as literary tradition. Because this force of creativity provides the indeterminate context out of which humanity establishes itself through language, it cannot serve as the basis of a philosophy of history. Indeed, as we have already seen, Herder treats such systematization as poetic and fictive anyway.

Insofar as this indeterminate context can be said to allow for both ontological and moral generation within history, though, it exhibits characteristics of God. In recounting the epics of the gods, the historian presents a physiology of a nation's linguistic experience in its ongoing genesis. In this way, Herder notes, "The God of nature is also the God of history," and the genesis of the world and mankind consists in the speech of God in and

31. See F. M. Barnard, "Herder's Treatment of Causation and Continuity in History," *Journal of the History of Ideas* 24 (1963): 198–200.

as history.[32]   The Book of Genesis, as such, is more than simply
a document recounting the origin of man.   It is, to use Herder's
1774 title, the "oldest document of the human race" because it
reveals, in hieroglyph and myth, the concurrent appearance of
word and deed, of divine revelation and living image, of document
and humanity.[33]   The fable or plot of history appears in the very
figuration of sensations, which Hamann refers to as the divine
creative *Logos*.

Indeed, in his response to Herder's *Essay on the Origin of Language* (1772), Hamann makes explicit the connection between the
force of divine creativity and linguistic expression: "Every
phenomenon of nature was a word—the sign, symbol, and pledge
of a new, inexpressible, but all the more intimate union, communication, and community of divine energy and ideas.   Everything
that man heard in the beginning, saw with his eyes, contemplated
and touched with his hands was a living word.   For God was the
word."[34]   Language was "as easy as child's play" because of its
immediacy: It required (and still requires) no advance beyond
the figuration in order to feel the moment of creativity, the
living word in fleeting speech.

For Hamann the force that harmonizes figuration has no
rational justification.   In its inception each linguistic performance
relies on faith as the power to generate historical determinateness
in language, reason, and even being.   Existence itself, for Hamann,
presumes already the determinate discrimination of things by
means of language—a discrimination that itself goes beyond all
rational support (because the discrimination is what is meant by
reason in the first place).   To Jacobi he writes, "For me the
question is not so much: What is reason? but rather What is
language? . . . In words and ideas no existence is possible.
Existence is attached solely to things."[35]   In the immediacy of

---

32. Herder, *Ideas on the Philosophy of the History of Mankind*, vol. 3 (1787), in
Sämtliche Werke, 14: 207; cf. Alexander Gillies, "Herder's Approach to the
Philosophy of History," *Modern Language Review* 35 (1940): 202.   Also note
Hamann's 1758 comment: "Nature and history are the two great commentaries on
the divine word" ("Biblical Reflections," in *Werke*, 1: 303; quoted in Smith,
Hamann, 78).

33. See Koepke, *J. G. Herder*, 29–30.

34. Hamann, *Last Will and Testament of the Knight of the Rose Cross on the Divine
and Human Origin of Language* (1772), in *Werke*, 3: 32.   See O'Flaherty, *Unity*, 38.

35. Hamann to Jacobi, 14 Nov. 1784, in *Briefwechsel*, 5: 264; cited in Smith,
Hamann, 249.   Cf. Alexander, *Hamann: Philosophy and Faith*, 163.   Remarks like
these are what endear Hamann to Kierkegaard.

figuration (in language and sensation) there is no question of truth or falsity, no possibility of the nonexistence of that which is immediately present. Only the displacement of language by a philosophy of being, the fall of/into man from the immediacy of divine creativity, would require a redemption of human creativity by the divine act of grace.

Benefiting from hints by Hume, both Hamann and Herder resist this more conservative reliance on divine intervention in the face of human impotence (expressed, for example, by Jacobi). Instead they suggest that within linguistic expression, and even prior to an awareness of our own determinate existence as beings, faith in the immediacy of figuration itself embodies the force of divine creativity. "I was full of Hume," Hamann remarks to Jacobi, "when I wrote the *Socratic Memorabilia* and the following passage of my little book has reference to that: 'Our own existence and the existence of all things outside us must be believed and can in no other way be determined'."[36] For the determination of being is not a determination of reason but a commitment of faith in the performance of mythopoesis. Thus when Hamann again writes to Jacobi three days later, he puts the matter simply: "What in your language is 'being' I should prefer to call 'word'."[37] In effect this says that the energy of divine creativity lost by the stagnation of philosophic reason can be retrieved by reassuming the birthright of mythopoetic expression.

This reintegration of reason and rhetoric in language reveals the mythological character of philosophy in highlighting its figural foundations in history. Even though language determines the possibility of thinking historically, the historical and temporal performance, along with the tradition of such engagements within figuration, establish the possibility of reason and philosophy. As Hamann says, "I am quite at one with Herder that all our reason and philosophy amount to tradition. . . . For me it is not a matter of physics or theology, but language, the mother of reason and revelation, their alpha and omega."[38] In its simplest form language constitutes a pattern, a history, a tradition of sensible figuration, just as thought or reason constitutes a revelation of a sequence of images. For Herder in particular this appeal to

---

36. Hamann to Jacobi, 27 Apr. 1787, in *Briefwechsel,* 7: 167.
37. Hamann to Jacobi, 30 Apr. 1787, in *Briefwechsel,* 7: 175.
38. Hamann to Jacobi, 28 Oct. 1785, in *Briefwechsel,* 6: 108; cited in Smith, *Hamann,* 252–53. Cf. Frank, "Herder's *Essay,*" 18.

tradition historicizes reason and identifies both language and reason as products of communal repetition.

The central place that Herder gives to literary traditions in his account of the philosophy of history reveals how the emphasis on the communal repetition of myths, stories, and folklore thoroughly revises previous concepts of historiography in terms of the mythopoetic character of language and sensation. In history experience becomes communal in terms of shared discourse, but the centrality of figuration remains. The historian's fiction or narration highlights and thus expresses linguistic forms that have achieved a certain redundancy and that therefore are displaced into past tenses by narrations suggesting providential creativity. These latter narrations constitute the philosophy of history, history seen from within the communal framework of language as a moral context.

Herder's philosophy of history elevates mythology and literary history to a preeminent status precisely because they display traditions of invitations to participate in the re-creation of worlds described in epic accounts. The rituals of poetic expression establish the contexts of meaning for understanding experience in communal terms; as such, they literally provide a philosophy tied to the immediacy of experience. "Even in its wildest lines and worst conceived features," he notes, "mythology is a philosophical attempt of the human mind, which dreams ere it wakes, and willingly retains its infant state."[39] Mythology thus expresses an authentic philosophic reticence to divorce thought from feeling—a divorce all too often willingly entered into by "cultivated" philosophy.

The sharing of vocabularies within mythic accounts, in turn, creates the family, society, and the sense of history in virtue of commonplaces of linguistic expression. As Herder notes, "Language expresses the collective experience of the group."[40] Indeed, language identifies individuals as a group in virtue of their experience of the order of figuration that constitutes that language as theirs.

For Herder, the continual extension of schematic interconnections allows poetic inventiveness to transcend differences in

39. Herder, *Ideas on the Philosophy of History*, cited in Feldman and Richardson, *Rise of Modern Mythology*, 233.

40. Herder, *On the Spirit of Hebrew Poetry* (1782; publ. 1787), in *Sämtliche Werke*, 11: 225. Cf. Isaiah Berlin, *Vico and Herder* (London: Hogarth Press, 1976), 168.

national linguistic heritage.   The creative force within such violations of rational boundaries of meaning is expressed in spontaneous allegories relating elements of different cultural experiences, just as the creative force continually appears in potential harmonies of sense from which new images emerge. The actional narration of this progressively collective and integrative epic is what Herder's philosophy of history identifies within its own fabular structure.

The moral of Herder's fable of history lies in its invitation to participate in the mutual development of individuals in societies— a creative cross-fertilization of experience and language that Herder calls *Humanität.* "Humanity" serves not as a standard for judging individuals or societies but as a guiding principle inviting the further development of creativity.[41]   Because it is a product of the mythic organization of language and experience, humanity (like reason) exists only within history.   But even within history it provides for the divine incentive for novel integration of expression and sensation, which characterizes mythic thought in general.

41. See Schütze, "The Fundamental Ideas in Herder's Thought: IV," *Modern Philology* 19 (1921): 382.

CHAPTER SEVEN

Historiography and the Retrospection of Romanticist Mythology

THIS FINAL CHAPTER RETURNS TO the historiographic presuppositions that underlie my treatment of myth in modern philosophy. It indicates how I have employed a Romanticist approach to historiography rather than the currently more common rationalistic approach, which overlooks or denigrates topics, themes, and thinkers I have taken as pivotal. This shift in perspective culminates in Romanticist philosophy's insistence on the importance of myth within absolute idealism. The absolute character of such a philosophy identifies procedures not only for tracing the development of mind and nature but also for doing the history of philosophy. In fact, the history of philosophy is the history of the reemergence of historiography into mythology.

THE SHIFT TO ROMANTICIST HISTORIOGRAPHY

By beginning this study with a discussion of the historiography of philosophy, I intended to draw attention to the fact that the history of philosophy can be presented either as an ongoing examination of the same recurring problems or as a continuously changing set of procedures that redefine the very nature of what constitutes philosophic issues. The first approach identifies topics in a way that carves out a place for "properly" philosophic inquiries as opposed to those of literary theory, rhetoric, anthropology, and even the history of ideas. The second approach permits cross-disciplinary investigations of topics, works, and individuals in an attempt to test the propriety of current descriptions of the tasks and methods of philosophy.

As such, this second approach does not presume from the start the appropriateness or inappropriateness of themes or thinkers for philosophic examination. Nor does it assume that topics discerned in the first (rationalistic) approach ought to be similarly discriminated in different historical epochs or thematic contexts. Even my organization of chapters around specific philosophers can be understood (in the second approach) as a heuristic device, an invitation to recognize how new readings of works redefine the meanings of author, genre, or period.

As the preceding chapters have exemplified, even the heuristic itself of such a contrast in philosophic methodology can raise significant questions both about how philosophers understand myth and about how the definition of myth can call for a new understanding of philosophy. In a broader sense, this contrast reveals how any historiography of philosophy that narrowly defines myth in terms of ancient fictions that do not continue to operate in philosophic development itself is blind to its own classical or neoclassical historicity. Such a historiographic program of determinate and rationally related topics reflects the stereotypic ahistorical attitude of Enlightenment philosophes and not the (perhaps equally stereotypic) organic and developmental emphases of the Romantics. Likewise, a rigid distinction between myth and fable or a preconceived ideal of myth vis-à-vis philosophy presumes a structuralist epistemology of historical thinking precisely within a domain in which such structures themselves are explicitly challenged.

In the modern period the distinction between the Enlightenment and Romanticist use of myth relies more or less on the degree to which thinkers acknowledge the presence of myth within philosophical discourse in general. Emphasis on the communicative, literary, and imaginative characteristics of early modern philosophy—especially in texts that appeal to the vocabulary of such ideas—reveals, however, how both groups of thinkers recognize the figural origins of language and thought and the basal unity of speculative reason and practical action within imagination. "Baconian" or "Cartesian" models of philosophy may underplay such themes; but Bacon and Descartes themselves open possibilities of such explorations. In this way the inclination to provide the stability and organization of a structure finds its dialectical opposition in the temporal move to historiography.

My earlier chapters on Bacon, Descartes, fable use in England, and Mandeville indicate the increasing sensitivity to myth within philosophy. With Vico (more specifically, with my treatment of Vico) sensitivity to the presence of myth within philosophy extends to rhetorical self-explication. Though only glimpsed as a halting possibility in those earlier discussions, the centrality of myth within even the act of historical exegesis erupts full-blown as the rhetorical premise for the possibility of meaning within the chapters on Vico, Herder and Hamann, and (now) more recognizably Romanticist thinkers.   In this self-explication all history of philosophy becomes reappropriated as historiography.   In the earlier, more classical, view, mythic interpretation is a possibility; in the Romanticist view a mythic interpretation is inescapable. The poststructuralist strategy outlined in the Introduction encompasses both positions in the necessarily dual historiography of modern philosophy.

It could be argued that certain thinkers (e.g., Descartes) lend themselves to rationalist rather than Romanticist historiography. Such a view, though, presumes from the beginning that these thinkers do not value the developmental, rhetorical, figural, or constitutive aspects of their own thought or writing.   And even when they explicitly discount the importance of mythopoetic features (as does Plato, for example), they repeatedly turn to such features despite themselves.

To rationalist historians of philosophy, Romanticist historiography historicizes philosophy, highlighting features of early modern philosophy otherwise overlooked or explained away as philosophically insignificant, "simply" stylistic, diplomatic, or prudential.   In addition, Romanticist historiography indicates how the Enlightenment-Romanticist distinction, while perhaps useful for heuristic purposes, rests on a shift in the assessment of the importance of history and historiography for philosophic activity.

The philosophes and deists of the eighteenth century often appear to argue that once they have shown that a certain belief or practice is based on what they call myth, it can be dispensed with as inappropriate for further philosophical treatment.   The Romantics, on the other hand, treat myth not as the end of discussion but rather as its beginning insofar as myth identifies the imaginative and creative matrix in which subsequent speech and thought emerge.[1]   In the Enlightenment view, emphasis on public linguistic figuration is more characteristic of rhetoric, sociology, or anthropology than of philosophy, in that philosophy studies instead the ideas behind expressions, the logic behind the grammar.   The Romantics, however, claim to retrieve philosophy's

---

1.   See Burton Feldman and Robert D. Richardson, *The Rise of Modern Mythology: 1680–1860* (Bloomington: Indiana University Press, 1972), 303.   Cf. Hayden V. White, *Metahistory: The Historical Imagination in Nineteenth-Century Europe* (Baltimore, Md.: Johns Hopkins University Press, 1974); and White, *Tropics of Discourse: Essays in Cultural Criticism* (Baltimore, Md.: Johns Hopkins University Press, 1978).

sensible ties to experience, reaffirming the essentially mythopoetic character of all discourse, including that of Absolute Mind.

THE EPISTEME OF MYTHOLOGY: BERKELEYAN RE/VISIONS

In order to understand how the shift from a rationalist perspective on myth to a rhetorical perspective occurs, we have to appeal to a more general schema of comparative historiographies. In each, words and ideas have distinctly different relationships to things. For example, for the Renaissance humanists Mussato, Bruni, Poliziano, Guarino, Pontano, and Valla, words have no rational, eternal meaning tied to some spiritual idea; rather, their meaning is determined only within particular performative and linguistic contexts.[2] Nature itself "speaks" in the visual and auditory signs or marks that we image as things, the works of nature. As Cicero had noted, nature is known to man through work, that is, as the focus of use-oriented attention. In like manner, the mind (ingenium) is revealed and known through its works; and its history is the history of the rhetoric of expressions.[3]

In this context language is the figuration that expresses the structure of nature, the visual and auditory grammar or sign system to which the mind is immediately related in knowing. To know the sign is thus to have access to nature itself, for the signs constitute the "primary speech" that lies at the basis of rational thought.[4] Such speech reveals instantaneously its own figuration as the generation of facticity. It is, as Ernesto Grassi notes, literally archaic in providing the principles by which rational thought is possible: "It does not lie within historical time; it is the origin and criterion of the movement of the rational process of clarification."[5] Figuration is not a historical origin of meaning because even historical origins are meaningful as origins only in virtue of a prior language, the metaphoric language of ingenuity/ *ingenium.*

2. See Ernesto Grassi, "Remarks on German Idealism, Humanism, and the Philosophical Function of Rhetoric," *Philosophy and Rhetoric* 19 (1986): 126–27.

3. Ernesto Grassi, *Rhetoric as Philosophy: The Humanist Tradition* (University Park: Pennsylvania State University Press, 1980), 9–10.

4. See Michel Foucault, *The Order of Things* (New York: Random House, 1970), 38, 42; and Murray Cohen, *Sensible Words: Linguistic Practice in England, 1640–1785* (Baltimore, Md.: Johns Hopkins University Press, 1977), xxiii, 21.

5. Grassi, *Rhetoric as Philosophy,* 19–20.

This is the language that does not point beyond itself to a truer meaning in relations of ideas; rather, as Baltasar Gracián (1601–58) writes, this language ciphers the world, and without it reality would remain unknown and mute. However, without the presupposition of an ulterior world behind that revealed in the work of ingenium, only the mask of figuration, the *persona* of performance, remains.

Indeed, authors of the seventeenth century often associate the preceding topics of metaphor, the origin of language, and creative ingenuity with theatrical performance. Emmanuele Tesauro (1591–1675), for example, notes that ingenious activity provides "a theatre full of wonders," the place in which public topics (*materia civile*) become identified and ordered.[6] Ingenium produces the wonderfully novel, the original, the prerational—all upon a stage on which characters (*personae*) develop in virtue of spoken or written characters (*littera*). The masks of figural sights and sounds, however, shield no other more ultimate truth, for even the face (*facies*) behind the mask itself expresses the dissemblance of pretense displacing character. In the theater nothing meaningful precedes the text.

Juan Luis Vives (1492–1540) provides the classic expression of the association of the theater with myth in his *Fabula de homine* (1518). Vives presents his fable about man within the context of a theater performance because, as he observes, "Man himself is a fable and a play."[7] Man displays himself in dis-play, the play that affirms the need to distance ourselves from the belief in the existence of the actor behind the mask: It calls for a willing suspension of disbelief in order to see the practical unity of the performance as a creative means for moral renovation.

In the typically mythic opening of Vives's fable, Jupiter commands the whole world to appear, a stage for the appearance of actors. Through the voice and sign (*signum*) of Jupiter's command, the actors appear on stage. But one of the creatures born out of Jupiter's primordial speech, man, adopts the masks of all the other creatures, finally even portraying Jupiter himself.

6. *Ibid.*, 15–16. For more on Gracián and Tesauro, cf. Michael Mooney, *Vico in the Tradition of Rhetoric* (Princeton, N.J.: Princeton University Press, 1985), 65–66, 143–48.

7. Vives, *Fable About Man*, tr. Nancy Lenkeith in *The Renaissance Philosophy of Man*, ed. Ernst Cassirer, P. O. Kristeller, and John Herman Randall (Chicago: University of Chicago Press, 1948), 387. Also see Grassi, *Rhetoric as Philosophy*, 11–12.

Man is then asked to join the gods unmasked, and at that point the gods themselves become players in a new fable whose moral centers around the marvels of human ingenuity.[8] In the process the line between human and divine ingenuity has been blurred, erased in the masked expressions *(littera)* that highlight the displacement or erasure *(litura)* of the embodied figure of man. The human mind, like the divine mind, cannot show itself immediately but only through different masks. In this way the divine language of natural figuration parallels the performances and linguistic pronouncements of human ingenuity.

In the seventeenth-century "classical" modern view, though, language is a "counter-discourse" that does not reflect the structure of nature but rather represents the order or pattern of ideas. Locke, for example, drives a wedge between word and thing by arguing that names refer to ideas, not things. The content or reference of language is mind, not nature. And even though Leibniz challenges Locke's account of the arbitrary origin of language, saying that there must be a sufficient reason why words developed as they did, he does relegate words to the status of signs "not only of thoughts but also of things."[9] Words and language thus take on an external significance, depending for their importance on their ability to refer beyond themselves; they are, as such, removed from nature proper.

Indeed, Locke's discussion of language is often presented as an afterthought, subordinate to the meat of Lockean epistemology. And perhaps, so it should be, considering Locke's indication that he turns to writing the third book of the *Essay Concerning Human Understanding* (1690) only when he recognizes how problems created by words impede the development of a theory of knowledge. Rhetorical flourishes, scholastic jargon, ambiguous terminology— all, for Locke, stand in the way of achieving clarity and dependability in thinking. Book III is to serve as an antidote to the invidious effects of words, a corrective to the impulse of thinking solely in linguistic rather than ideational terms.

This contrast between words and ideas undergirds the problematic scheme Locke adopts—a scheme in which words are arbitrary

---

8. Vives, *Fable About Man*, 388–92. Cf. Grassi, *Rhetoric as Philosophy*, 11–12.

9. G. W. Leibniz, *Die Unvorgrieflichen Gedanken* (late 1690s, publ. 1717), cited in Ronald Callinger, *G. W. Leibniz* (Troy, N.Y.: Rensseleer Polytechnic Institute, 1976), quoted in Hans Aarsleff, *From Locke to Saussure: Essays on the Study of Language and Intellectual History* (Minneapolis: University of Minnesota Press, 1982), 88.

signs of ideas, and ideas are natural signs of things. Since we supposedly have access only to our ideas, knowledge resides in the ordering of ideas. Language, in turn, serves as the means by which we communicate our ideas and knowledge. To the extent that language facilitates the ordering of ideas and the communication of such order, it is useful; to the extent that it frustrates such goals, it is superfluous and harmful.[10]

Both Berkeley and Condillac object to this model and do so by highlighting the importance of language as central in the formation of ideas and in the organization of knowledge. Berkeley notes that Locke should have begun his *Essay* with the discussion of language, and Condillac observes that Locke should have addressed the role of language within the context of ideas in the second book of the *Essay*.[11] But both thinkers make such claims because they believe that Locke fails to extend empiricist principles to the study of language. For Berkeley, it is Locke's metaphysics that denigrates language; for Condillac, the problem lies in how Locke's epistemology ignores language. In both cases, language emerges as a central feature extending, and even recharacterizing, the empiricist project.

In one sense, however, Berkeley shares Locke's concerns about the use of figurative language in philosophizing, for in his *Philosophical Commentaries* (1707–08), Berkeley proclaims that "the chief thing I do or pretend to do is onely to remove the mist or veil of Words."[12] For Locke this means that we should concentrate on ideas and grudgingly accept the fact that language provides obstacles rather than assets for philosophical reflection. Berkeley, on the other hand, doubts that the problem is with

10. See John Locke, *An Essay Concerning Human Understanding*, ed. Peter H. Nidditch (Oxford: Clarendon Press, 1975), 504 (III.10.23), 561 (IV.3.30). Also see Cohen, *Sensible Words*, xxiii–xxv, 40, 80.

11. See George Berkeley's *Philosophical Commentaries*, entry 717, in *The Works of George Berkeley*, ed. A. A. Luce and T. E. Jessup, 9 vols. (Edinburgh: Thomas Nelson and Sons, 1948–57), 1: 87; and William McGowan, "Berkeley's Doctrine of Signs," in *Berkeley: Critical and Interpretive Essays*, ed. Colin M. Turbayne (Minneapolis: University of Minnesota Press, 1982), 241. Also see Étienne Bonnot de Condillac, *An Essay on the Origin of Human Knowledge* [1746; English tr. 1756] (New York: AMS Press, 1974), 10 (Introduction); and Stephen K. Land, *The Philosophy of Language in Britain: Major Theories from Hobbes to Thomas Reid* (New York: AMS Press, 1986), 32.

12. Entry 642, in *Works*, 1: 78; and McGowan, "Berkeley's Doctrine," 241. Cf. McGowan, "George Berkeley's American Declaration of Independence," *Studies in Eighteenth-Century Culture* 12 (1983): 108.

words as such but rather is with the view that treats words and language as a mist or veil to be penetrated through to their ideational ground. As his recurring interest in the language of vision and in the languages of the other senses indicates, he feels we cannot ignore the inherent linguistic (i.e., significatory) character of the world as experienced. When he says that the world we see and feel is the language of God, he means literally that everything has meaning in virtue of its signifying and signified function within a system of discourse that permits no extrasystematic referent.

Perhaps the most overlooked feature of Berkeley's celebrated rejection of Locke's belief in material objects is his rejection of Locke's very division of things into independently existing objects, ideas, and words. Berkeley does not simply drop material things from the immaterialist program and leave the other two categories intact. Rather, he incorporates all three into a system in which the existence of an entity or the meaning of an experience is defined in terms of its deferential character, its affirmation of itself as only one-half of a signifying-signified relationship. This linguistic aspect of metaphysics is indispensable, a mist or veil that cannot be removed and thus hardly a mist or veil.

So widespread is the Lockean distinction of object-idea-word and the belief that Berkeley uses the same distinction (with the exception that he finally absorbs things into ideas), that Berkeley's remarks about the language of nature are often understood simply as a metaphor for a semiotic system of ideas. In this common view, the language of nature, the language by which God speaks to us, has a grammatical character and structure such that the study of linguistics proves beneficial in guiding thought without at the same time challenging the independence of thought from language.[13] Berkeley, it is argued, certainly could not have meant to say that things are words, much less that ideas are words.

Suppose, though, that we take Berkeley's remarks about the language of nature seriously. Nature, then, would be a system of

13. See, for example, Colin M. Turbayne, "Berkeley's Metaphysical Grammar," in *A Treatise Concerning the Principles of Human Knowledge, with Critical Essays*, ed. Colin M. Turbayne (Indianapolis, Ind.: Bobbs-Merrill, 1970), 11–29. Turbayne's *The Myth of Metaphor*, 2d ed. (Columbia: University of South Carolina Press, 1970) also employs the distinction between Berkeley's language "model" and his metaphysical theory.

signs, but one in which not all signs are part of any particular language, "not even significant signs, such as the natural cries of animals, or the inarticulate sounds and interjections of men." Berkeley continues: "It is the articulation, combination, variety, copiousness, extensive and general use and easy application of signs . . . that constitute the true nature of language."[14] All signs signify something, but not all signs are parts of determinate languages. Each language (e.g., the language of sight, the language of touch) contains "steady consistent" methods that identify the grammar of nature particular to that language. Without such a grammar, the language in which nature speaks— that is, the sign system in which ideas are associated—lacks the regularity needed as the basis for human social interaction and moral stability.[15]

However, those "significant" signs that do not yet lend themselves to the general usage and easy application found in grammar-guided languages reveal the gaps between structurally determinate languages. Aboriginally inarticulate cries or uncountenanced juxtapositions of visual ideas disrupt the grammatical tranquility of the languages of nature in ways that productively resist the temptation to specify formal equivalences among signs from different regions of discourse. To try to reduce or translate the language of sight into that of touch ignores the fact that sign relations hold only within a particular language: They point to no other languages. In like manner, ideas cannot be correlated with things; as Berkeley likes to say, ideas signify only other ideas.

This difference, free play, or slippage in codes of signification permits the transcendence of the grammars of articulate languages necessary for the ongoing re-creation of the mind. In providing for such gaps, Berkeley aims away from a semiotic description of nature that is structurally uniform and precise and toward one that prizes the beauty and harmony of variety opened by a poetic reading of nature.

14. Berkeley, *Alciphron* (1732), in *Works*, 3: 157.
15. See *A Treatise Concerning the Principles of Human Knowledge* (1710), in *Works*, 2: 89 (secs. 108–109), especially the first-edition version; and *Siris* (1744), in *Works*, 5: 121. Also see John Herman Randall, *The Career of Philosophy*, vol. 1: *From the Middle Ages to the Enlightenment* (New York: Columbia University Press, 1962), 620–26; and Paul J. Olscamp, "Does Berkeley Have an Ethical Theory?" in Turbayne (ed.), *Treatise*, 184–88.

As, in reading other books, a wise man will choose to fix his thoughts on the sense and apply it to use, rather than lay them out in grammatical remarks on the language, so, in perusing the volume of nature, it seems beneath the dignity of the mind to affect an exactness in reducing each particular phenomenon to general rules, or showing how it follows from them. We should propose to ourselves nobler views, such as to re-create and exalt the mind with a prospect of the beauty, order, extent, and variety of natural things.[16]

The appeal to the Book of Nature in terms of language calls attention to its "sense," the meanings available in, and in virtue of, the immediate sensibility of phenomena. A reductionist explanation of nature, just like a grammatical critique of a love letter, misses nature's valuational structure and frustrates the mind's growth in moral/aesthetic sensibility. The figuration of the languages of nature both identifies a temporary order (which through redundancy becomes grammatical) and highlights the discrepancies among the regions of discourse (such as the languages of sight or touch) that compose the sign system of nature. Without the different established by contrasts in vocabularies and semantic and syntactic structures—all brought to prominence by the significance of signs outside those languages—prospects for the aesthetic renovation of the mind and nature disappear.

As long as words are understood as signifying ideas, that is, as long as we accept the Lockean contrast between words and ideas, a "curtain of words" creates the possibility of the gap, the delusion, the dissimulation. As Berkeley comments in the *Principles*, this "embarrassment and delusion of words" can be avoided only by considering ideas "bare and naked," undisguised by the attempt to make them represent things.[17] Ideas must be considered without the veil that deludes and embarrasses, hides and yet reveals, tantalizes by covering with displacement. The nudity of ideas themselves excludes the distancing word. Here no disguise is countenanced, no unfulfilled substitution is permitted as a surrogate. The distinction between words and ideas becomes suspect, the word-as-distinct-from-idea onerous, deceptive. Only the idea is left, but it will be an idea that has meaning only as a signifier. Ideas can signify only ideas because they exist as

16. Berkeley, *Principles*, in *Works*, 2: 89 (sec. 109).
17. See Berkeley's introduction to *Principles*, in *Works*, 2: 38–40 (secs. 21–25).

meaningful only in relation to one another, that is, in habitual connection in experience.[18]

This assertion of "embarrassed figuration" (as Roland Barthes phrases it) or differed referentiality (in Derrida's term) is crucial for providing the impulse of discourse, the means by which reason proceeds beyond the solipsism and skepticism implicit within the Cartesian and Lockean epistemologies.[19]   In rejecting Locke's primary-quality groundings for ideas, Berkeley undermines the skeptical challenge to a representationist epistemology; but he does not ignore the necessity of describing how reason still employs a dynamic of referentiality.

In order to avoid the skeptical implications of a divorce between idea and object, Berkeley maintains that ideas signify one another as elements of a language that cannot permit a distinction between the material and the immaterial—except, perhaps, as an anachronistic holdover from Locke's commonsensical (i.e., unphilosophic) vocabulary.   In order to have discourse, one must have the difference between the signifying and the signified; but in order to avoid skepticism, one cannot leave the language of nature.

The vocabulary of ideas might be used to replace that of words in order to accommodate a Lockean mentality.   But such a replacement succeeds only insofar as that vocabulary is qualified by a revision of the semiotic character of ideas themselves (something Locke fails to do).   In order to understand the full import of Berkeley's position, then, we have to *think* as philosophers (in linguistic/semiotic terms) and speak in terms of the vulgar (i.e., in terms of ideas).   Once words are excluded, ideas become the new signifiers, but they do so only by becoming new components in the semiotic system of nature: that is, they become words in the vocabulary of God.

When combined with his discussion of vision as God's language, and his identification of things and ideas, Berkeley's semiotics reunites thought and thing in a linguistic and embodied affront to common idealism by means of a semiotic that challenges the distinction of thought and thing, of idealism and materialism, in

18. See Berkeley's *Essay Toward a New Theory of Vision* (1709), in *Works*, 1: 231; and *Principles*, in *Works*, 2: 69 (sec. 65). Cf. Jonathan Dancy, *Berkeley: An Introduction* (Oxford: Basil Blackwell, 1987), 109, 117–22.

19. See Roland Barthes, *The Pleasure of the Text* (1973), tr. Richard Miller (New York: Hill and Wang, 1975), 56–57; Jacques Derrida, *Of Grammatology*, tr. Gayatri C. Spivak (Baltimore, Md.: Johns Hopkins University Press, 1976), lxix, 89, 110, 139–40.

virtue of a reunderstanding of the role of difference. To differ means not to point beyond one domain (e.g., that of ideas or of language) to another (e.g., that of things), but rather to posit figurally a self-effacing reference to another component in the same system (the signified). Ideas, things, and (now, in the current context, most important) language all become parts of the same semiotically linked system. If ideas can refer only to other ideas, and words only to other words, then the distinction between things, ideas, and words becomes superfluous.

Insofar as mind is understood later in the eighteenth century as responsive to social and environmental development, and thus not restricted to eternally fixed laws of logic, language is further removed, in the classicist (now Enlightenment) view, from its ties to reality.[20] This, in turn, sets up the specific dilemma with which the Romanticist thinkers have to deal: As meaning is distanced from the immediacy of figuration, reasoning has less of an impact on the emotionally felt world to which individuals long to be morally and epistemologically tied. The same rigor that guarantees a method for truth accordingly also undermines noetic and moral certainty.

The only way to retrieve the unity of immediate expression in word, deed, and thing, from the Romanticist view, is to reinstate the conditions that exhibit the emergence of reason. That is, the passional and cognitive impact of mythology must be relearned as the foundation of philosophy. Such a move transforms philosophy, in Hegel's words, into a "mythology of *Reason.*" "We must have a new mythology," Hegel notes late in the 1790s; "mythology must become philosophical . . . and philosophy must become mythological, in order to make philosophers sensible [*sinnlich*]."[21] In order to overcome the metaphysical, noetic, and moral chasm created by the incision of insensible mind as a disruption of the unity of word and thing, Hegel calls for a renewal of myth within philosophy. At the same time, Friedrich Schlegel

20. See Cohen, *Sensible Words*, xxiv, 40, 80; Foucault, *Order of Things*, 43–44; and Elizabeth Sewell, *The Orphic Voice: Poetry and Natural History* (New York: Harper and Row, 1971), 38.
21. "Earliest Systematic Program of German Idealism," quoted in Donald P. Verene, *Hegel's Recollection: A Study of Images in the 'Phenomenology of Spirit'* (Albany: State University of New York Press, 1985), 25–26. Also see Philippe Lacoue-Labarthe and Jean-Luc Nancy, *The Literary Absolute: The Theory of Literature in German Romanticism*, tr. Philip Barnard and Cheryl Lester (Albany: State University of New York Press, 1988), 36.

points out that "mythology and poetry are one and inseparable," and that philosophy as well as physics needs mythology in order to overcome the subjectivism implicit within idealism.[22]   For idealism risks the same skeptical divorce from immediately felt reality as its rationalist predecessors.   At that point we are but one step away from Schelling's philosophy of mythology, a philosophy that brings together nature and spirit in a metaphysics of the Absolute.   By the end of the eighteenth century, then, recurring themes in the discussion of myth and philosophy come together in a way that challenges the rationalistic distinctions among poetics, philology, moral philosophy, and metaphysics.

SHAFTESBURY, DIDEROT, CONDILLAC

The turn to mythology in philosophy stems from the same longing for harmonious integration that prompts the poet to reject the canons of established grammars, which maintain the order of the linguistically structured cosmos.   Without such restraints on linguistic performances, meaning changes in every act: Every spoken word, uttered sound, or visual sign threatens the laws of rational thought; every figuration becomes an invitation to promiscuity in being.   As Condillac notes in his *Essay on the Origin of Human Knowledge* (1746), every attempt at originality obliges a writer to contribute to the ruin of a language.[23]   But such ruination simply undercuts the belief that the meaning, the beauty, and the truth of a language exist independent of its expression.   This the poet constantly recalls for us: He or she invites the disruption that literally shows the emergence of being and identifies power, beauty, and truth not in terms of fixed results but in terms of procedures of action.

Because Shaftesbury approaches the question of genius precisely in these terms, it is no wonder that, in spite of his close tutorial relationship with Locke, he ignores almost all of the Lockean epistemological enterprise.   Locke's plain, historical method of

22. See Schlegel's "Discourse on Mythology" (1800), cited in Feldman and Richardson, *Rise of Modern Mythology*, 307.   Also see A. Leslie Willson, "Romantic Neomythology," in *Myth and Reason: A Symposium*, ed. Walter D. Wetzels (Austin: University of Texas Press, 1973), 49, 59, 62; and Hans Blumenberg, *Work on Myth*, tr. Robert M. Wallace (Cambridge: MIT Press, 1985), 570–71, 576–84.

23. Condillac, *Origin of Human Knowledge*, 297 (II.1.158).

presenting a genetic epistemology lacks, from Shaftesbury's view-point, a sensitivity to the narration crucial for unearthing this so-called history.

Because this narration identifies meaning in the display of the self-constitution of poetic beauty, it enervates the mind by appealing to the heart. Fabular creativity exhibits the mind in a moment of self-revelation concerning its own power, the power implicit in the unity of sensible, passional expression and propor-tionality or rationality. In his *Characteristics* (1711), Shaftesbury refers to literature's ability to produce such a self-revelation as "moral magic." The figurations of poetic expression appeal to the mind almost completely unnoticed as such. In doing so, they make truth (rationality, proportionality) accessible within the mutually self-defining activity of the "characters" of sensible expression and the praxic character of mind engaged in its own moral education.

Nothing affects the heart like that which is purely from itself, and of its own nature; such as the beauty of sentiments, the grace of actions, the turn of characters, and the proportions and features of a human mind. This lesson of philosophy, even a romance, a poem, or a play may teach us; whilst the fabulous author leads us with such pleasure through the labyrinth of the affections, and interests us, whether we will or no, in the passions of his heroes and heroines.[24]

The poetic, fabular author draws us back to the sensibility of sentiment, action, and figural characters as revelations of the pleasing immediacy of self-expressive, and therefore self-educative, narration. Just as literature distinguishes the characters of a narrative in terms of heroic affections and passions, so also the figural characters (the written marks, the uttered sounds) effect a moral education by means of the surreptitious affects (or "affec-tions") of figuration. The fabular author thus molds moral char-acter in fashioning figural characters in sensual ("sentimental") sequences of narration. Here, truly, the medium establishes the message, where the "turn of characters" applies equally to figural as well as moral organization.

In fable, as Joseph Addison's 1712 *Spectator* article reminds us, the mind revels in its own self-constitution and self-education.

24. Earl of Shaftesbury (Anthony Ashley Cooper), *Characteristics of Men, Manners, Opinions, Times*, ed. John M. Robertson, 2 vols. in 1 (Indianapolis, Ind.: Bobbs-Merrill, 1964), 1: 90. See also 2: 283–84.

The revelry or playful enthusiasm embodied in the revelation of the self in its character (and characterization) as figural permits the emergence of the morally determinate. The possibility of the presentation of a moral within a fable determines narration, demanding some form of closure. It directs attention to the passional in virtue of—not in spite of—the pleasurable magic of the presentation, the invitation to meaningfulness embodied (as Vico would note) in the figures or "characters" of heroes and heroines. In this way the ultimate tragic flaw of a hero or heroine lies in not knowing (the characters of) his or her own name, because the name is precisely the figural ground for the possibility of having a character in the first place.

Shaftesbury extends this notion of the simultaneous creation of the figure and the self to include the process of the artistic re-creation of the universe. This further emphasis on the dynamic character of being emerges most clearly in Shaftesbury's claim that the beautiful is not that which simply fulfills some transcendent and static ideal of reason; rather it is that which expresses harmoniously the distinctive character of becoming that is implicit within a processive understanding of reality. The beautiful reveals the true in its own instantiation, that is, in its own particular immediate way of showing the emergence of harmony especially in its diachronic form. Poetry elevates the act of creativity to a position of epistemological preeminence in that it reunites the essentially developmental character of the beautiful and the true with a processive appreciation of creative reason. The poetic impulse highlights the fabular nature of meaning as emergent and figurally constituted.

However, truth—the beauty and proportionality of such figuration—remains the goal of poetic fabulation. As Shaftesbury remarks, "In poetry, which is all fable, truth still is the perfection."[25] Truth fulfills creativity in that truth displaces the process of fabling with the static arrival at definition. Truth within poetry serves as the fossil structure to which fable aspires, the order of frozen harmony that lacks its essential ingredient of movement.

Shaftesbury thus raises the issues of creativity, ingenuity, and genius within a context that he identifies distinctly as romantic,

---

25. *Ibid.*, 1: 94. Shaftesbury follows this remark with a reference to Le Bossu's *Treatise of the Epick Poem.*

fictionally appealing, and unrestricted by mundane (nonheroic) reason. For Shaftesbury, though, the romantic also resonates in a worrisome way with hints of enthusiasm, the blinding of reason by prejudicial judgments. Like Locke, Shaftesbury fears the dissipation of reason by undisciplined improvisation. The task of a romantic understanding of genius, he maintains, is to highlight the process by which entities and meanings come to exist before they become objects of judgment (especially prejudicial judgments). Beauty and artistry reside in this power of the act of becoming, insofar as artistic genius refers specifically to the process of, not the product of, action and reason.[26] Only in the realization of the creative particular as archetype is there ground for the coalescence of genius and genesis. And this is possible only by understanding reason in its harmonic (both synchronic and diachronic) characters.

Diderot (Shaftesbury's French translator) attempts to provide a bridge between Shaftesbury's concern for the dynamic character of reason/meaning/language and the rationalistic identification of genius as abbreviated or rapid reasoning. Typically this contrast appears as the distinction between imagination and reason. But Diderot confounds the contrast by portraying the two in terms of the unresolved tension set up in appeals to dreams and hieroglyphs.

To appeal to such devices has two effects. First, it highlights the fact that reason cannot achieve clarity without the aid of imagination. While it seems paradoxical to say that imagination clarifies rather than clouds reason, with Diderot just such tactics provide the matrix that makes inspiration both possible and acceptable to reason.[27] Reason can explain imaginative genius only by pointing beyond itself to the extravagances of dreams or hieroglyphs as explicit examples of presences that point to the avowed absence of reason. As instanced in Diderot's *Dream of d'Alembert* (1769), in which delirium becomes the occasion for philosophic speculation, dreams and hieroglyphs cannot be reduced to or take the place of reason; but neither can reason

---

26. See Cassirer, *The Philosophy of the Enlightenment,* tr. Fritz C. A. Koelln and James P. Pettegrove (Princeton, N.J.: Princeton University Press, 1979), 84–85, 314–18.

27. See Kineret S. Jaffe, "The Concept of Genius: Its Changing Role in Eighteenth-Century French Aesthetics," *Journal of the History of Ideas* 41 (1980): 594; and Herbert Dieckmann, "Diderot's Conception of Genius," *Journal of the History of Ideas* 2 (1941): 173–74.

proceed without the images they bring to figural prominence. Revelations to reason emerge from the body in dreams. In fact, only in the blind, deaf, and mute presentations of supposedly unthinking matter does the body speak, guiding the definition of the self in terms of such figural metaphors.[28]   Dreams and hieroglyphs indicate a breach in reason's ability to provide immediate access to discourse. Or more specifically, they reveal the displacement of reason, which itself prevents the resolution of tension implicit in discourse suspended between possible significations or different semantic fields.[29]

The figural displacement of reason by means of imaginative constructs normally assumes the priority of a meaningful (rational) context to be expressed. But the second effect of Diderot's turn to dreams and hieroglyphs shows how the intrusion of images (characters) as narration interferes and yet coincides with the events narrated.[30] The possibility of signification or representation arises only in the emergence of the facticity of the figuration, without which the gap between thought and language cannot exist. It is this memory of images that brings into being not only the poet but also the philosopher, the reasonable being, even man himself.[31] For without such signs the appropriation of the absence that is filled by human discourse fails to identify the creative character of the author engaged in the enterprise.

This is the human paradox: Man becomes himself only in the imaging of language, only in becoming other than himself. In Diderot's own *Paradox of Acting* (1778), he speaks of the "great play, the play of the world" in which the actors on the stage are fiery souls, unreflective in their performance; those in the pit, men of genius, achieve the distance to comment on the behavior of those on the stage. Here, genius gains access to reason by

28. Cf. Michael Moriarty, "Figures of the Unthinkable: Diderot's Materialist Metaphors," in *The Figural and the Literal: Problems of Language in the History of Science and Philosophy, 1630–1800*, ed. Andrew Benjamin, Geoffrey N. Cantor, and John R. R. Christie (Manchester, Eng.: Manchester University Press, 1987), 161, 169.

29. See Marc Eli Blanchard, "Writing the Museum: Diderot's Bodies in the Salons," in *Diderot: Digression and Dispersion*, ed. Jack Undank and Herbert Josephs (Lexington, Ky.: French Forum, 1984), 29.

30. See Jeffrey Mehlman, *Cataract: A Study in Diderot* (Middletown, Conn.: Wesleyan University Press, 1979), 23–26, 31; and James Creech, *Diderot: Thresholds of Representation* (Columbus: Ohio State University Press, 1986), 111, 118.

31. See Denis Diderot's *On Dramatic Poetry*, quoted in Margaret Gilman, "Imagination and Creation in Diderot," *Diderot Studies* 2 (1952): 203.

means of the displacement of the author from himself or herself, just as the author of the *Paradox* becomes distanced from himself in his dialogue and can retrieve his authorial character only in the interaction (the gap-filling) of the two speakers of the dialogue.[32] The world as a play serves as the metaphor by which the actors can establish a discourse of displacement, distancing themselves from roles without which no reflection or reason is generated. The metaphor thus stands in place of no prior, actually existing world of meaning, for no thought exists prior to the language of the performance.

In his earlier works, the *Letter on the Blind* (1749) and the *Letter on the Deaf and Dumb* (1751), Diderot explains this epistemology of displacement by noting (following Condillac) that perceptions or sensations should not be confused with ideas. Our perceptions lack a prior determinate rationale, and, as such, our first experience of figuration includes no presupposition of ordered meaning lurking behind the immediately given masks of imaging. For example, we do not see when we first use our eyes: "During the first moments of sight we only receive a mass of confused sensations, which are only disentangled after a time and by a process of reflection."[33] Sight provides a language by which a discourse of visible imagery makes possible a meaning for, or an ordering of, such perceptions.

More striking, though, is the fact that such a language of visible imagery makes possible a meaning for blindness, without which the distancing of a language of vision from some derivative rational organization is unthinkable. Blindness, like deafness, permits the distancing essential to the emergence of a meaning of sight or sound as distinct elements in the vocabulary of sensible imagery. Because "every sense has its own language," no diction based on one sense alone (e.g., vision) serves as the paradigm for intellection.[34] No idea or rational meaning of a sensation exists independently of figuration, for without the immediate accessibility

32. See Diderot, *The Paradox of Acting* [1778, first publ. 1830], tr. Walter H. Pollock (New York: Hill and Wang, 1957), 18; and Lionel Gossman and Elizabeth MacArthur, "Diderot's Displaced *Paradoxe*," in *Diderot: Digression and Dispersion*, 115–17.

33. *Letter on the Blind*, in *Diderot's Early Philosophical Works*, tr. and ed. Margaret Jourdain (1916; reprint, New York: AMS Press, 1973), 126–27; and Moriarty, "Diderot's Materialist Metaphors," 154–55. Cf. Condillac, *Origin of Human Knowledge*, 134 (I.4.25).

34. See Diderot's *Salon of 1767*, quoted in Creech, *Diderot*, 108.

of figuration, found especially in dream or hieroglyph, no guide-lines are provided for the imaginative organization of the elements of perception.

Diderot's letters on the blind and the deaf thus identify the crucial moment at which perception becomes rational and sensations become ideas: namely, at the point when the possibility of the absence of sensation is recognized. This gap or lack is more than simply covered over by metaphor; it does not exist before metaphor begins its temporal dissemblance, its attempt to provide a figure in place of, and thus distinct from, others. The absence of sensation in blindness or deafness embodies, then, the figure of the absence of a figure, and it is the emergence of the possibility of this absence that permits the distinction between perception and ideation, sensation and thought.

Diderot's fascination with the figural sensibility of the languages of the senses appears at first to reinstate the classical emphasis on the priority of sense experience. But, as Condillac makes clear, this form of empiricism, unlike that of Locke but closer to that of Berkeley, takes seriously the linguistic character of figural sensation. In this regard imagination regains its appropriate position as the foundation for intellection, insofar as the sequences of images immediately available for organization into thought constitute the guidelines for reasoning. In Condillac's view Locke mistakenly treats imagination as subservient to reason without considering the imaginal basis for reason itself. This accounts for Locke's dismissal of language and of figuration in general in his treatments of cognition. But for Diderot and Condillac the immediate confrontation with the languages of the senses in the primordial masks of performance and figuration requires a more rigorous empiricism than that adopted by Locke and addressed only indirectly in Berkeley's semiotic appeal to nature as God's language of signs.

Whereas Shaftesbury and Diderot hint at the fabular or mythic nature of this understanding of imagination, Condillac makes it explicit. In doing so, he unites all of the major themes that cluster around the topic of myth: imagination, the origin of language, the figural centrality of sensible signs in defining the reason, genius, and character of a nation. Instead of simply giving a more thoroughgoing analysis than Locke of the implications of empiricism, Condillac challenges the very metaphysics of mind implicit within empiricist epistemology. Sensations do not simply occasion the activity of reason; rather, the order of sensations defines the activity of reason. Because of its imagistic character, language serves a crucial role in the emergence and development of reason. Insofar as the appeal to fable and myth self-consciously recognizes how the genesis of meanings resides in story/history, it reveals the "good metaphysics" of sensibility, which antedates the attempt to dismiss imagination in favor of a cognition whose logic attempts to transcend its narrative origins.

In *An Essay on the Origin of Human Knowledge* (1746) Condillac points out that to reason is to express relations between propositions. From the beginning, these relations needed to be specified not in actions but "fixed by particular circumstances, and a great many different times."[35] This, he notes, accounts for the origin of fable, in that fable/myth specifies the precise relationships among the elements of thought in a culture. The propriety of such relationships emerges in the course of numerous recountings of the myths, for propriety itself—the "truth" of the myth—is precisely what the myth establishes: "And indeed, truth is the property of fable; not that things are absolutely as imagination represents them, because imagination exhibits them under clear and familiar images, such as please us of course, without leading us into error."[36] Imagination provides the images and signs that amuse and instruct us in the truths of practical affairs, the affairs of "sentiment" or immediate import that lend themselves to the clarity found in the signs related immediately before us in mythic accounts.

Myth and fable appear problematic only to those who seek some further meaning behind the text or recital. But for those who recognize that the true task of fabling presumes no such ulterior meaning, the function of pleasing instruction becomes tantamount. Here the appeal to the senses is central to the effect of the account because the sensible account defines what is sensible (reasonable) in the necessarily particular and immediate settings of the fable's ordering of signs.

The more a language abounds in analogous expressions and employs signs that invite figural association, the more it assists memory and imagination because memory and imagination depend on the connection of ideas, which itself is formed by the relation and analogy of signs.[37] Such signs include words, geo-

---

35. Condillac, *Origin of Human Knowledge*, 254 (II.1.105).
36. *Ibid.*, 90–91 (I.2.90).
37. *Ibid.*, 287 (II.1.146); and 119 (I.4.7).

metrical symbols, and hieroglyphics. Good sense, wit, and reason all result from the connection of ideas with one another, but this connection is produced by the use of such signs.[38] Only by means of signs are we able to think most ideas, and only in their ordering in fabling do we learn how to reason. To learn the signs or words of a culture, then, is essential for thought, for "we think only by the help of words."[39] Without such signs no guide exists for showing how thought supposedly proceeds, no connectors point to the next step in argumentation, narration, or action.

Like Berkeley, Condillac challenges Locke's narrow focus on language as simply a means for communicating our ideas. Again, Locke's assumption that we have ideas first and then want to communicate them is the focal point of dispute. In his *Logic* (1780) Condillac extends the notion of language to include action by speaking of the language of action that precedes verbal language. "Men begin to speak the language of action as soon as they feel, and they then speak it without designing to communicate their thoughts; . . . in the beginning they contemplate nothing, because they have not yet observed any thing. Therefore all is in a confused state to them as to their language, and they discern in it nothing."[40] In much the same way that Mandeville had argued, Condillac points out that the language of action exhibits meaning without referring to mental meanings, for the mental does not exist as yet for such a language. Nothing is contemplated because nothing is observed, noted, or cognized. Only the immediately accessible figures or expressions (e.g., facial expressions) have meaning in terms of the sequences that characterize with determinate precision the relations of sensible signs.

Condillac's celebrated reduction of reflection to sensation does not simply accept, then, Locke's distinction between sensation and reflection without at the same time questioning the Lockean division of word and idea. For when Condillac claims that "to speak, to reason, to form general or abstract ideas, is ultimately

---

38. *Ibid.*, 102 (I.2.107).

39. Condillac, *The Logic of Condillac* (1780, publ. 1792), tr. Joseph Neef, ed. Daniel N. Robinson (Washington, D.C.: University Publications of America, 1977), 53.

40. *Ibid.*, 54.

the same thing," he really means it.[41] Speaking is really and aboriginally thinking, and in no way does any real distinction exist between them, for any such distinction raises doubts about the communicative and expressive ability of experienced behavior.

The language of action or gesture is natural, innate, immediate, because it is that which creates the affective as well as cognitive conditions that could permit the discrimination of ideas by means of figural identification. Prior to action, there is no thought; that is, prior to engagement in a system of signs, there is no cognitive element needing an external medium for its embodiment. The body is all there is.

This language of aboriginal embodiment precedes verbal language. In fact, insofar as language is understood as derivative or parasitic, it conceals the nature of reality and prohibits access to thought that is truly sensible. "Good metaphysics," Condillac concludes, "began before languages."[42] Before languages are distinguished from one another and from ideas and things, the vocabulary of gesture and action reveals in its immediacy the identity of word and thing, idea and word.

Instead of treating figural expressions as signs of ideas, such an aboriginal language focuses on the structure of figurations themselves. Figurations reveal their origins in their very sensibility and, as such, provide the metaphysical foundations for all subsequent ideas. "There are, therefore, no ideas which the language of action cannot express; and it will express them with so much the more clearness and precision."[43] The juxtaposition of signs in the sensible action of expression cannot fail to achieve the greatest precision and clarity because the immediacy of the performance refers to nothing beyond itself. In order to analyze our own thought we first have to appeal to these signs as the devices by which distinction is made possible. The good metaphysics of sensible figuration places all insight before us in a way that removes the doubts of ambiguity in meaning implicit within the intrusion of the distinction between sign and idea.

---

41. *Ibid.*, 66. See Jacques Derrida, *The Archeology of the Frivolous: Reading Condillac*, tr. John P. Leavey, Jr. (Pittsburgh: Duquesne University Press, 1980), 59, 62, 65.

42. Condillac, *Logic*, 63.

43. *Ibid.*, 56.

Thus, language is innate and immediate in a way ideas cannot be.[44] It is no wonder that Locke worries about innate ideas because he cannot avoid assuming their prior existence as long as he thinks of ideas, reason, and thought as independent of language. The significance of Book I of Locke's *Essay* becomes apparent, then, only when we see the difficulties that occasion the writing of Book III. But even Locke himself does not recognize the problem built into the word-idea-thing distinction, so he is unable to defend his position against Leibniz's doubts about his attack on innate ideas.

This is precisely the reformulation of the innate-idea problem that Condillac's discussion opens. Before verbal language exhibits the order and systematic character typical of what we normally identify as thinking and reasoning, the innate language of action provides the best means we have for reasoning. Instead of treating names as signs of ideas—a move that distances us from the immediacy of the real feeling of figurative expressions—aboriginal language reveals the true empirical character of thinking and reason in the actual arrangement of sensations linked as signs to other sensations.

Here the Lockean afterthought of language is turned on its empiricist head. In order to communicate an idea, one must first know what the idea is of. But this already recognizes a semiotic, signifier-signified relationship, a system in which a word, sound, or gesture is not simply a sign having a referent (either thing or idea). As Barthes reminds us (following Saussure), a sign is not the same as a signifier, but rather the *union* of signifier and signified.[45] Condillac, accordingly, challenges Locke's notion of language precisely because Condillac recognizes the rationalist prejudice implicit in Locke's analysis, namely, that ideas are what we first know. While it may be true that one can reason within the logical structures outlined by Descartes' Port Royal followers, this by no means exhausts the possibilities for what constitutes order and reason. From Condillac's perspective, Locke falls into the mistaken belief that reasoning can occur only by means of an appeal to a system that invites the skeptical attacks about which Berkeley warns us.

44. *Ibid.*, 53. Cf. Land, *Philosophy of Language*, 33.
45. See Barthes, *Elements of Semiology*, tr. Annette Lavers and Colin Smith (New York: Hill and Wang, 1968), 39. Cf. T. K. Seung, *Structuralism and Hermeneutics* (New York: Columbia University Press, 1982), 125.

What is worrisome about Locke's treatment, from Condillac's standpoint, is Locke's belief that thought can occur without signs.[46] Words, like hieroglyphics, are linked as signs whose relata are joined by their analogies to one another as figural expressions.[47] They are related not in what they mean, for what they mean is a function of their places within the sign system. Nor are they related in terms of the connections their ideas exhibit, for such connections are not based on analogies but rather, as Locke points out, on their "agreement or disagreement" with one another.[48] However, because the agreement of ideas with one another is supposedly grounded in the real things ideas represent, only the claim that *things* agree with or conform with one another could establish the basis for arguing that ideas can be dependable as the vehicles of thought. But Locke's representationist model cannot appeal to such a claim about things; it must only assume such relatedness in virtue of Locke's positing of a divine involvement in linking ideas of human concernment to external reality.[49] In Condillac's view, this makes the connections of ideas merely arbitrary when compared to the relations based on analogies found in words and other signs.[50] Speech, reason, and even abstract thought are based on the presupposition that perceptions can signify other perceptions and thus can guide intellectual activity; but such activity cannot occur apart from this character of implicit intentionality embodied in the sign feature of language.

When Condillac says, then, that "we think only by the help of words," what he means is that thought and reasoning express a systematic use of figuration.[51] Words are perceptual, experiential, and, most important, elements in a system of signs; it is this functional definition of language that undermines the metaphysics of word-thought-object with which Locke struggles. Problems about whether words always must refer to an idea evaporate for Condillac because, for him, the question of the ontological status of words vis-à-vis ideas and objects misses the essential point

---

46. See Condillac, *Origin of Human Knowledge*, 136 (I.4.27).
47. *Ibid.*, 275 (II.1.127) and 280 (II.1.138).
48. See Locke, *Essay* (Nidditch ed.), 395 (II.33.5).
49. *Ibid.*, 372–73 (II.30.2) and 598–99 (IV.7.11). Cf. Land, *Philosophy of Language*, 35, 94.
50. See Condillac, *Origin of Human Knowledge*, 102 (I.2.107), 287 (II.1.146); and Condillac, *Logic*, 56.
51. *Logic*, 53, 66.

about how thought and meaning are experientially based. Condillac's functional resolution refocuses attention on experience and thus precludes the possibility of addressing the implicit metaphysics of language that burdens Locke's account.[52]

Locke's worry about such a functional move (already apparent in Hobbes's treatment of names) lies in his recognition that, once the associations of words are released from the restraint of the associations of ideas, all connections in thinking can be taken as signs. And Berkeley concedes that the universally semiotic character of the world could be rather arbitrary were it not for the divinely maintained structures in the language of nature.

Hobbes himself notes that only in *ordered* speech do we recognize words or things as signs; that is, until something can be incorporated into a systematic framework of signification, it cannot even be identified.[53] Prior to such incorporation human beings can only make an unsuccessful effort to speak. The effort fails, in Condillac's words, because at that point "human beings contemplate nothing, because they have not yet observed any thing. Therefore, all is in a confused state to them as to their language, and they discern nothing in it."[54] Only the repetition of such associations, formalized in the myths or commonplaces of a culture, establishes the structure of relations between signs that achieve the status of canons of logic and reason.[55]

In each renewed narration, a new speech (and thus a new logic) traces a new history of the meaning of the language of figuration. To know the history or story (narration) of the sign system legitimizes in memory the expression, which otherwise threatens the stability of the community's linguistic heritage. Contained within the imaginative expressions of a nation is the logic of the nation, the revealed accounts of the history of how words and signs appear in relationships accepted as reasonable. Adopting a theme that Herder later uses in his defense of the need for a distinctly German literature, Condillac points out how logic is born out of the speech and poetry of a nation. Only in the repetitive environment or collective memory (i.e., fables or

52. On how this parallels Hobbes's treatment, see Land, *Philosophy of Language*, 244.

53. See *De Corpore*, in *The English Works of Thomas Hobbes*, ed. William Molesworth, 11 vols. (London: John Bohn, 1839–45), 1: 17.

54. *Logic*, 54. On Hobbes and Locke, see Land, *Philosophy of Language*, 15–18.

55. See Condillac, *Origin of Human Knowledge*, 254 (II.1.105).

myths) of society do signs emerge as literally *pictured* in the language of a nation (especially in its poetry).[56]

The character and genius of a culture, then, reside (for Condillac) in the sensitivity of the culture to the figural and metaphorical transformations open to it in terms of its willingness to adopt the stance of the fabular. He recognizes that his entire account of the history of language development itself resembles just such a story (*roman*), but it is precisely this reorientation toward the expressive history of the figural that allows for the imaginative legitimation of a logic of discovery within fabling.[57]

For Locke, this social psychologizing of reason is too much to take. It is not that he does not trust God to make sure that the structure of reason is justified and that the canons of logic apply to the world of objects. Indeed, he feels he avoids skeptical attacks because it seems obvious to him that ideas are natural signs of objects. What is not so obvious to him, and what fuels the advances of Berkeley and Condillac, is the recognition that ideas can signify only ideas, and words can signify only words. This development of empiricism restricts the extension of semiotic analysis to one order of reality at a time. For both Berkeley and Condillac, it is an appropriate restriction.

In particular, Condillac's assault on the preeminence of abstract reason over imagination-based sensation amounts to an attack on the propriety of rationalist presuppositions within empiricism. He retrieves the priority of the sign over idea, and in doing so clears the way for the appreciation of the harmonic union of beauty and truth as the developmental process of creativity that Shaftesbury describes. The identification of beauty as essentially a moment of irreducible sensibility does not dissolve under reason's attempt to discover truth, because the true now needs to be understood in predominantly developmental terms.

But without an eternally fixed truth behind the activity of the creative artist, we are left only with the veil of dialogic and performative imagination to establish and reveal the rational. This is Diderot's insight into the role of fabulation within philosophy. For without the act of sensible figuration, no displacement of reason occurs within imagination. And without the poetic

---

56. *Ibid.*, 299 (II.1.161–62); and 134 (I.4.25).
57. See *ibid.*, 299 (II.1.163); and Derrida, *Archeology of the Frivolous*, 68, 76–79.

affirmation of the propriety of violence to grammatical and rational canons, imagination remains merely a shadow of a system of intellection unable to account for its origin.

THE POETIC IMPULSE WITHIN PHILOSOPHY

As early as 1735 Thomas Blackwell warns about the ramifications of such twists of epistemological order. In the imaginative, the mythic, or the metaphoric, he notes, we find threats not only to grammatical order but also to social order. Because a metaphor is susceptible of infinite meanings, it can lead to madness.[58] The heroic frenzy of the poet is a rebellion against the regulation of thought over word, of philosophic determinateness over mythic power. The metaphor stands as an affront to the order of the mind; indeed, it affirms that figuration precedes the very existence of individual minds, for mind (like idea) depends on figural expression for its determinate identification.

In a more general way, the beginning of poetry is the cancellation of the progression and laws of rational thought. As Schlegel comments, poetry transplants us again "into the beautiful confusion of imagination, into the original chaos of human nature."[59] Prior to the mythopoetic performance, human nature does not exist. Re-creation of (and in) a philosophy of human nature is possible only in challenging the very starting points of philosophy, which define humanity in the first place.

As one of the seminal writers influencing Herder and the German Romantics, Blackwell makes this precise point about how mythology reintroduces us to the chaotic underpinnings of human nature itself. Mythology returns us to a state before humanity, reason, mind. Only a rationalized misapprehension of myth assumes that mankind is capable of thinking or of even existing independently of some mythic organization.

In his *Enquiry Into the Life and Writings of Homer* (1735), for example, Blackwell notes that mythology has two forms. "Artificial mythology" is a rational science, a dispassionate comparison of harmony and discord found in the powers of the universe. This

58. See Blackwell, *An Enquiry into the Life and Writings of Homer* (1735), in Feldman and Richardson, *Rise of Modern Mythology*, 106.
59. "Lecture on Mythology," from Schlegel, *Dialogue on Poetry*, tr. Roman Struc (University Park: Pennsylvania State University Press, 1968), 86.

is the mythology easily dismissed by rationalist critics as euhemeristic fantasies. "Natural mythology," on the other hand, expresses itself in terms of those powers or feelings we experience but over which we ultimately do not exercise control. This mythology describes the chaotic world of proto-man, the condition in which meaning is possible but not yet determinate, the state in which nature is still a place of magic.

According to Blackwell, Homer's gods combine both features: They are powers of the universe that we also recognize as operating in us, calling forth from us improvement, harmony, balance. In short, they provide the opportunity for an ordering of the chaos of aboriginal nature into a distinctly human nature.[60] In Homer's mythology the powers of the universe influence both mind and body because Homeric mythology assumes no distinction between intellect and passion. All nature, including human nature, embodies a unity often ignored (though longed for) in disparaging evaluations of myth. "I am very sensible," Blackwell complains, "that *Homer's Mythology* is but little understood; or, to express it better, is *little felt.*"[61] It is no wonder, he notes, that mythology rationally understood appears as little more than fiction without import, for the type of apprehension most appropriate to myth questions the very attempt to understand myth rationally: Only a prerational, imaginative, heartfelt sensibility appreciates the force and immediacy of such accounts.

Blackwell thus brings together several of the themes that later crystallize in Romanticist philosophy: the unity of the harmony of reason and the impact of sensibility; the power of imagination in the poetic determination of order; the historical and developmental character of mind's emergence from chaos into higher forms of integration. In his *Letters Concerning Mythology* (1748) he agrees with Shaftesbury in reiterating the passional centrality of fable in mythology by identifying poetry in terms of fable: "All Fable is *Poetry,* and the truest Species of it is *Fable.*"[62] Since poetry is historically conditioned, though, myth or fable most properly expresses the truth implicit within poetry insofar as myth or fable expresses nature as the condition for history itself.

---

60. See Blackwell, *Homer,* in Feldman and Richardson, *Rise of Modern Mythology,* 105.

61. *Ibid.*

62. *Letters Concerning Mythology* (London: n.p., 1748), 310. Also see Feldman and Richardson, *Rise of Modern Mythology,* 102.

Myth highlights the aboriginal unity of fabular narration (plot) and fabular moral exhortation (apologue) by establishing historicity in the performance of linguistic figuration.

The visual and auditory sign sequences of poetic expression point most obviously to their own self-constitution as meaning generators within mythic accounts; and in this way, myth or fable expresses the central feature of poetry better than all other poetic forms. Poetry creates meaning in expression itself. Insofar as poetry is mistakenly understood to reveal something within the mind or within nature apart from this creative constitution of sensible order, it loses the immediacy or emotive impact consonant with poetry's self-referential activity. Human nature and ordered nature in general exist in virtue of poetic incorporation. Myth makes this point explicit in a self-conscious way. To interpret the Romanticist fascination with myth, poetry, or imagination as a renewed attempt to breach the gap between man and nature or between mind and world erroneously presumes the rationalist insertion of language as a functioning reminder of the distinction between idea and thing. By indicating how poetic expression creates the very possibility for the interiority of mind or the exteriority of thing, the Romanticists recapture for figuration the power of harmonious integration without having to overcome some aboriginal alienation that reason alone cannot hope to correct.

Here, then, already are contained the seeds of the connections between myth and poetry, language, morality, and metaphysics, which come to fruition in Romanticist champions of myth, imagination, and genius. Insofar as poetry is treated as a figural, linguistic performance of the passional introduction of order into the chaos of proto-experience, it carves out a history, a sequence of reality. The philological investigations of William Warburton, Edward Young, L. D. Nelme, John Cleland, and C. G. Heyne reveal how myth reidentifies this historicity of language and in so doing counters the Lockean dissociation of words and things.[63] Vico and Herder, in their turn, also elevate language within the context of myth in emphasizing the historical character of emergent depictions of reality as products of the languages or poetic traditions of peoples.

63. See, for example, Cohen, *Sensible Words*, 133–34; and Feldman and Richardson, *Rise of Modern Mythology*, 113–16, 215–18.

The Romanticist theorists extend such treatments of the social constitution of the humanly experienced and humanly expressed world to the moral integration of nature on the grand scale. Wordsworth, for example, suggests that the spontaneity of the speech of common folk captures the universal mythic impulse toward creativity. Working under the same impulse, the poet counteracts the tendency to interpret nature in terms of static laws of rational thought. Like Mark Akenside, Wordsworth argues that the poet reunites the moral and corporeal powers of the world by re-creating the world as a matrix of passional interest.[64] Because the world described by Enlightenment rationalism and empiricism stands as determinate, intransigent, and apparently devoid of inherent valuation, the poet's only recourse is to oppose the actual physical world of rational artistry with the free exercise of imaginative nature in order to recapture the sense of moral immediacy. As long as moral dictates are tied to a world ordered by a hand other than one's own, the imperative to care is only contingent.

For Coleridge, on the other hand, mythopoesis is the activity of nature: The poet, as the expression or performance of nature, is not limited by anything other than himself or herself. But this does not mean that nature has no laws or rules of grammar, logic, or psychology by which poetic creativity is regulated.[65] Quite the contrary: The primary imaginative act in virtue of which minds develop (i.e., perception) sets up the condition for a secondary act of imagination, namely, that of the poetic re-creation of the world as historical. In agreement with Herder, Coleridge points out how nature's own organic development itself establishes the rules of the grammar of being; but—and this is what distinguishes Coleridge from Spinoza and Wordsworth—such rules are the products of the *historical* development of nature.

64. See M. H. Abrams, *The Mirror and the Lamp: Romantic Theory and the Critical Tradition* (New York: Oxford University Press, 1953), 123–24; and Feldman and Richardson, *Rise of Modern Mythology*, 140.

65. See James Engell, *The Creative Imagination: Enlightenment to Romanticism* (Cambridge: Harvard University Press, 1981), 344–46; Abrams, *Mirror and the Lamp*, 283; and Gene M. Bernstein, "The Mediated Vision: Eliade, Lévi-Strauss, and Romantic Mythopoesis," in *The Binding of Proteus: Perspectives on Myth and the Literary Process*, ed. Marjorie W. McCune, Tucker Orbison, and Philip Withim (Lewisburg, Pa.: Bucknell University Press, 1980), 168–69.

To F. W. J. Schelling, this means that the mythopoetic activity of the Absolute appears as the work of genius.[66]   But genius is unconscious of its contribution to the development of the laws of historical reason until such innovations are incorporated into the linguistic consciousness of a people as an embodiment of the Absolute.   As the creative, public, and linguistic performance of increasing social integration, myth expresses the tentative character of history becoming realized; it thus brings together nature and spirit in a metaphysics of the Absolute.

In Schelling's "philosophy of mythology," mythology achieves its highest stature, a posture that incorporates and then makes thematic the features of mythopoesis that characterize the writings of the classical modern philosophers.   Within Schelling's approach, all other philosophy and religion is incorporated into myth.   The discussion of all determinate reality and even of the chaos out of which the contrast between nature and spirit emerges falls under the transcendental heuristic of mythology.   Myth thus subsumes all possible topics in a way that removes from it every discriminating feature.   As such, it provides us less with yet another philosophy than with an invitation to historiographic or, more generally, metaphilosophic conversion.

66. See Engell, *Creative Imagination*, 308; and Feldman and Richardson, *Rise of Modern Mythology*, 315–19.

Bibliography

Aarsleff, Hans. *From Locke to Saussure: Essays on the Study of Language and Intellectual History.* Minneapolis: University of Minnesota Press, 1982.

_____. "The Tradition of Condillac: The Problem of the Origin of Language in the Eighteenth Century and the Debate in the Berlin Academy before Herder." In *Studies in the History of Linguistics,* edited by Dell Hymes. Bloomington: Indiana University Press, 1974.

Abraham, William E. "The Origins of Myth and Philosophy." *Man and World* 11 (1978): 165–85.

Abrams, M. H. *The Mirror and the Lamp: Romantic Theory and the Critical Tradition.* New York: Oxford University Press, 1953.

Ainsworth, Edward G., and Noyes, Charles E. *Christopher Smart: A Biographical and Critical Study.* Columbia: University of Missouri Press, 1943.

Alexander, Richard W. "The Myth of Power: Hobbes's *Leviathan.*" *JEGP* 70 (1971): 31–50.

Alexander, W. M. *Johann Georg Hamann: Philosophy and Faith.* The Hague: Martinus Nijhoff, 1966.

Allen, Don Cameron. *Mysteriously Meant: The Rediscovery of Pagan Symbolism and Allegorical Interpretation in the Renaissance.* Baltimore, Md.: Johns Hopkins Press, 1970.

Alquié, Ferdinand. *La Découverte metaphysique de l'homme chez Descartes.* 2d ed. Paris: Presses Universitaires de France, 1966.

Armens, Sven. *John Gay: Social Critic.* New York: King's Crown Press, 1954.

Arwaker, Edmund. *Truth in Fiction: or, Morality in Masquerade.* London: J. Churchill, 1708.

Attridge, Derek. "Language as History/History as Language: Saussure and the Romance of Etymology." In *Post-structuralism and the Question of History,* edited by Derek Attridge, Geoff Bennington, and Robert Young. Cambridge: Cambridge University Press, 1987.

Avis, Paul. *Foundations of Modern Historical Thought: From Machiavelli to Vico.* London: Croom Helm, 1986.

Bacon, Francis. *The Works of Francis Bacon.* Edited by J. Spedding et al. 7 vols. London: Longman and Co., 1857–59.

Ball, Albert. "Swift and the Animal Myth." *Transactions of the Wisconsin Academy of Sciences, Arts, and Letters* 48 (1959): 239–48.

Banier, Antoine. *The Mythology and Fables of the Ancients Explain'd from History.* 4 vols. London: A. Millar, 1739–40.

Barchilon, Jacques. "Uses of the Fairy Tale in the Eighteenth Century." *Studies on Voltaire and the Eighteenth Century* 24 (1963): 111–38.

Barnard, F. M. "Herder's Treatment of Causation and Continuity in History." *Journal of the History of Ideas* 24 (1963): 197–212.

Barthes, Roland. *Elements of Semiology.* Translated by Annette Lavers and Colin Smith. New York: Hill and Wang, 1968.

_____ . *The Pleasure of the Text.* Translated by Richard Miller. New York: Hill and Wang, 1975.

Baumann, Sally E. "The Individual in the *Fables* of La Fontaine." Ph.D. diss., University of Chicago, 1976.

Baynes, Kenneth; Bohman, James; and McCarthy, Thomas, eds. *After Philosophy: End or Transformation?* Cambridge: MIT Press, 1985.

Beck, L. J. *The Method of Descartes: A Study of the "Regulae."* Oxford: Clarendon Press, 1952.

Belaval, Yvon. "Vico and Anti-Cartesianism." In *Giambattista Vico: An International Symposium,* edited by Giorgio Tagliacozzo and Hayden V. White. Baltimore, Md.: Johns Hopkins University Press, 1969.

Benjamin, Andrew E. "Descartes' Fable: The *Discours de la Méthode.*" In *The Figural and the Literal: Problems of Language in the History of Science and Philosophy, 1630–1800,* edited by Andrew E. Benjamin, Geoffrey N. Cantor, and John R. R. Christie. Manchester, Eng.: Manchester University Press, 1987.

Benjamin, Andrew E.; Cantor, Geoffrey N.; and Christie, John R. R., eds. *The Figural and the Literal: Problems of Language in the History of Science and Philosophy, 1630–1800.* Manchester, Eng.: Manchester University Press, 1987.

Benjamin, Walter. *The Origin of German Tragic Drama.* Translated by John Osborne. London: New Left Books, 1977.

Berkeley, George. *A Treatise Concerning the Principles of Human Knowledge, with Critical Essays.* Edited by Colin Turbayne. Indianapolis, Ind.: Bobbs-Merrill, 1970.

_____ . *The Works of George Berkeley.* Edited by A. A. Luce and T. E. Jessup. 9 vols. Edinburgh: Thomas Nelson and Sons, 1948–57.

Berlin, Isaiah. *Vico and Herder.* London: Hogarth Press, 1976.

Bernstein, Gene M. "The Mediated Vision: Eliade, Lévi-Strauss, and Romantic Mythopoesis." In *The Binding of Proteus: Perspectives on Myth and the Literary Process,* edited by Marjorie W. McCune, Tucker Orbison, and Philip Withim. Lewisburg, Pa.: Bucknell University Press, 1980.

Bidney, David. "Myth, Symbolism, and Truth." In *Myth: A Symposium,* edited by Thomas A. Sebeok. Bloomington: Indiana University Press, 1958.

Blackwell, Richard J. "Scientific Discovery and the Laws of Logic." *New Scholasticism* 50 (1976): 333–44.

Blackwell, Thomas. *Letters Concerning Mythology.* London: [n.p.], 1748.

Blanchard, Marc Eli. "Writing the Museum: Diderot's Bodies in the Salons." In *Diderot: Digression and Dispersion,* edited by Jack Undank and Herbert Josephs. Lexington, Ky.: French Forum, 1984.

Bloom, Harold. *A Map of Misreading.* New York: Oxford University Press, 1975.

Blumenberg, Hans. *Work on Myth.* Translated by Robert M. Wallace. Cambridge: MIT Press, 1985.

Bogel, Fredric V. "Fables of Knowing: Melodrama and Related Forms." *Genre* 11 (1978): 83–108.

Bond, Donald F., ed. *The Spectator.* 5 vols. Oxford: Clarendon Press, 1965.

Booth, Wayne C. "Metaphor as Rhetoric: The Problem of Evaluation." In *On Metaphor,* edited by Sheldon Sacks. Chicago: University of Chicago Press, 1979.

Brown, Warren R. "An Introduction to Mandeville's *The Fable of the Bees.*" Ph.D. diss., Claremont Graduate School, 1977.

Bush, George E. "The Fable in the English Periodical, 1660–1800." Ph.D. diss., St. John's University, 1965.

Cambon, Glauco. "Vico as Poet." *Forum Italicum* 2 (1968): 326–31.

Cantelli, Gianfranco. "Myth and Language in Vico." In *Giambattista Vico's Science of Humanity,* edited by Giorgio Tagliacozzo and Donald P. Verene. Baltimore, Md.: Johns Hopkins University Press, 1976.

Caponigri, A. Robert. "Philosophy and Philology: The 'New Art of Criticism' in Giam Battista Vico." *Modern Schoolman* 59 (1982): 81–116.

Cassirer, Ernst. *Language and Myth.* Translated by Susanne Langer. New York: Dover, 1946.

_____. *The Philosophy of Symbolic Forms.* Vol. 1: *Language.* Translated by Ralph Mannheim. New Haven, Conn.: Yale University Press, 1953.

_____. *The Philosophy of the Enlightenment.* Translated by Fritz C. A. Koelln and James P. Pettegrove. Princeton, N.J.: Princeton University Press, 1979.

Caton, Hiram. *The Origin of Subjectivity: An Essay on Descartes.* New Haven, Conn.: Yale University Press, 1973.

Champigny, Robert. "The Theatrical Aspect of the Cogito." *Review of Metaphysics* 12 (1959): 370–77.

Chase, Richard. *Quest for Myth.* New York: Greenwood Press, 1949.

Chiasson, Elias J. "Bernard Mandeville: A Reappraisal." *Philological Quarterly* 49 (1970): 489–519.

Christie, John R. R. "Introduction: Rhetoric and Writing in Early Modern Philosophy and Science." In *The Figural and the Literal: Problems of Language in the History of Science and Philosophy, 1630–1800,* edited by Andrew E. Benjamin, Geoffrey N. Cantor, and John R. R. Christie. Manchester, Eng.: Manchester University Press, 1987.

Clarke, Robert T. *Herder: His Life and Thought.* Berkeley: University of California Press, 1955.

_____. "Herder's Conception of 'Kraft'." *PMLA* 57 (1942): 737–52.

Cohen, Murray. *Sensible Words: Linguistic Practice in England, 1640–1785.* Baltimore, Md.: Johns Hopkins University Press, 1977.

Cohen, Percy. "Theories of Myth." *Man,* new series 4 (1969): 337–53.

Collingwood, Robin G. *The Idea of History.* Edited by T. M. Knox. Oxford: Oxford University Press, 1956.

Collins, James D. *Descartes' Philosophy of Nature.* Oxford: Basil Blackwell, 1971.

_____. *Interpreting Modern Philosophy.* Princeton, N.J.: Princeton University Press, 1972.

Colman, John. "Bernard Mandeville and the Reality of Virtue." *Philosophy* 47 (1972): 125–139.

Condillac, Étienne Bonnot de. *An Essay on the Origin of Human Knowledge.* Anonymous English translation, 1756. Reprint. New York: AMS Press, 1974.

_____. *The Logic of Condillac.* Translated by Joseph Neef. Edited by Daniel N. Robinson. Washington, D.C.: University Publications of America, 1977.

Corti, Maria. *An Introduction to Literary Semiotics.* Translated by Margherita Bogat and Allen Mandelbaum. Bloomington: Indiana University Press, 1978.

Crawford, Donald. "Kant's Theory of Creative Imagination." In *Essays in Kant's Aesthetics,* edited by Ted Cohen and Paul Guyer. Chicago: University of Chicago Press, 1982.

Creech, James. *Diderot: Thresholds of Representation.* Columbus: Ohio State University Press, 1986.

Croxall, Samuel. *Fables of Aesop and Others.* London: J. Tonson, 1722.

Dancy, Jonathan. *Berkeley: An Introduction.* Oxford: Basil Blackwell, 1987.

Daniel, Stephen H. "Civility and Sociability: Hobbes on Man and Citizen." *Journal of the History of Philosophy* 18 (1980): 209–15.

_____. "Descartes' Treatment of 'Lumen Naturale'." *Studia Leibnitiana* 10 (1978): 92–100.

_____. "The Nature of Light in Descartes' Physics." *The Philosophical Forum* 7 (1976): 323–44.

_____. "A Philosophical Theory of Literary Continuity and Change." *Southern Journal of Philosophy* 18 (1980): 275–80.

_____. "Reading Places: The Rhetorical Basis of Place." In *Commonplaces: Essays on the Nature of Place,* edited by David W. Black, Donald Kunze, and John Pickles. Lanham, Md.: University Press of America, 1989.

de Corte, Marcel. "La dialectique poétique de Descartes." *Archives de Philosophie,* vol. 13, no. 2 (1937): 101–68.

de Grazia, Margreta. "The Secularization of Language in the Seventeenth Century." *Journal of the History of Ideas* 41 (1980): 319–29.

De Mas, Enrico. "Vico's Four Authors." In *Giambattista Vico: An International Symposium*, edited by Giorgio Tagliacozzo and Hayden V. White. Baltimore, Md.: Johns Hopkins University Press, 1969.

de Witt, Johan. *Fables Moral and Political.* 2 vols. London: [n.p.], 1703.

Derrida, Jacques. *The Archeology of the Frivolous: Reading Condillac.* Translated by John P. Leavey, Jr. Pittsburgh: Duquesne University Press, 1980.

_____. *Dissemination.* Translated by Barbara Johnson. Chicago: University of Chicago Press, 1981.

_____. "The Ends of Man." Translated by Edouard Morot-Sir et al. *Philosophy and Phenomenological Research* 30 (1969): 31–57.

_____. *Of Grammatology.* Translated by Gayatri C. Spivak. Baltimore, Md.: Johns Hopkins University Press, 1976.

_____. "White Mythology: Metaphor in the Text of Philosophy." Translated by F. C. T. Moore. *New Literary History* 6 (1974–75): 5–74.

_____. *Writing and Difference.* Translated by Alan Bass. Chicago: University of Chicago Press, 1978.

Descartes, René. *Correspondance de Descartes.* Edited by Charles Adam and Gaston Milhaud. 8 vols. Paris: Presses Universitaires de France, 1936–63.

_____. *Descartes' Conversation with Burman.* Translated by John Cottingham. Oxford: Clarendon Press, 1976.

_____. "Descartes's Olympica." Translated by John F. Benton. In "Somnio Ergo Sum: Descartes' Three Demands," by W. T. Jones. *Philosophy and Literature* 4 (1980): 145–66.

_____. *Le Monde.* Translated and edited by Michael S. Mahoney. New York: Abaris Books, 1979.

_____. *Oeuvres.* Edited by Charles Adam and Paul Tannery. 13 vols. Paris: Cerf, 1897–1913.

_____. *The Philosophical Works of Descartes.* Translated by Elizabeth S. Haldane and G. R. T. Ross. 2 vols. Cambridge: Cambridge University Press, 1967.

_____. *Règles utiles et claires pour la direction de l'esprit en la recherche de la verité.* Translated and annotated by Jean-Luc Marion. The Hague: Martinus Nijhoff, 1977.

Diderot, Denis. *Diderot's Early Philosophical Works.* Translated and edited by Margaret Jourdain. 1916. Reprint. New York: AMS Press, 1973.

_____. *The Paradox of Acting.* Translated by Walter H. Pollock. New York: Hill and Wang, 1957.

Dieckmann, Herbert. "Diderot's Conception of Genius." *Journal of the History of Ideas* 2 (1941): 151–82.

Dodsley, Robert. *An Essay on Fable.* Introduction by Jeanne K. Welcher and Richard Dircks. Los Angeles: William Andrews Clark Memorial Library, 1965.

Doolittle, James. "Hieroglyph and Emblem in Diderot's *Lettre sur Les Sourds et Les Muets.*" *Diderot Studies* 2 (1952): 148–67.

Dorfles, Gillo. "Myth and Metaphor in Vico and Contemporary Aesthetics." In *Giambattista Vico: An International Symposium*, edited by Giorgio Tagliacozzo and Hayden V. White. Baltimore, Md.: Johns Hopkins University Press, 1969.

Dronke, Peter. *Fabula: Explorations into the Uses of Myth in Medieval Platonism.* Leiden: E. J. Brill, 1974.

Eaves, T. C. Duncan. *Samuel Richardson: A Biography.* Oxford: Clarendon Press, 1971.

Eco, Umberto. *A Theory of Semiotics.* Bloomington: Indiana University Press, 1976.

Engell, James. *The Creative Imagination: Enlightenment to Romanticism.* Cambridge: Harvard University Press, 1981.

Farrington, Benjamin. *The Philosophy of Francis Bacon: An Essay on Its Development from 1603 to 1609.* Liverpool, Eng.: Liverpool University Press, 1964.

Feldman, Burton, and Richardson, Robert D. *The Rise of Modern Mythology: 1680–1860.* Bloomington: Indiana University Press, 1972.

Fisch, Max H. "Vico and Pragmatism." In *Giambattista Vico: An International Symposium*, edited by Giorgio Tagliacozzo and Hayden V. White. Baltimore, Md.: Johns Hopkins University Press, 1969.

Fish, Stanley. "Literature in the Reader: Affective Stylistics." *New Literary History* 2 (1970): 123–61.

Flores, Ralph. "Cartesian Striptease." *SubStance* 12 (1983): 75–88.

Foucault, Michel. *The Archaeology of Knowledge.* Translated by A. M. Sheridan Smith. New York: Harper and Row, Harper Torchbooks, 1972.

_____ . *The Order of Things.* Translation of *Les Mots et les choses* (1966). New York: Random House, 1970.

Frank, Luanne. "Herder's *Essay on the Origin of Language:* Forerunner of Contemporary Views in History, Aesthetics, Literary Theory, Philosophy." *Forum Linguisticum* 7 (1982): 15–26.

Frankel, Margherita. "Vico and Rousseau Through Derrida." *New Vico Studies* 1 (1983): 51–61.

Fugate, Joe K. *The Psychological Basis of Herder's Aesthetics.* The Hague: Mouton, 1966.

Gallie, W. B. *Philosophy and the Historical Understanding.* New York: Schocken Books, 1964.

Gardner, Howard, and Winner, Ellen. "The Development of Metaphoric Competence: Implications for Humanistic Disciplines." In *On Metaphor*, edited by Sheldon Sacks. Chicago: University of Chicago Press, 1979.

Gasché, Rodolphe. "Of Aesthetic and Historical Determination." In *Post-structuralism and the Question of History*, edited by Derek Attridge, Geoff Bennington, and Robert Young. Cambridge: Cambridge University Press, 1987.

Gillies, Alexander. "Herder's Approach to the Philosophy of History." *Modern Language Review* 35 (1940): 193–206.

Gilman, Margaret. "Imagination and Creation in Diderot." *Diderot Studies* 2 (1952): 200–220.

Gilson, Étienne. *René Descartes, Discours de la Méthode: Texte et Commentaire.* Paris: J. Vrin, 1925.

Ginsberg, Robert, ed. *The Philosopher as Writer: The Eighteenth Century.* Selinsgrove, Pa.: Susquehanna University Press, 1987.

Gossman, Lionel, and MacArthur, Elizabeth. "Diderot's Displaced *Paradoxe.*" In *Diderot: Digression and Dispersion,* edited by Jack Undank and Herbert Josephs. Lexington, Ky.: French Forum, 1984.

Gouhier, Henri. *Les premières pensées de Descartes.* Paris: J. Vrin, 1958.

Gould, Eric. *Mythical Intentions in Modern Literature.* Princeton, N.J.: Princeton University Press, 1981.

Graham, Albert Edwin. "John Gay's *Fables,* Edited with an Introduction on the Fable as an Eighteenth-Century Literary Genre." Ph.D. diss., Princeton University, 1960.

Grassi, Ernesto. "Critical Philosophy or Topical Philosophy? Meditations on the *De nostri temporis studiorum ratione.*" In *Giambattista Vico: An International Symposium,* edited by Giorgio Tagliacozzo and Hayden V. White. Baltimore, Md.: Johns Hopkins University Press, 1969.

_____ . "Humanistic Rhetorical Philosophizing: Giovanni Pontano's Theory of the Unity of Poetry, Rhetoric, and History." *Philosophy and Rhetoric* 17 (1984): 135–55.

_____ . "The Priority of Common Sense and Imagination: Vico's Philosophical Relevance Today." *Social Research* 43 (1976): 552–80.

_____ . "Remarks on German Idealism, Humanism, and the Philosophical Function of Rhetoric." *Philosophy and Rhetoric* 19 (1986): 125–33.

_____ . *Rhetoric as Philosophy: The Humanist Tradition.* University Park: Pennsylvania State University Press, 1980.

_____ . "Vico, Marx, and Heidegger." In *Vico and Marx: Affinities and Contrasts,* edited by Giorgio Tagliacozzo. Atlantic Highlands, N.J.: Humanities Press, 1983.

Greene, Robert A. "Whichcote, Wilkins, 'Ingenuity,' and the Reasonableness of Christianity." *Journal of the History of Ideas* 42 (1981): 227–52.

Greenleaf, W. H. *Order, Empiricism and Politics.* Westport, Conn.: Greenwood Press, 1980.

Grimaldi, Alfonsina Albini. *The Universal Humanity of Giambattista Vico.* New York: S. F. Vanni, 1958.

Hamann, Johann Georg. *Briefwechsel.* Edited by Walther Ziesemer and Arthur Henkel. 7 vols. Wiesbaden: Insel, 1955–75.

_____ . *Hamann's "Socratic Memorabilia": A Translation and Commentary.* Translated and edited by James C. O'Flaherty. Baltimore, Md.: Johns Hopkins University Press, 1967.

_____ . *Sämtliche Werke.* Edited by Josef Nadler. 6 vols. Vienna: Herder, 1949–57.

Harland, Richard. *Superstructuralism.* New York: Methuen, 1987.

Harries, Karsten. "Metaphor and Transcendence." In *On Metaphor*, edited by Sheldon Sacks. Chicago: University of Chicago Press, 1979.

Harth, Philip. Introduction to *The Fable of the Bees*, by Bernard Mandeville. Edited by Philip Harth. Harmondsworth, Eng.: Penguin, 1970.

_____. "The Satiric Purpose of *The Fable of the Bees*." *Eighteenth-Century Studies* 2 (1969): 321–39.

Hartman, Geoffrey H. *Criticism in the Wilderness*. New Haven, Conn.: Yale University Press, 1980.

_____. *The Fate of Reading*. Chicago: University of Chicago Press, 1975.

_____. *The Unmediated Vision*. New Haven, Conn.: Yale University Press, 1954.

_____. "Words, Wish, Worth: Wordsworth." In *Deconstruction and Criticism*. New York: Seabury Press, 1979.

Hassan, Ihab, and Hassan, Sally, eds. *Innovation/Renovation*. Madison: University of Wisconsin Press, 1983.

Hausman, Carl R. "Philosophical Creativity and Metaphorical Philosophy." *Philosophical Topics* 12 (1981): 193–211.

Hawkes, Terence. *Structuralism and Semiotics*. Berkeley: University of California Press, 1977.

Hayek, F. A. "Dr. Bernard Mandeville." *Proceedings of the British Academy* 52 (1966): 125–41.

Heidegger, Martin. *What Is Called Thinking?* Translated by J. Glenn Gray. New York: Harper and Row, 1968.

Henning, E. M. "Archaeology, Deconstruction, and Intellectual History." In *Modern European Intellectual History: Reappraisals and New Perspectives*, edited by Dominick LaCapra and Steven L. Kaplan. Ithaca, N.Y.: Cornell University Press, 1982.

Herder, Johann Gottfried. *Essay on the Origin of Language*. Translated by Alexander Gode in *On the Origin of Language*. New York: Frederick Ungar, 1966.

_____. *Sämtliche Werke*. Edited by Bernhard Suphan et al. 33 vols. Berlin: Weidmannsche Buchhandlung, 1877–1913.

Hobbes, Thomas. *The English Works of Thomas Hobbes*. 11 vols. Edited by William Molesworth. London: John Bohn, 1839–45.

Horne, Colin J. " 'From a Fable form a Truth': A Consideration of the Fable in Swift's Poetry." In *Studies in the Eighteenth Century*, edited by R. F. Brissenden. Canberra: Australian National University Press, 1968.

Horne, Thomas A. *The Social Thought of Bernard Mandeville*. London: Macmillan, 1978.

Huete, Sylvia Ballard. "John Gay's *Fables I* and *II*: A Study in the Eighteenth Century Fable." Ph.D. diss., University of Southern Mississippi, 1973.

Hundert, E. J. "Bernard Mandeville and the Rhetoric of Social Science." *Journal of the History of the Behavioral Sciences* 22 (1986): 311–20.

Hurd, Richard. *Letters on Chivalry and Romance.* 1762. Edited by Hoyt Trowbridge. Augustan Reprint Society Publication No. 101–102. Los Angeles: William Andrews Clark Memorial Library, 1963.

Hutton, Patrick H. "The *New Science* of Giambattista Vico: Historicism in Its Relation to Poetics." *Journal of Aesthetics and Art Criticism* 30 (1971–72): 359–67.

Irving, William H. *John Gay: Favorite of the Wits.* Durham, N.C.: Duke University Press, 1940.

Jaffe, Kineret S. "The Concept of Genius: Its Changing Role in Eighteenth-Century French Aesthetics." *Journal of the History of Ideas* 41 (1980): 579–99.

James, E. O. "The Nature and Function of Myth." *Folk-Lore* 68 (1957): 474–82.

Janik, Linda Gardiner. "A Renaissance Quarrel: The Origin of Vico's Anti-Cartesianism." *New Vico Studies* 1 (1983): 39–50.

Jardine, Lisa. *Francis Bacon: Discovery and the Art of Discourse.* Cambridge: Cambridge University Press, 1974.

Johnson, Mark, ed. *Philosophical Perspectives on Metaphor.* Minneapolis: University of Minnesota Press, 1981.

Jones, W. T. "Somnio Ergo Sum: Descartes' Three Demands." *Philosophy and Literature* 4 (1980): 145–66.

Judovitz, Dalia. "Autobiographical Discourse and Critical Praxis in Descartes." *Philosophy and Literature* 5 (1981): 91–107.

_____. *Subjectivity and Representation in Descartes.* Cambridge: Cambridge University Press, 1988.

Kaye, F. B. "Mandeville on the Origin of Language." *Modern Language Notes* 39 (1924): 136–42.

Keeling, S. V. *Descartes.* 2d ed. London: Oxford University Press, 1968.

Kennington, Richard. "Descartes' 'Olympica'." *Social Research* 28 (1961): 171–204.

Kirk, G. S. *Myth: Its Meaning and Function.* Cambridge: Cambridge University Press, 1970.

Kishler, Thomas C. "The Satiric Moral Fable: A Study of an Augustan Genre with Particular Reference to Fielding." Ph.D. diss., University of Wisconsin, 1959.

Knight, Isabel F. *The Geometric Spirit: The Abbé de Condillac and the French Enlightenment.* New Haven, Conn.: Yale University Press, 1968.

Kockelmans, Joseph J. "On Myth and Its Relationship to Hermeneutics." *Cultural Hermeneutics* 1 (1973): 47–86.

Koepke, Wulf. "Herder's Craft of Communication." In *The Philosopher as Writer: The Eighteenth Century,* edited by Robert Ginsberg. Selinsgrove, Pa.: Susquehanna University Press, 1987.

_____. *Johann Gottfried Herder.* Boston: Twayne Publishers, 1987.

_____. "Truth and Revelation: On Herder's Theological Writings." In *Johann Gottfried Herder: Innovator Through the Ages,* edited by Wulf Koepke and Samson Knoll. Bonn: Bouvier, 1982.

Koepke, Wulf, and Knoll, Samson, eds. *Johann Gottfried Herder: Innovator Through the Ages.* Bonn: Bouvier, 1982.

Kraus, Pamela A. "From Universal Mathematics to Universal Method: Descartes' 'Turn' in Rule IV of the *Regulae.*" *Journal of the History of Philosophy* 21 (1983): 159–74.

Kristeller, Paul O. " 'Creativity' and 'Tradition'." *Journal of the History of Ideas* 44 (1983): 105–13.

Krupnick, Mark. Introduction to *Displacement: Derrida and After,* edited by Mark Krupnick. Bloomington: Indiana University Press, 1983.

Kuhns, Richard. "Metaphor as Plausible Inference in Poetry and Philosophy." *Philosophy and Literature* 3 (1979): 225–38.

Kuspit, Donald B. "Epoché and Fable in Descartes." *Philosophy and Phenomenological Research* 25 (1964): 30–51.

LaCapra, Dominick. "Intellectual History and Defining the Present as 'Postmodern'." In *Innovation/Renovation,* edited by Ihab Hassan and Sally Hassan. Madison: University of Wisconsin Press, 1983.

——————. "Rethinking Intellectual History and Reading Texts." In *Modern European Intellectual History: Reappraisals and New Perspectives,* edited by Dominick LaCapra and Steven L. Kaplan. Ithaca, N.Y.: Cornell University Press, 1982.

——————. *Rethinking Intellectual History: Texts, Contexts, Language.* Ithaca, N.Y.: Cornell University Press, 1983.

Lacoue-Labarthe, Philippe, and Nancy, Jean-Luc. *The Literary Absolute: The Theory of Literature in German Romanticism.* Translated by Philip Barnard and Cheryl Lester. Albany: State University of New York Press, 1988.

Lamprecht, Sterling. "The Fable of the Bees." *Journal of Philosophy* 23 (1926): 561–79.

Land, Stephen K. *The Philosophy of Language in Britain: Major Theories from Hobbes to Thomas Reid.* New York: AMS Press, 1986.

Lang, Candace. "Aberrance in Criticism?" *SubStance* 41 (1983): 3–16.

Langer, Susanne K. *Philosophical Sketches.* Baltimore, Md.: Johns Hopkins University Press, 1962.

Le Bossu, René. *Treatise of the Epick Poem.* 1695. In *Le Bossu and Voltaire on the Epic.* Facsimile reproduction. Introduction by Stuart Curran. Gainesville, Fla.: Scholar's Facsimiles and Reprints, 1970.

LeFèvre, Roger. *La vocation de Descartes.* Paris: Presses Universitaires de France, 1956.

Leland, Dorothy. "On Reading and Writing the World: Foucault's History of Thought." *Clio* 4 (1975): 225–43.

Lemmi, Charles W. *The Classic Deities in Bacon.* Baltimore, Md.: Johns Hopkins University Press, 1933.

Leroy, Maxime. *Descartes: le philosophe au masque.* Paris: Editions Rieder, 1929.

L'Estrange, Sir Roger. *Fables and Storyes Moralized.* London: R. Sare, 1699.

_____. *Fables of Aesop and other Eminent Mythologists: With Morals and Reflexions.* 2d ed., rev. London: R. Sare et al., 1694.

Locke, John. *Aesop's Fables.* London: A. & J. Churchil, 1703.

_____. *The Educational Writings of John Locke.* Edited by James Axtell. Cambridge: Cambridge University Press, 1968.

_____. *An Essay Concerning Human Understanding.* Edited by Peter H. Nidditch. Oxford: Clarendon Press, 1975.

_____. *An Essay Concerning Human Understanding.* 2 vols. Edited by John W. Yolton. New York: Dutton, 1964.

Luft, Sandra Rudnick. "A Genetic Interpretation of Divine Providence in Vico's *New Science.*" *Journal of the History of Philosophy* 20 (1982): 151–69.

Lyons, John D. "Subjectivity and Imitation in the *Discours de la Méthode.*" *Neophilologus* 66 (1982): 508–24.

Lyotard, Jean-François. "Answering the Question: What is Postmodernism?" In *Innovation/Renovation,* edited by Ihab Hassan and Sally Hassan. Madison: University of Wisconsin Press, 1983.

_____. *The Postmodern Condition.* Translated by Geoff Bennington and Brian Massumi. Minneapolis: University of Minnesota Press, 1984.

McGowan, Margaret M. "Moral Intention in the Fables of La Fontaine." *Journal of the Warburg and Courtauld Institutes* 29 (1966): 264–81.

McGowan, William. "Berkeley's Doctrine of Signs." In *Berkeley: Critical and Interpretive Essays,* edited by Colin M. Turbayne. Minneapolis: University of Minnesota Press, 1982.

_____. "George Berkeley's American Declaration of Independence." *Studies in Eighteenth-Century Culture* 12 (1983): 105–14.

McNamee, Maurice B., S.J. "Literary Decorum in Francis Bacon." *St. Louis University Studies,* series A: Humanities, vol. 1, no. 3 (1950): 1–52.

Major-Poetzl, Pamela. *Michel Foucault's Archaeology of Western Culture.* Chapel Hill: University of North Carolina Press, 1983.

Mandeville, Bernard. *An Enquiry into the Origin of Honour.* London: J. Brotherton, 1732.

_____. *The Fable of the Bees.* Edited by F. B. Kaye. 2 vols. Oxford: Clarendon Press, 1924.

_____. *A Letter to Dion.* Edited by Bonamy Dobree. Liverpool, Eng.: University Press of Liverpool, 1954.

_____. *Typhon: or the Wars between the Gods and the Giants.* London: J. Nutt, 1704.

Manuel, Frank E. *The Eighteenth Century Confronts the Gods.* Cambridge: Harvard University Press, 1959.

Marchand, James W. "Herder: Precursor of Humboldt, Whorf, and Modern Language Philosophy." In *Johann Gottfried Herder: Innovator Through the Ages,* edited by Wulf Koepke and Samson Knoll. Bonn: Bouvier, 1982.

Marion, Jean-Luc. *Sur la théologie blanche de Descartes*. Paris: Presses Universitaires de France, 1981.

Mechanic, Leslie B. "John Dryden's *Fables*: A Study in Political Subversion." Ph.D. diss., University of Pennsylvania, 1975.

Mehlman, Jeffrey. *Cataract: A Study in Diderot*. Middletown, Conn.: Wesleyan University Press, 1979.

Milhaud, Gaston. *Descartes Savant*. Paris: Felix Alcan, 1921.

Millet, J. *Histoire de Descartes avant 1637*. Paris: Didier, 1867.

Miner, Earl. *Dryden's Poetry*. Bloomington: Indiana University Press, 1967.

Monro, Hector. *The Ambivalence of Bernard Mandeville*. Oxford: Clarendon Press, 1975.

Mooney, Michael. "The Primacy of Language in Vico." *Social Research* 43 (1976): 581–600.

_____. *Vico in the Tradition of Rhetoric*. Princeton, N.J.: Princeton University Press, 1985.

Moriarty, Michael. "Figures of the Unthinkable: Diderot's Materialist Metaphors." In *The Figural and the Literal: Problems of Language in the History of Science and Philosophy, 1630–1800*, edited by Andrew E. Benjamin, Geoffrey N. Cantor, and John R. R. Christie. Manchester, Eng.: Manchester University Press, 1987.

Morton, Michael M. "Herder and the Possibility of Literature: Rationalism and Poetry in Eighteenth-Century Germany." In *Johann Gottfried Herder: Innovator Through the Ages*, edited by Wulf Koepke and Samson Knoll. Bonn: Bouvier, 1982.

Nancy, Jean-Luc. *Ego Sum*. Paris: Flammarion, 1979.

_____. "Larvatus Pro Deo." *Glyph* 2 (1977): 14–36.

_____. "Mundus est Fabula." *MLN* 93 (1978): 635–53.

Nisbet, H. B. "Herder and Francis Bacon." *Modern Language Review* 62 (1967): 267–83.

_____. *Herder and the Philosophy and History of Science*. Cambridge: Modern Humanities Research Association, 1970.

Noel, Thomas. *Theories of the Fable in the Eighteenth Century*. New York: Columbia University Press, 1975.

Norris, Christopher. *The Deconstructive Turn*. New York: Methuen, 1983.

Noxon, James. "Dr. Mandeville: A Thinking Man." In *The Varied Pattern*, edited by Peter Hughes and David Williams. Toronto: A. M. Hakkert, 1971.

Oakeshott, Michael. *Hobbes on Civil Association*. Berkeley: University of California Press, 1975.

O'Flaherty, James C. *Hamann's "Socratic Memorabilia": A Translation and Commentary*. Baltimore, Md.: Johns Hopkins University Press, 1967.

_____. *Johann Georg Hamann*. Boston: Twayne, 1979.

_____. *Unity and Language: A Study in the Philosophy of Johann Georg Hamann*. 1952. Reprint. New York: AMS Press, 1966.

Olscamp, Paul J. "Does Berkeley Have an Ethical Theory?" In *A Treatise Concerning the Principles of Human Knowledge, with Critical Essays*, edited by Colin M. Turbayne. Indianapolis, Ind.: Bobbs-Merrill, 1970.

Olson, Alan M. "Myth, Symbol, and Metaphorical Truth." In *Myth, Symbol, and Reality*, edited by Alan M. Olson. Notre Dame, Ind.: University of Notre Dame Press, 1980.

Owen, Joan Hildreth. "The Choice of Hercules and Eighteenth Century Fabulists." Ph.D. diss., New York University, 1969.

Perelman, Chaim. *The New Rhetoric and the Humanities*. Translated by William Kluback. Boston: D. Reidel, 1979.

Perelman, Chaim, and Olbrechts-Tyteca, L. *The New Rhetoric: A Treatise on Argumentation*. Translated by John Wilkinson and Purnell Weaver. Notre Dame, Ind.: Notre Dame University Press, 1969.

Perry, Ben Edwin. "Fable." *Studium Generale* 12 (1959): 17–37.

Pierce, David C. "Claude Lévi-Strauss: The Problematic Self and Myth." *International Philosophical Quarterly* 19 (1979): 381–406.

Pocock, J. G. A. *Politics, Language and Time*. New York: Atheneum, 1973.

Polanyi, Michael. *Personal Knowledge*. Chicago: University of Chicago Press, 1958.

Polanyi, Michael, and Prosch, Harry. *Meaning*. Chicago: University of Chicago Press, 1975.

Pope, Alexander. *The Poems of Alexander Pope*. Vol. 7. Edited by Maynard Mack. London: Methuen, 1967.

Poster, Mark. "The Future According to Foucault: *The Archaeology of Knowledge* and Intellectual History." In *Modern European Intellectual History: Reappraisals and New Perspectives*, edited by Dominick LaCapra and Steven L. Kaplan. Ithaca, N.Y.: Cornell University Press, 1982.

Poulet, Georges. "The Dream of Descartes." In *Studies in Human Time*. Translated by Elliott Coleman. Baltimore, Md.: Johns Hopkins University Press, 1956.

Price, Martin. *To the Palace of Wisdom*. Carbondale: Southern Illinois University Press, 1964.

Primer, Irwin, ed. *Mandeville Studies*. The Hague: Martinus Nijhoff, 1975.

Pritchard, Mary H. "Fables Moral and Political: The Adaptation of the Aesopian Fable Collection to English Social and Political Life, 1651–1722." Ph.D. diss., University of Western Ontario, 1976.

Randall, John Herman. *The Career of Philosophy*. Vol. 1: *From the Middle Ages to the Enlightenment*. New York: Columbia University Press, 1962.

Reagan, Charles E. "Hermeneutics and the Semantics of Action." *Pre/Text* 4 (1983): 239–55.

_____. "Psychoanalysis as Hermeneutics." In *Studies in the Philosophy of Paul Ricoeur*, edited by Charles E. Reagan. Athens: Ohio University Press, 1979.

Reiss, Timothy. "Cartesian Discourse and Classical Ideology." *Diacritics* vol. 6, no. 4 (Winter 1976): 19–27.

_____ . *The Discourse of Modernism.* Ithaca, N.Y.: Cornell University Press, 1982.

Richardson, Samuel, ed. *Aesop's Fables.* 1740. Facsimile Reprint. New York: Garland, 1975.

Ricoeur, Paul. "Creativity in Language: Word, Polysemy, Metaphor." In *The Philosophy of Paul Ricoeur,* edited by Charles E. Reagan and David Stewart. Boston: Beacon Press, 1978.

_____ . "Discussion of Nelson Goodman's *Ways of Worldmaking.*" *Philosophy and Literature* 4 (1980): 107–20.

_____ . *Hermeneutics and the Human Sciences.* Edited and translated by John P. Thompson. Cambridge: Cambridge University Press, 1981.

_____ . "Metaphor and the Main Problem of Hermeneutics." *New Literary History* 6 (1974–75): 95–110.

_____ . "The Metaphorical Process as Cognition, Imagination, and Feeling." In *On Metaphor,* edited by Sheldon Sacks. Chicago: University of Chicago Press, 1979.

_____ . "The Model of the Text: Meaningful Action Considered as a Text." *New Literary History* 5 (1973–74): 91–117.

Righter, William. *Myth and Literature.* London: Routledge and Kegan Paul, 1975.

Rogers, A. K. "The Ethics of Mandeville." *International Journal of Ethics* 36 (1925–26): 1–17.

Romanowski, Sylvie. *L'Illusion chez Descartes: La structure du discours cartésien.* Paris: Klincksieck, 1974.

Rorty, Richard. "The Historiography of Philosophy: Four Genres." In *Philosophy in History: Essays on the Historiography of Philosophy,* edited by Richard Rorty, Jerome B. Schneewind, and Quentin Skinner. Cambridge: Cambridge University Press, 1984.

_____ . *Philosophy and the Mirror of Nature.* Princeton, N.J.: Princeton University Press, 1979.

Rorty, Richard; Schneewind, Jerome B.; and Skinner, Quentin; eds. *Philosophy in History: Essays on the Historiography of Philosophy.* Cambridge: Cambridge University Press, 1984.

Rossi, Paolo. *The Dark Abyss of Time: The History of the Earth and the History of Nations from Hooke to Vico.* Translated by Lydia C. Cochrane. Chicago: University of Chicago Press, 1984.

_____ . *Francis Bacon: From Magic to Science.* Translated by Sacha Rabinovitch. Chicago: University of Chicago Press, 1968.

Ruthven, K. K. *Myth.* London: Methuen, 1976.

Sacks, Sheldon, ed. *On Metaphor.* Chicago: University of Chicago Press, 1979.

Schlegel, Friedrich. *Dialogue on Poetry.* Translated by Roman Struc. University Park: Pennsylvania State University Press, 1968.

Schneider, Louis. *Paradox and Society: The Work of Bernard Mandeville.* Edited by Jay Weinstein. New Brunswick, N.J.: Transaction Books, 1987.

Schütze, Martin. "The Fundamental Ideas in Herder's Thought: II, III, IV." *Modern Philology* 18 (1920): 289–303; 19 (1921): 113–30, 361–82.

_____ . "Herder's Conception of 'Bild'." *Germanic Review* 1 (1926): 21–35.

Scott-Taggart, M. J. "Mandeville: Cynic or Fool?" *Philosophical Quarterly* 16 (1966): 221–32.

Sebeok, Thomas, ed. *Myth: A Symposium.* Bloomington: Indiana University Press, 1958.

Seung, T. K. *Structuralism and Hermeneutics.* New York: Columbia University Press, 1982.

Sewell, Elizabeth. "Bacon, Vico, Coleridge, and the Poetic Method." In *Giambattista Vico: An International Symposium,* edited by Giorgio Tagliacozzo and Hayden V. White. Baltimore, Md.: Johns Hopkins University Press, 1969.

_____ . *The Human Metaphor.* Notre Dame, Ind.: University of Notre Dame Press, 1964.

_____ . *The Orphic Voice: Poetry and Natural History.* New York: Harper and Row, 1971.

Shaftesbury, earl of (Anthony Ashley Cooper). *Characteristics of Men, Manners, Opinions, Times.* Edited by John M. Robertson. 2 vols. in 1. Indianapolis, Ind.: Bobbs-Merrill, 1964.

Shea, John S. Introduction to *Aesop Dress'd,* by Bernard Mandeville. Augustan Reprint Society Publication No. 120. Los Angeles: William Andrews Clark Memorial Library, 1966.

_____ . "Studies in the Verse Fable from La Fontaine to Gay." Ph.D. diss., University of Minnesota, 1967.

Sherbo, Arthur. *Christopher Smart: Scholar of the University.* East Lansing: Michigan State University Press, 1967.

Skarsten, A. Keith. "Nature in Mandeville." *JEGP* 53 (1954): 562–68.

Skinner, Quentin. "The Idea of Negative Liberty: Philosophical and Historical Perspectives." In *Philosophy in History: Essays on the Historiography of Philosophy,* edited by Richard Rorty, Jerome B. Schneewind, and Quentin Skinner. Cambridge: Cambridge University Press, 1984.

Smith, M. Ellwood. "A Classification for Fables, Based on the Collection of Marie de France." *Modern Philology* 15 (1917–18): 477–89.

_____ . "The Fable as Poetry in English Criticism." *Modern Language Notes* 32 (1917): 466–70.

Smith, Ronald G. *J. G. Hamann, 1730–1788.* New York: Harper and Bros., 1960.

Stephens, James. *Francis Bacon and the Style of Science.* Chicago: University of Chicago Press, 1975.

Sutherland, James. *English Literature of the Late Seventeenth Century.* Oxford: Clarendon Press, 1969.

Swift, Jonathan. *Poems of Jonathan Swift.* Edited by Harold Williams. Oxford: Clarendon Press, 1937.

Tagliacozzo, Giorgio, and Verene, Donald P., eds. *Giambattista Vico's Science of Humanity.* Baltimore, Md.: Johns Hopkins University Press, 1976.

Tagliacozzo, Giorgio, and White, Hayden V., eds. *Giambattista Vico: An International Symposium.* Baltimore, Md.: Johns Hopkins University Press, 1969.

Taylor, Charles. "Philosophy and Its History." In *Philosophy in History: Essays on the Historiography of Philosophy,* edited by Richard Rorty, Jerome B. Schneewind, and Quentin Skinner. Cambridge: Cambridge University Press, 1984.

Tedlock, Denis. "The Spoken Word and the Work of Interpretation in American Indian Religion." In *Myth, Symbol, and Reality,* edited by Alan M. Olson. Notre Dame, Ind.: University of Notre Dame Press, 1980.

Thiher, Allen. *Words in Reflection: Modern Language Theory and Postmodern Fiction.* Chicago: University of Chicago Press, 1984.

Turbayne, Colin M. "Berkeley's Metaphysical Grammar." In *A Treatise Concerning the Principles of Human Knowledge, with Critical Essays,* edited by Colin M. Turbayne. Indianapolis, Ind.: Bobbs-Merrill, 1970.

_____. *The Myth of Metaphor.* 2d ed. Columbia: University of South Carolina Press, 1970.

Turbayne, Colin M., ed. *Berkeley: Critical and Interpretive Essays.* Minneapolis: University of Minnesota Press, 1982.

_____, ed. *A Treatise Concerning the Principles of Human Knowledge, with Critical Essays.* Indianapolis, Ind.: Bobbs-Merrill, 1970.

Ulmer, Gregory. "*Op Writing*: Derrida's Solicitation of *Theoria.*" In *Displacement: Derrida and After,* edited by Mark Krupnick. Bloomington: Indiana University Press, 1983.

Undank, Jack, and Josephs, Herbert, eds. *Diderot: Digression and Dispersion.* Lexington, Ky.: French Forum, 1984.

Uphaus, Robert W. "Satire, Verification, and *The Fable of the Bees.*" *Papers on Language and Literature* 12 (1976): 142–49.

Vaughan, Frederick. "*La Scienza Nuova*: Orthodoxy and the Art of Writing." *Forum Italicum* 2 (1968): 332–58.

Verene, Donald P. *Hegel's Recollection: A Study of Images in the 'Phenomenology of Spirit.'* Albany: State University of New York Press, 1985.

_____. "The New Art of Narration: Vico and the Muses." *New Vico Studies* 1 (1983): 21–38.

_____. "Vico and Marx on Poetic Wisdom and Barbarism." In *Vico and Marx: Affinities and Contrasts,* edited by Giorgio Tagliacozzo. Atlantic Highlands, N.J.: Humanities Press, 1983.

_____. "Vico's Philosophy of Imagination." *Social Research* 43 (1976): 410–33.

_____ . *Vico's Science of Imagination.* Ithaca, N.Y.: Cornell University Press, 1981.

_____ . "Vico's Science of Imaginative Universals and the Philosophy of Symbolic Forms." In *Giambattista Vico's Science of Humanity,* edited by Giorgio Tagliacozzo and Donald P. Verene. Baltimore, Md.: Johns Hopkins University Press, 1976.

Vico, Giambattista. *The Autobiography of Giambattista Vico.* Translated by Max H. Fisch and Thomas G. Bergin. Great Seal Books. Ithaca, N.Y.: Cornell University Press, 1963.

_____ . "A Factual Digression on Human Genius, Sharp, Witty Remarks, and Laughter." Translated by Antonio Illiano, James D. Tedder, and Piero Treves. *Forum Italicum* 2 (1968): 310–14.

_____ . *The New Science of Giambattista Vico.* Translated by Thomas Bergin and Max Fisch. Ithaca, N.Y.: Cornell University Press, 1968.

_____ . *On the Most Ancient Wisdom of the Italians.* Translated by L. M. Palmer. Ithaca, N.Y.: Cornell University Press, 1988.

_____ . *On the Study Methods of Our Time.* Translated by Elio Gianturco. Indianapolis, Ind.: Bobbs-Merrill, 1965.

_____ . *Opere.* Edited by Giovanni Gentile and Fausto Nicolini. 8 vols. in 11. Bari, Italy: Laterza, 1911–41.

_____ . *Vico: Selected Writings.* Translated and edited by Leon Pompa. Cambridge: Cambridge University Press, 1982.

Vives, Juan Luis. *Fable About Man.* Translated by Nancy Lenkeith. In *The Renaissance Philosophy of Man,* edited by Ernst Cassirer, P. O. Kristeller, and J. H. Randall. Chicago: University of Chicago Press, 1948.

Wallace, Karl R. "Aspects of Modern Rhetoric in Francis Bacon." *Quarterly Journal of Speech* 42 (1956): 398–406.

_____ . *Francis Bacon on the Nature of Man.* Urbana: University of Illinois Press, 1967.

Watt, Ian. *The Rise of the Novel: Studies in Defoe, Richardson and Fielding.* London: Chatto and Windus, 1957.

Wells, George A. "Condillac, Rousseau, and Herder on the Origin of Language." *Studies on Voltaire and the Eighteenth Century* 230 (1985): 233–46.

_____ . "Vico and Herder." In *Giambattista Vico: An International Symposium,* edited by Giorgio Tagliacozzo and Hayden V. White. Baltimore, Md.: Johns Hopkins University Press, 1969.

White, Hayden V. *The Content of the Form: Narrative Discourse and Historical Representation.* Baltimore, Md.: Johns Hopkins University Press, 1987.

_____ . "Foucault Decoded: Notes from Underground." *History and Theory* 12 (1973): 23–54.

_____ . "The Irrational and the Problem of Historical Knowledge in the Enlightenment." In *Irrationalism in the Eighteenth Century,* edited by Harold E. Pagliaro. Studies in Eighteenth-Century Culture, vol. 2. Cleveland, Ohio: Case Western University Press, 1972.

_____ . *Metahistory: The Historical Imagination in Nineteenth-Century Europe.* Baltimore, Md.: Johns Hopkins University Press, 1974.

_____ . *Tropics of Discourse: Essays in Cultural Criticism.* Baltimore, Md.: Johns Hopkins University Press, 1978.

White, Howard B. "Bacon's Wisdom of the Ancients." *Interpretation* 1 (1970): 107–29.

Willson, A. Leslie. "Romantic Neomythology." In *Myth and Reason: A Symposium,* edited by Walter D. Wetzels. Austin: University of Texas Press, 1973.

Wray, William R. "The English Fable, 1650–1800." Ph.D. diss., Yale University, 1950.

Index